LANFORD WILSON

LANFORD WILSON
Collected Works
1970–1983

CONTEMPORARY PLAYWRIGHTS SERIES

SK
A Smith and Kraus Book

A Smith and Kraus Book
Published by Smith and Kraus, Inc.
PO Box 127, Lyme, NH 03768

The Library of Congress Cataloging-In-Publication Data
Wilson, Lanford, 1937–
[Plays. Selections]
Lanford Wilson: collected full-length plays vol.ii, 1970–1983. —1st ed.
p. cm. — (Contemporary playwrights series, issn 1067-9510)
ISBN 1-57525-119-1 *paper,* 1-57525-190-6 *cloth*
I. Title. II. Series.
PS3573.I458A6   1996   1998
812.54—dc20   96-1909
            CIP

Cover and Text Design by Julia Hill Gignoux, Freedom Hill Design

First Edition: November 1998
10 9 8 7 6 5 4 3 2 1

CONTENTS

THE HOT L BALTIMORE

For Marshall W. Mason

*Conchata Ferrell in the Circle Repertory Company production
of* The Hot L Baltimore. *
Photograph © by Frederick Eberstadt.*

INTRODUCTION

The Circle Repertory Company began with a meeting on July 14, 1969. I didn't get around to writing *The Hot L Baltimore* for the company until about December, 1972. I was in the middle of a massive writer's block and had been working nearly a year on a play that just wouldn't come. It was to be based on an incident that took place in the early 18th century. I had tried to tackle it as a collage, as a trial play, as a musical, as a minstrel show; I had just about thrown in the towel and decided that whatever the damned play should be, I wasn't the one to write it.

Marshall and I were at the theater in the middle of the night, varnishing the audience risers — the huge black plywood platforms that stack to elevate the audience, one row above the other. Every fifteen minutes or so we ran to the front of the airless room where there was a small balcony overlooking Broadway, to gasp like drowning swimmers, filling our lungs with more or less fresh oxygen. Varnishing huge surfaces in a close room must be like sniffing glue. The radio was blasting. In that commercial building (above a Thom McAn shoe store) we could turn the theater's excellent sound system to full volume at that hour with nobody around to complain. When Arlo Guthrie's "The City of New Orleans" came on I said, "I love this song; I've always been going to write a long aching lament for the vanishing railroads." And Marshall said something like, "Well, why don't you do it then, instead of that dumb thing you've been trying to work on for the past year."

I'm not really a railroad freak, or not as freaky as the Girl in this play. I ride trains because I don't like to fly. Anyway, it turns out the play is more a lament for our vanishing architecture, and I *am* passionate about the loss of some of our country's great buildings. I arrived in Chicago just as they were tearing down every Louis Sullivan building they could get their hands on.

In '71 Circle Rep did an evening of my one acts. The next logical move was to write a full-length play for the company. The block, the respite, the struggle with that stupid minstrel show, had served me well. I had the opportunity to see the company in a number of plays, I knew the actors' strengths, I knew what they felt comfortable with and what would challenge them, which is what interested me—throwing them into a different direction (yes, you can cry, can you make me laugh — or you can make me laugh but can you make me cry — which actually isn't that difficult, I cry at TV commercials). And with that noble goal of challenging the actor stated, sometimes you just flat-out take advantage of what he does really well.

Circle Rep used to do short plays for weekend runs in workshop — anything a director or some of the actors wanted to develop. Circle, especially in the early years, was always about learning. When Conchata Ferrell arrived from West Virginia I said she was perfect for Agnes in my one act *Ludlow Fair*. She and Trish Hawkins did the play in workshop. She was not only perfect, she was a wonder and so was this Trish Hawkins, a gal I had never seen before. People had to know these two women. So the one thing I knew when I began *The Hot L Baltimore* was that I wanted to take advantage of Chatti's sardonic comic delivery — enter April. And for Trish, the freshest, truest, most vital actress I had seen — enter the Girl. I hadn't written for specific actors before, but the process was fascinating. When another character entered the play (the character came first) I would say, O.K.: Who in the company is right for this? Then develop the character for that actor. Or sometimes I just asked. Stephanie Gordon said she had been playing so many classy ladies, she wanted to play someone really trashy for a change. Enter Suzy, the romantic prostitute.

When I finished the second act I asked Marshall and some of the guys to read to me what I had so far. I listened in amazement. I called my agent and said, "Bridget, it's charming." I had told her something of the play. She said, "With all those whores?" And all I could say was, I know, and I don't know how it happened, but it's *charming*. I was crestfallen; I had thought I was writing a daring, in-your-face exposé. But I was also excited — it sounded like a play. At least the first two acts of a play. I had no idea where the beast was going. I knew only that Jamie was abandoned, probably to April. I asked all my friends what happens in third acts. They were no help at all. However, Marshall had said the play sounded a little Chekhovian. O.K. I reread *The Cherry Orchard*. In the last act, when they leave, they have champagne, they have a party. So Suzy will be leaving and, given Suzy, she'll throw herself a going-away party. This seemed right for a Rite of Spring play.

I had at first imagined the play would go all over the place like *Balm in Gilead*: the street outside, into the rooms of the many tenants, locations all over Baltimore. Half-way through the first act, when the characters steadfastly refused to move from the lobby, I knew I was stuck with one set. The hotel was becoming the lead.

Marshall and I wanted to convey the rhythms of the play to the actors. We divided the sixteen parts between us, (there was a mail man, the part was cut) gathered the cast together in Stephanie's apartment and read it to them. They later told us they hadn't understood a word. At the first rehearsal the actors sat in a huge circle for the first reading of the play. Marshall and I listened to see if we had the casting right. John Hogan, just arrived two weeks earlier from Chicago, had stepped into the part I had written for Brad Douriff as Brad was at a school that disallowed acting during the first year. Judd Hirsch was perfect for Bill, the only part I had written without a company actor in mind. I had met him the previous year when the Washington Theatre Club did *Lemon Sky*. He was going with the girl who played Carol. He visited, came over to Davey Marlin Jones' house with his girlfriend; we rolled around on the carpet, drinking and talking most of the night. I remembered only one of the biggest, butchest, funniest actors I'd ever met. He picked up the script the week before rehearsal, read it, told his girlfriend he had to walk and think about it. When he got back to the apartment, she had read the play and said, "You're doing this." The part of the little lesbian that I had begun writing for Tanya Berezin (she was unthinking enough to get pregnant, so much for that idea) was taken up by Mari Gorman. Tanya had said, "If for any reason I can't do something, get Mari Gorman." Mari won every acting award she was eligible for and one where I think they bent the rules. Only one actor was totally wrong for the part I had written for her; she was too young by half and, though I hadn't noticed it much before, or maybe I thought it would work for the part, she had a very slight European accent. What was called for was an elegant, mildly batty southern lady. I remembered Helen Stenborg who had stood out so prominently in *Rimers* years earlier. Helen became one of the most important and most supportive members of the company. We paid little attention to the play itself, just sensing that, yes, it was a play and, yes, it would probably work. Richard Steel, another Circle director, was our only audience. He went bouncing around the theater yelling, "Oh, my God, do you know what you've got? I can't believe we get to do this here! Oh, God, this is so great!" We thought he was crazy.

The production turned out to be a phenomenon. Marshall directed it beautifully, the cast rose to the occasion with an ensemble performance the likes of which I had never seen before. Not even my memories of Littlefield's *The Hostage* could touch it. Harold Clurman, in his review for *The Nation*, had to define what "ensemble" really means instead of what critics are forever calling ensemble. He said you could not tell where the script ended and the acting began. Since I had little to do with that, I will freely admit it's true. The wonderful producer Kermit Blumgarten, one of the greatest Men of the Theater I will ever know, transferred the production (the first of three Circle Rep plays that year to move to a larger theater) to the downtown Circle in the Square, compounding forever the confusion of those two companies. I went by the box office every afternoon to ask if anyone had bought a ticket. Finally, after a month of sold-out houses, that man said, "Lanford, you don't have to check on it every day, the play is going to run a year." It ran three years; first breaking the record for a play at that theater, then for any non-musical play off-Broadway.

ORIGINAL PRODUCTION

The Hot L Baltimore was first presented on February 4, 1973, at the Circle Repertory Company, 2307 Broadway, New York City. Producers Kermit Blumgarten and Roger Ailes transferred the Circle Rep production to the Circle-in-the-Square Theatre, where it reopened on March 22, 1973, with the following cast:

BILL LEWIS	Judd Hirsch
GIRL	Trish Hawkins
MILLIE	Helen Stenborg
MRS. BELLOTTI	Henrietta Bagley
APRIL GREEN	Conchata Ferrell
MR. MORSE	Rob Thirkield
JACKIE	Mari Gorman
JAMIE	Zane Lasky
MR. KATZ	Antony Tenuta
SUZY	Stephanie Gordon
SUZY'S JOHN	Burke Pearson
PAUL GRANGER III	Jonathan Hogan
MRS. OXENHAM	Louise Clay
CAB DRIVER	Peter Tripp
DELIVERY BOY	Marcial Gonzales

The play was directed by Marshall W. Mason, with sets by Ronald Radice, costumes by Dina Costa, and sound by Chuck London.

The author expresses his thanks to the John Simon Guggenheim Memorial Foundation for their support during the writing of this play.

THE PEOPLE

MR. KATZ The hotel manager. Thirty-five, balding a little but hiding it. Firm and wary and at times more than a little weary. Dark, in an inexpensive dark suit.

MRS. OXENHAM The day desk clerk–phone operator. Forty-five and firm; quick-speaking with no commerce.

BILL LEWIS The night clerk. Thirty, large-featured, well-built in a beefy way, a handsome but not aggressive face. He covers his difficulty in communicating his feelings for the Girl with a kind of clumsy, friendly bluster.

PAUL GRANGER III A student, twenty. Blond, angular, and taut. His tenor voice is constrained by anxiety, he speaks and moves sporadically. Clear, lightly tanned complexion.

MRS. BELLOTTI The mother of a former tenant, fifty-five. Round and thin-voiced; complains to get her way, she is a whining fighter. Neatly but not expensively dressed. A sigher.

THE RESIDENTS

MR. MORSE Seventy, craggy, with a high, cracking voice. Morse moves slowly, with great energy and a sense of outrage.

MILLIE A retired waitress, sixty-eight, with good carriage and a lovely voice. Elegance marred by an egocentric spiritualism.

THE GIRL A call girl, nineteen. Light, blond, maddeningly curious; a romantic enthusiasm and a youthful ebullience, which is perhaps unconsciously exaggerated for its appeal in her trade.

APRIL GREEN A prostitute, over thirty. A large and soft pragmatist with a mellow alto laugh and a beautiful face.

SUZY A prostitute, thirty. She is hopelessly romantic and hard as nails.

JACKIE Twenty-four. Jeans, boots, her name written on the back of her denim jacket. Her manner, voice, and stance are those of a young stevedore. To her humiliation, she is, under the manner, both femininely vulnerable and pretty.

JAMIE Jackie's brother. Pale, small, and wiry. A little slow (one suspects browbeaten). Alert but not quick. Always listening to his sister. Nineteen.

CAB DRIVER

DELIVERY BOY

SUZY'S JOHN

THE SCENE

Once there was a railroad and the neighborhood of the railroad terminals bloomed (boomed) with gracious hotels. The Hotel Baltimore, built in the late nineteenth century, remodeled during the Art Deco last stand of the railroads, is a five-story establishment intended to be an elegant and restful haven. Its history has mirrored the rails' decline. The marble stairs and floors, the carved wood paneling have aged as neglected ivory ages, into a dull gold. The Hotel Baltimore is scheduled for demolition.

The theater, evanescent itself, and for all we do perhaps itself disappearing here, seems the ideal place for the representation of the impermanence of our architecture.

The lobby is represented by three areas that rise as the remains of a building already largely demolished: the Front Desk, the Lounge, and the Stairway.

Much of the action of the play is in the area behind the Front Desk. It should be open to the audience so we can follow the routine of the staff. Above this inner sanctum is a Rivera-style mural depicting the railroad's progress westward. Against the mural are stacked dozens of record books, boxes of files, and letters. A broken TV is used as a table for paperbacks, a hot plate, and a radio. There is a card table; folding chairs where the hookers congregate; the usual switchboard (which should be practical); pigeonholes; and a sweeping desk that faces the Lounge.

The Lounge: A sofa and three or four chairs, none original to the hotel, are all re-covered in plastic fabric. There is a table large enough to set up a checkerboard. From the Lounge the marble Stairway rises and curves, leading off to one side.

There could be an elevator with a barricade across the doors. There is a door to a broom closet and the skeletal indication of the front door.

Over the center of the lobby is a nonworking and almost unseen bronze chandelier that serves as the source of power, via two extension cords, for the tinny radio and the office hot plate.

About the radio: The play is designed to incorporate music popular during production. The music plays in the theater before the acts, and as the lights dim, the sound fades into the radio on stage. At the end of the acts the radio music builds again, moving into the house. The first and third acts should end with a positive song with an upbeat, a song that one has heard in passing a dozen times but never listened to closely.

The time is a recent Memorial Day.

The Hot L Baltimore

ACT ONE

Paul Granger III is asleep in a chair. Bill and Girl are behind the desk, he is at the switchboard, she is sitting beside, watching the operation. Six lines are plugged into the board. A radio is just audible.

BILL. *(Into the mouthpiece.)* It's seven o'clock. *(He disconnects one line.)* It's seven o'clock. *(He disconnects another.)*

GIRL. How do you do that? You plug everybody in at once, then just keep ringing until everybody answers, huh?

BILL. It's seven o'clock. *(Starts to disconnect the line.)* I don't know; I ain't been out, I got no idea.

GIRL. *(Impulsively into the phone.)* Miserable. Terrible; it's raining and cold and —

BILL. *(Quickly disconnecting the line.)* Don't do that. I told you, you can't do that if you're gonna sit back here.

GIRL. I want to find out what you're doing all the time.

BILL. You see why I don't have time to talk in the morning — *(Into the phone.)* It's seven o'clock.

GIRL. I just answer the —

BILL. You don't answer, you ask questions. *(Ringing.)* Come on.

GIRL. It helps me get awake.

BILL. It doesn't help me any when I'm trying to —

GIRL. — When you wake up, don't you like a pleasant little —

BILL. *(Into the phone.)* It's seven o'clock. Seven o'clock. *(Leaving the switchboard, turning off the radio.)* When I wake up, I get up.

GIRL. *(Taking up the call sheet.)* Six different people having to get up at seven o'clock. I'd hate it. *(Bill looks at her disapprovingly then notices something on the stairs.)*

9

BILL. Who's there? Who's up on the —

MILLIE. *(Overlapping.)* Good morning, Billy; don't let me frighten you. *(She starts a slow descent into the light.)*

BILL. Morning, Millie.

MILLIE. *(To herself.)* I don't know why it should tire me going down the stairs. I believe my body's metabolism can't get it through its head that I'm in retirement. You'd think after six months I'd be able to sleep past six-thirty; but I can't even manage to get back to sleep in the morning.

BILL. *(Overlapping from "head" — ringing.)* Son of a bitch.

GIRL. Who's that? Maybe they didn't get in till late last night.

BILL. No, he's like that every morning. Same thing every morning. *(To Millie — who has reached the desk.)* You see what they're doing to the Pioneer? I drive by.

GIRL. That was such a beautiful place! Why do they tear everything down?

MILLIE. *(She takes a morning paper and goes to the sofa.)* No, no, what would I care now?

BILL. They really built that old place; they're having a hell of a time getting it down. *(Behind Girl's back.)* That's not the only building going under the ball, you know. *(Indicating this hotel.)*

MILLIE. So I hear. Well…

GIRL. *(Overlapping "well.")* Where do you live?

BILL. *(To Millie.)* Don't you want to —

GIRL. Where do you live? You said you drive by the Pioneer.

BILL. Uptown; don't poke me.

GIRL. Who do you live with? Are you married?

BILL. Come on! *(Turning to the switchboard, disconnecting the last line.)* It's seven o'clock.

GIRL. What are you doing? He didn't answer.

BILL. I'm giving up on him. What's the matter, Millie, kinda hate to see it go?

MILLIE. No, I have no feelings about it either way. They couldn't afford the staff to keep it up any more. I long ago gave up being sentimental about losing propositions.

GIRL. Don't; I'm just going to get depressed. I really hate it that nobody cares about any — This used to be the most exclusive medium-sized hotel anywhere on the Eastern Seaboard line. This place was built —

BILL. How'd you suddenly get onto talking about —

GIRL. — in eighteen hundred and something.

BILL. What's this place got to do with the Pioneer?

GIRL. Oh, dummy. I can recognize a picture of my own hotel when it's on the front page of the newspaper.

BILL. Yeah, when was that?

GIRL. They used a picture from its grand opening.

MILLIE. I didn't realize it was this place, but I don't suppose I've looked at the building, really, in years.

GIRL. Oh, it looks just like it used to, only dirty.

BILL. *(As Mrs. Bellotti enters.)* That's some news, huh?

MRS. BELLOTTI. *(At the desk, to Bill.)* Excuse me, is Mr. Katz in?

GIRL. He comes in at seven-thirty.

BILL. *(To the Girl.)* Just never — No, he comes in — ain't in yet.

MRS. BELLOTTI. I don't think I've talked to you; I'm Mrs. Bellotti. Horse Bellotti's mother. Mr. Katz is gonna give him another chance, ain't he? He ain't gonna kick him out, is he? *(As she starts to come behind the desk. Bill jumps at her, leaving the board.)*

BILL. Here, you can't come back here. Don't come back here. That gate ain't supposed to be left open.

MRS. BELLOTTI. *(Overlapping.)* I can talk from here, this is fine; you'll talk to him, to Mr. Katz, won't you? You look like a nice young man. 'Cause I don't know what his daddy and me are going to do if he don't —

BILL. *(Cutting in.)* — I don't know nothin' about it. I got nothin' to do with it.

GIRL. *(Answering the phone.)* Hotel Baltimore, good morning.

BILL. *(Returning to the chair, shooing her out.)* He'll do what he wants to about it. Come on.

GIRL. I'll connect you.

MRS. BELLOTTI. Only he can't kick him out. I don't want him coming back to some strange place somewhere else. Does he want more money? Is that what it is? Does he want more money? 'Cause Horse's bill is always paid full on the first of every week; he's never been a day late with it. Is that what he wants?

BILL. *(Ignoring her. He has replugged a line. Ringing.)* Damn it.

GIRL. You gonna try him again? *(Reaching.)* Let me ring him.

BILL. No! Come on — make us a — why don't you make us a cup of tea?

GIRL. Millie, you want a cup of tea?

MILLIE. *(Looking up from the paper.)* No, thank you, Martha.

GIRL. *(Wincing.)* Ohhh, it's not Martha any more; I hate it.

MILLIE. I thought you had decided to settle on Martha.

GIRL. No! I mean I did, but I hate it. Where's the mailman? It's after —

MILLIE. On Memorial —

GIRL. Oh, I can't bear days when there's no mail delivery. Week days. What's this stuff?

BILL. That's something for you to do; those go in the boxes.

GIRL. *(Taking up the stack of thirty-five envelopes.)* Terrific. Oh, no. You know what is it? It's our — Oh, that's horrible, I certainly am not. It's our things. Eviction notices. "Newgate Development and Management" —

MILLIE. Let me see.

GIRL. Oxenham can do it; she'll love it. Just tell me how long a notice they're giving us. *(Her attention now is on the pigeonholes.)* Can you imagine people not picking up their mail? How can they bear it? Two-twelve. Must be a salesman. *(Takes four or five letters from the box.)* Baltimore, Baltimore. Boring. Denver. Something Idaho. *(To Bill.)* What does that say?

BILL. Don't take people's mail out of their —

GIRL. I'm gonna put it back — what does that say?

BILL. If you can't read it, I can't.

GIRL. *(Categorizing it.)* Some sloppy town in Idaho. Washington, D.C. I've been over every inch of Idaho twice. Sugar beets, potatoes, and cows. *(Going on — another box.)*

BILL. Don't mix those up.

GIRL. I'm not. Don't bother me. Annapolis — nowhere. Baltimore. New York, Baltimore. Here's one I don't know. Franklin, Louisiana. No idea. Millie, you ever heard of Franklin, Louisiana?

MILLIE. Down on the Gulf, I believe.

GIRL. In the heel or the toe? You know.

MILLIE. Well. The ball of the foot.

GIRL. Around Saint Martinville?

MILLIE. South of there; right on the Gulf.

GIRL. Right. *(Disposes of it.)* Swamp City. No wonder. *(As Mrs. Bellotti starts to move away, ignored.)* You come back at seven-thirty — quarter to eight, and he'll be here.

MRS. BELLOTTI. *(Immediately drawn back.)* Has he said anything? To you? 'Cause I don't think he really has it in for Horse. He just doesn't understand him. He shouldn't have gone in, really. And he's only been in for five months, so you know it wasn't anything bad; he's a nice boy. He's just different. He's been to a psychiatrist and he gave him a complete examination and he said there wasn't anything wrong with David mentally; he's just shy. I tell him — Horse…you should meet someone. He's too adult to live with us. He's thirty-six. He and his dad don't get along.

I tell him he has to *try* to meet people — to meet a girl, and he says how would I do that? And I don't know what to tell him…

GIRL. *(As Bill disconnects the plug.)* You giving up on him again?

BILL. He'll call down to Oxenham at ten o'clock, mad as the devil.

MRS. BELLOTTI. You think he'll let him stay?

BILL. Mr. Katz is in by eight o'clock, you come back then.

MRS. BELLOTTI. I just came by on my way to — I'm supposed to be home with Frank 'cause he's on morphine and God knows what condition he might be in. We're all the way out in — You think he'll be to work by eight o'clock? Is there a place where I can get a cup of coffee or something? Or I'll just sit here and wait till he comes in if he's going —

BILL. There's a place on the corner's got real good coffee. *(Girl punches him — it has notoriously bad coffee.)*

MRS. BELLOTTI. That's what I'll do; 'cause I can't afford to go all the way home and come back. And I can't talk to him on the phone 'cause he won't come to — *(Fades off and listens.)*

BILL. That Pioneer used to be a pretty slick place, did it?

MILLIE. *(Putting the notice in her purse.)* Oh, yes…thirty years ago or more, people found it a pleasant enough place to spend their money.

BILL. President Taft used to go there?

MILLIE. President Coolidge. The father of the "constructive economy"! I served him quite often. He always sat his party in my station. *(Mrs. Bellotti wanders off and out.)*

GIRL. Does she have a son that lives here?

BILL. I don't know *who* she was. You can't come back here if you don't close that gate. *(To Millie.)* He a pretty good tipper, was he?

MILLIE. President Coolidge? Not at all.

BILL. No?

MILLIE. No tip at all. He didn't pay and he didn't tip. I think the pleasure was supposed to be mine.

BILL. You're a hard one, Millie.

MILLIE. *(Pleased.)* No, no…not really.

GIRL. Did it have ghosts? I mean it had been there so long…probably not, though, huh? In a restaurant?

MILLIE. Oh, yes. There were a number of *spirits*. One or two who never left the dining room. They were almost as much a fixture as I was. One particularly.

BILL. Didn't nobody sit on him?

MILLIE. Oh, *she* never sat. She was very shy; she just stood about, near the doorway. We often saw her when we were cleaning up.

GIRL. Who was she?

MILLIE. Someone who liked the restaurant, it would seem.

GIRL. Are there ghosts here? There are, aren't there?

MILLIE. They don't like to —

GIRL. I *knew* it! I *knew* it!

MILLIE. They don't like to be talked about; it would only upset them.

GIRL. Well, Lord knows I'm not going to upset them! Could you tell my fortune? Because I believe in — Oh! Listen! *(In the beat of silence there is the echo of a train, not far off.)* Oh, no! *(In a rage of disappointment.)* That's the Silver Star! Oh, damn! Doesn't that just make you want to cry? How can they do that!?

BILL. I think she's got the schedules and bells and whistles all memoriz —

GIRL. *(Angry.)* There's no schedule involved in it. I don't think they have schedules any more. Silver Star is due in at four-nineteen; she's more than three damn hours late. I get so mad at them for not running on time. I mean it's their own damn schedule, I don't know why they can't keep to it. They're just miserable. The service is so bad and hateful, and the porters and conductors, you just can't believe it isn't deliberate. I think they're being run by the airlines. *(To Millie.)* Do you have stock in the railroads? Could you do something? Write somebody?

MILLIE. Oh, no; I don't have much stock. Certainly not in the railroads. I can't imagine anyone with any business sense just now —

GIRL. Where will they go?

MILLIE. Who?

GIRL. The ghosts? When they tear the hotel down? What'll happen to them?

MILLIE. Oh…they'll stay around for a while wondering what's become of everything. Then they'll wander off with people. They form attachments.

BILL. *(As the board lights up.)* Now what does he want? *(Phone.)* Yeah? Front desk.

APRIL. *(Entering, from off.)* All right, all right, what's the story this time? Last week it was a plumber in the basement; two weeks before that he said the boiler was busted; the time before that, the coldest fuckin' day of the year, he's got some excuse so stupid I can't even remember it.

BILL. *(Phone.)* You put in a call for seven o'clock. It's seven o'clock. *(Disconnects.)* Whadda you want, April?

APRIL. *(Overlapping.)* Seven o'clock? Who you tellin' — it's no goddamned seven o'clock — it's not been light more than —

GIRL. I told you two weeks ago; spring ahead fall back.

APRIL. What kind of monkey language is that supposed to —

BILL. — Don't you listen to the radio or read a —

APRIL. — The fuckin' daylight savings. *(Turning to go.)* Fall back on my ass; it's too scratchin' much. I don't know what anyone expects —

BILL. *(Overlapping.)* It's been almost a month, April, you oughtta be used to it by now.

APRIL. *(Returning.)* Hey, come on, I gotta get to sleep — whatta you gonna do about the water?

BILL. What's wrong with it?

GIRL. It's cold.

APRIL. No. Last night it was cold. Tonight it's cold — and it's orange.

BILL. They're probably workin' on the pipes.

APRIL. Yeah, well, I'm gonna work on somebody's pipes. *(Hikes her leg up on his chair looking and scratching.)* Things aren't wicked enough around here with —

BILL. *(Overlapping exchange.)* — Come on, I'm not in your way, am I? What are you doing?

APRIL. — I'm not bothering you —

BILL. — What have you got your leg up in the air —

APRIL. — You're not going to see anything —

BILL. *(Getting up.)* — What are you getting on me? —

APRIL. — Whadda you think, I'm lousy? *(Shaking her hair on him.)* Waaaaaaa!

BILL. Come on, whatta you doing? What the hell's wrong with you?

APRIL. *(Laughing.)* You really are an ass acher, you know it?

BILL. Whadda you want, April?

APRIL. Don't start with me. What I want, this hotel don't offer.

BILL. I'm trying to work here.

APRIL. What are you doing about the water? *(He starts to speak.)* Tell me you just work here.

BILL. *(Beat.)* What're you coming down here in your nightgown?

APRIL. What nightgown? This is a silk — Dacron kimono. This is a perfectly respectable garment. Whadda you think, I'm trying to turn you on? You're not my type.

BILL. I didn't know you had a type.

APRIL. *(Abstracted.)* Yeah...well...I've got several types. Give me a cigarette *(Helping herself; chuckling.)* A guy — yesterday — said, you sure smoke an awful lot — asked did I smoke in bed — I said...try me. *(Laughs.)*

GIRL. That's dangerous. Smoking in bed.

BILL. *(Phone.)* Front desk. Yeah. Hold on. Hand me that book.

APRIL. Morning, Millie.

MILLIE. Good morning. I don't know whether to say good morning to you or good night.

GIRL. What number?

BILL. Two-eighteen. Just see if he's up on his bill.

GIRL. What does he pay — weekly?

BILL. Let me see it.

APRIL. Say good night to me and I'll curl up right here on the floor.

GIRL. He paid half and then the rest yesterday.

BILL. *(Into the phone.)* Yeah. What was that number? *(He writes it down — Girl begins to dial before he is finished.)* O.K.

APRIL. Thanks for the butt. Put a note in my hole I don't want to be rung till after four o'clock.

GIRL. Is that an eight or a zero?

BILL. Come on — three-eight-six-oh.

GIRL. *(To April.)* Don't forget to turn your clock up.

APRIL. I don't keep clocks. Clocks and dogs. My clock's outside my window on the front of the terminal. Says a quarter after five. Twenty-four hours a day. *(Laughing.)* I figger that's a good enough time for just about any-thing. *(Laughing.)* Guy came up to me last week — couldn't think of anything to say — said — "Uh, uh, excuse me, you don't happen to know what time it is, do you?" I said, "Sure, it's a quarter after five." The son of a bitch was so surprised he looked at his goddamned watch. *(Laughs.)*

GIRL. *(Pause.)* What time was —

APRIL. I don't want to hear it. Whatever you're going to say. You're a real bring-down, you know it? I'd give a hundred bucks for her hair; I wouldn't turn a nickel for her brain.

GIRL. No, I got the joke, I just wondered what —

APRIL. Listen, don't listen to me. Kids now are a different breed. If I was six-teen I'd be just as — How old are you?

GIRL. Nineteen.

APRIL. Nineteen. Jesus. If I was nineteen and looked like that —

BILL. And know what you know now.

APRIL. Fuck what I know now. Give me the rest of it — I'll learn. You want to know the sad truth? If I looked like that I wouldn't have to know what I know now.

GIRL. Did you ever take a ride on a —

APRIL. What? On a what? *(Beat.)* Probably I did.

GIRL. Nothing. I don't want to know what you'd say.

APRIL. Yeah, well, I got that problem. Listen, I'm going to bed before I get bitter. *(Takes another cigarette.)* You tell Katz I'm after his balls if he ain't got hot water when I get up.

MR. MORSE. *(Overlapping a word or two — entering.)* I have a complaint. Who's here? I have a complaint.

BILL. What's yours, Mr. Morse?

APRIL. Lay it on us, Mr. Morse.

GIRL. *(Simultaneous.)* Morning, Mr. Morse.

MORSE. *(Simultaneous.)* Listen to me.

BILL. Yeah.

MORSE. Listen to me!

BILL. I hear you.

MORSE. I'm going to hold the hotel responsible.

BILL. Why's that?

MORSE. Listen to my voice.

BILL. I hear you, Mr. Morse.

MORSE. Listen to my voice. I can't afford to get a cold and I'm getting one.

BILL. That's your complaint? *(April laughs.)*

MORSE. My window won't close. It's swelled tight and there is an inch crack that won't close all the way.

APRIL. That's just advancing age, Mr. Morse.

GIRL. You got the same complaint, huh?

APRIL. I wouldn't go that far.

JACKIE. *(Entering, followed by Jamie, who goes immediately to the sofa and sits. To April.)* Listen, April, could I ask you a personal thing — one thing.	MORSE. I put a towel into the crack and I wrapped up my chest and neck, and it still didn't help. And I — I am going
APRIL. I'm just trying to get to bed, lady.	to hold the hotel responsible, I got very little sleep. You're
JACKIE. Sure, right, that's cool. *(To Girl.)* Bitch of a day, ain't it? *(To Bill.)* Listen, Hal — er uh — Bill: I pay my bill, right? I mean, you know the way I do things; like I haven't caused any problems around here —	responsible if something isn't done. Because there's *dampness* in my room. And if I'm taken to the hospital, I'm going to hold the hotel responsible for the bill!

nothing like that — right? That's
not the way I operate…

BILL. *(Overlapping.)* Hold it, I can't hear you both at once. I'll send someone up to close it for you, Mr. Morse. It just needs some weight behind
it. *(To Jackie.)* What is it now?

JACKIE. You're still not calling me Jackie. You know better than that. I like
everything out front. First name.

BILL. I can't remember everybody's name here.

JACKIE. I been a friend here,   MR. MORSE. *(Slight retard.)*
right? To you and these people.   That window should be re-
We don't trespass on people's   paired. If it just needed to be
feelings. Me and my brother   closed, I could close it myself.
don't bother anybody. I mean,   I'm capable of closing my own
we been here what? Nearly a   window. You send a man up
month: You got the rent receipts   there with hammer and nails
there. We been here, we ain't   and tools. I'd do it myself if I
complainers. That ain't the way   had the proper tools. And I'm
we live. We don't have peo-   coming down with a cold. With
ple up to our rooms. *(As Bill*   a severe cold.
is showing no interest.) Second
thought, skip it, I'll wait for Katz.

APRIL. What's the matter, Mr. Morse, lose your tools?

MORSE. There's *dampness* in my *room*

BILL. I'll send someone up to close it.

JACKIE. Sure ain't gettin' any warmer, is it? It's the East Coast. It's bad for
your lungs to live this close to the ocean. It's bad for you.

MORSE. It's bad.

JACKIE. Your throat and chest.

GIRL. I didn't know that.

MORSE. And my health is on the point of breaking.

JACKIE. What's he got? You got a problem with your window? I'll shut it
down for you. Give me your keys; it's no trouble.

BILL. No, no — *(He starts to get up as the phone buzzes.)*

JACKIE. People got to help one another, don't they?

MORSE. *(Taking out his keys.)* I'm coming down with a severe cold and I'm
going to hold this hotel responsible. And my neck is getting stiff.

JACKIE. *(Taking the keys.)* I   BILL. *(Phone.)* Front desk.
believe in helping each other   Yeah. What's that? Nine, three?
where you can. It just needs   *(Writing.)* Is that in Baltimore?

somebody to put a few calories *(Starts to dial, notices Jackie.)*
into it. It's no problem. *(She
goes upstairs.)*

GIRL. Probably just needs a good push.

BILL. *(Phone.)* Hold it. *(Yelling after Jackie.)* Come on! *(To phone.)* Hold it.
(To Jackie.) You! What the hell's her name? Don't go up there. Hey! *(Sotto
voce.)* Son of a bitch. *(Back to phone.)* Yeah?

MORSE. You have no right to object if that young man wants to help me.

APRIL. Mr. Morse, you gotta throw away the mustard plaster and take something worthwhile to bed with you. *(He mutters and heads to the lounge.)*
You want to volunteer, Lilac?

BILL. She's a little young for him, don't you think?

APRIL. That's all right; by the time he gets it up, she'll be old enough.

BILL. *(Phone.)* Four-three-oh-seven. Yeah. Been pretty quiet. No, she paid —

MORSE. There's somebody sleeping in my chair.

APRIL. They eat your porridge you're shit out of luck, ain't you, baby?

GIRL. He's waiting to see Mr. Katz. *(To April.)* You want a cup of tea?

APRIL. Whatta you got? I'd kill for a chicken broth.

BILL. Come on! *(Turning to phone.)* Him too, the both 'em paid: receipts in
the book. Naw. Naw, it's been pretty quiet. O.K. *(Disconnects as Jamie
starts for the stairs.)* Here! Where you going?

JAMIE. *(Freezing.)* I wasn't going any place.

BILL. You just stay down here till she comes back down here. Katz'll be here
in a few minutes.

MORSE. Here. Boy. Where's our board? *(Jamie shrugs hangdog, mumbles.)*
Either you want to play or you don't want to play.

JAMIE. I'll play. *(They look for the board.)*

GIRL. *(To Morse.)* Did you know they were going to tear down the —

MORSE. *What?*

GIRL. *(Louder.)* They're tearing down the hotel; they're gonna tear down this
building.

MORSE. Good!

GIRL. Listen!

APRIL. What? *(A not too distant train bell.)*

GIRL. It's pullin' out.

APRIL. You got the ears of a bat.

GIRL. Holy — it's three hours late now; by the time it gets to Miami, it'll be
six hours overdue again.

BILL. She knows what she's talking about; she's been on all of 'em.

APRIL. Trains give me a pain.

GIRL. I used to live right by a railroad track. I never waved to a single person who didn't wave back to me.

APRIL. The tracks I can take or leave.

GIRL. — If you saw something important to you neglected — like that. They've let the road beds go to hell. You have to close your eyes on a train. Or look out the window. That's still beautiful; some of it. In the country.

MORSE. Where's the board? Bill?

APRIL. The one time I remember taking —

BILL. What? Be quiet a minute. What?

MORSE. Somebody took the checkerboard.

BILL. I got it back here; you left it out. Nobody put it away last night. *(He hands it to the Girl, who takes it to the lounge where Mr. Morse and Jamie begin setting it up.)*

GIRL. Can I watch? *(Nothing.)*

MILLIE. When I was a girl I used to ride back and forth between Columbia and Baton Rouge on the Gulf Raider.

GIRL. I don't think I know that one.

MILLIE. Oh, it's not running any more, I'm sure. It was a wonderfully elegant coach. They had a shower, they had —

GIRL. They had a shower?

APRIL. On a train?

MILLIE. Oh, yes — I'd seen it a number of times. I decided once to take a shower before I retired. I walked the full length of the train in my bathrobe and slippers and shower cap, carrying a towel and my soap. Through the dining cars with everyone having dinner. I'm sure I'm the only person who ever took advantage of the shower. It was a marvelous train, very modern — Art Deco then — chrome and steel. Quite the thing.

GIRL. They used to keep on schedule, didn't they?

MILLIE. Well, I know the service was excellent; and one went from one wonderful terminal to another —

GIRL. — Only you should see them now —

MILLIE. — But the schedules? Oh…they *(Drifting away.)* may have. Maybe not during the war when so many servicemen rode the trains; it seems they used to. It didn't matter so much if you came in a few hours late. I don't know. I've always thought of myself as a bit outside society; I never seem to understand what other people expect.

APRIL. I took a train once, and let me tell you I —

GIRL. — I don't want to hear it. Whatever you did. Whatever it was, I don't want to know.

APRIL. I was eight years old. What could I do?

GIRL. I don't care. Something. You probably got raped. I don't want to hear it.

APRIL. I most certainly did not get raped! I have never been raped! I'd say there was little likelihood of me *ever* getting raped.

MORSE. There's one missing. There's a red checker missing. *(As Katz enters, walking straight to the office.)* Somebody didn't put them back properly.

GIRL. Good morning.

KATZ. *(Taking off his coat.)* Morning. Who's the boy in the lobby?

BILL. Guy says he wants to see you.

KATZ. How long's he been there?

GIRL. Since about four.

BILL. Came in about four; said he'd wait.

MORSE. *(Coming to desk.)* There's a red checker missing from that box.

KATZ. — We've had complaints about your singing in the lobby again.

MORSE. *(Furious.)* Who? Who said anything? I have already complied with those complaints. I ought to do those exercises in my room but I moved to this lobby because people sleep during the day. Those exercises are important to my health. Prescribed by my physician and I —

KATZ. I'm just telling you — you create a scene.

MORSE. Who said it? I have a right to know who said it.

APRIL. Mr. Morse, for a seventy-year-old man with his voice going, you got a healthy set of pipes when you need 'em, ain't you?

MORSE. That singing is necessary to —

APRIL. Honey, I don't mind the singing; I just wish you'd learn the words to the song.

MORSE. — I have a right! —

APRIL. All right, Katz. Speaking of pipes — you know the hot water in this hotel?

KATZ. Yeah?

APRIL. Well, I hate to be the one to tell you, but I think it's coming down with hepatitis.

BILL. Damn it! Here, cover the board. I almost forgot that girl went up to Morse's room.

KATZ. What girl?

BILL. That girl with the brother. She — *(Jackie comes down before he can leave the desk area.)* Don't go up to rooms here. Like that.

MORSE. Those exercises are important to my health.

JACKIE. His window was stuck. I helped him out. He ought to sleep with it open anyway; you can't talk to him about it. *(To Katz.)* Look at this here, now. I been waiting for you to get in. Did you see that Bel-air out there?

KATZ. I don't know, no.

JACKIE. Parked right in front of the door.

KATZ. I didn't see it.

JACKIE. Well, that's my wheels. I bought it two weeks ago. Paid cash. That's the way I like to do things —

JACKIE. Only I can't put it on the road till I get plates. See, I was driving it, but a cop stopped me; 'cause the plates on it don't belong to it.

MORSE. *(Yelling back hoarse-ly.)* People...are not... considerate...of other... people...is my complaint! *(Sits at checkerboard.)*

KATZ. Stopped for what?

JACKIE. For the plates. The plates was expired. Some pig. You're not listening to me —

KATZ. — What do you want? Say what you want. You and your brother both. You've always got angles — angles — I don't have the — *(Shuts up as she rides over him.)*

JACKIE. *(Cued by "brother both.")* Could I have just three minutes of your time? That's all I'm asking, just three minutes of your time. See, the title's clear; it's clear and paid for cash. I got the inspection sticker — never mind what I had to go through — but I can't put it on the road without the plates and the thing is you got to get your insurance to get your plates. I didn't know anything about that 'cause I ain't had wheels in my name before.

KATZ. I don't know nothing about it; I don't drive a car.

JACKIE. *(Overlapping some.)* That's what they told me. I just kept it out of the yard 'cause I told them I was getting the plates. And I went around — never mind where I had to go — what I have to have is Ten, Twenty, and Five. That's what they call it. Ten thousand for a single injury; twenty thousand for a multiple, and five for damages. Collision you don't have to have.

APRIL. I don't know why people have cars.

JACKIE. *(With a glance to her but no pause.)* — 'Course every place has a different price right there you know what kind of a racket they're running. Like the ones you've heard of are way-out-of-sight, off-the-wall clip joints. But the minimum I need for Ten, Twenty, and Five is $165; that's all it'd take to —

KATZ. I can't help you with it —

JACKIE. What with? With what? I'm not asking you for money. I'm not a borrower. I don't take a penny from nobody I don't know. I wouldn't have to pay the hundred, I'd just need sixty-five down and quarterly, if I hadn't got canned from the pet shop — only I wasn't canned. I saw what was coming and walked out on them. The pansy manager was trying to get me fired so his little friend could have my job. I hit him with a birdcage and walked out on the bastard. He kept live snakes as pets, if you want to know the sort of person he was. Let them run loose in the shop at night.

GIRL. You hit him with a birdcage?

JACKIE. He was mincing down the aisle with this stack of birdcages, he made a crack I won't repeat; and I took one of 'em and slapped it alongside his head.

APRIL. I don't know why but I believe that.

JACKIE. He called me up, tried to tell me I owed him for a myna bird. There wasn't no goddamned myna bird in that cage. Where you going? — I'm trying to tell you something.

KATZ. I don't know what you're talking about. I'm working here. I got no time.

JACKIE. *(As Suzy and a client enter.)* I'm telling you. If you'd stop interrupting. I need a friend. I'm in a bind. Straight out — that's the way I deal: I need a friend. That's what I'm saying; I need a pal.

KATZ. *(To Suzy's John who precedes her upstairs.)* Here! Here! Where you going? Has he got a room?

SUZY. I hope you don't mean —

KATZ. — You! Hey, come down here!

SUZY. — What are you doing? Are you crazy? He's a friend of mine! We're going to have a little drink. *(Katz retires.)* If you please. I'd appreciate it if you'd cool down. A little bit here.

SUZY'S JOHN. *(Whispered.)* Come on, Christ.

SUZY. I'm trying to clear up a misunderstanding, here. *(To Katz.)* I don't like to be prosecuted.

APRIL. You don't like what?

SUZY. *(Laughing with her.)* First thing you ever heard me say I didn't like, huh? *(Laughs.)* How about this crummy *weather?*

APRIL. *(Laughing.)* Those are the ugliest shoes I ever saw! *(Both laugh.)*

JACKIE. What's funny about them?

SUZY. She gave me those shoes —

SUZY AND APRIL. Last night. *(They laugh.)*

SUZY. You're three-nineteen.

JACKIE. We're tryin' to transact some business here.

SUZY. Ain't ya? Three-nineteen?

JACKIE. Yeah; me and my brother.

SUZY. I'm four-nineteen. I'm right over you.

SUZY'S JOHN. *(A whisper.)* You're on the fourth goddamned floor of a walk-up?

SUZY. I hope I don't keep you awake.

SUZY'S JOHN. Come on, would you?

JACKIE. You eat good food, you eat natural products, you don't have trouble sleeping.

SUZY. With the noise!

JACKIE. I never noticed no noise.

SUZY. Whadda you mean you never noticed no noise?

JACKIE. I never noticed no noise.

SUZY. *(Furious.)* Well, what the hell, are you deaf? *(April laughs.)* What the hell are you laughing at?

SUZY'S JOHN. Come on, goddamn it. I ain't got all day. Get on with it. *(Touches her lightly.)*

SUZY. Just don't assault me, if you please.

SUZY'S JOHN. I said, I don't have all day. Come on, now, or forget it.

SUZY. *(To others.)* Are you going to allow me to be assaulted?

SUZY'S JOHN. All right, then, forget it.

SUZY. I'm coming. Just don't rush me. These people are friends of mine. Learn to live at a leisurely pace. You live longer.

GIRL. Did you know they're tearing down the hotel?

SUZY. Tonight?

GIRL. We're all going to have to move before long. It's been sold.

SUZY. What do you mean, move?

KATZ. Go on up — not now; everybody does. They're tearing it down. You'll have to find another place.

SUZY. When? What is this? Who said? I don't move for nobody. To hell with it; find another place, where? I got eleven-foot ceilings in my room. Where am I going to find something like that?

KATZ. What do you care what your ceilings are?

APRIL. If you spent as much time looking at the ceilings as she does, you'd care what they looked like.

GIRL. I wonder what's gonna be where my room is? I mean, in that space of air? That space will still be up there where I lived. We probably walk right under and right past the places where all kinds of things happened. A tepee or a log cabin might have stood right where I'm standing. Wonderful things might have happened right on this spot.

APRIL. Davy Crockett might have crapped on the stairs. Pocahontas might of got laid by —

SUZY. *(Overlapping.)* You're horrible! You have no human soul! I thought that was a beautiful thought.

APRIL. People who get Suzy's space are gonna wonder why it's so hot.

SUZY. People who get yours are gonna wonder why it stinks. I hope they do tear it down; this place is disgusting! *(Pushing the john ahead of her.)* I suppose you'll use this as an excuse not to fix the elevator. *(Exits.)*

APRIL. *(To Suzy's john.)* Hey, keep your business out of her filthy mouth, up there!

KATZ. Every morning she's drunk and she acts up like that! *(Beat.)* People! *(Pause.)*

JACKIE. So what I did was, I went to the bank. And they're willing to give me the money, even without the job, if I can get someone to co —

KATZ. *(Overlapping.)* No! No! Can't do it. I'm not in the business. The hotel won't do it and I won't do it personally. Not even if I knew you, and I don't know you.

JACKIE. *(Simultaneously.)* I'm not asking you for anything. It's not costing — I only want you to sign a paper. All I need is a signature. On a paper; your name on a paper.

KATZ. No. No. No.

JACKIE. *(Taking a pear from a paper bag, biting into it furiously.)* Your fuckin' name on a fuckin' piece of paper.

KATZ. Watch your voice.

JACKIE. Forget it. Skip it. I don't need it. Just come out and look at the car. Just see it — see if you —

KATZ. *(Re: a receipt — to Bill.)* What is this? Who signed this?

JACKIE. You got a head harder than a bull's dick, you know that?

KATZ. Go on, don't hang around here with that talk.

JACKIE. We're not bothering nobody. *(Mrs. Bellotti enters and crosses to desk.)*

KATZ. Eat outside.

JACKIE. Eat out, my ass! *(She goes to the lounge.)*

MRS. BELLOTTI. Excuse me, are you Mr. Katz? I expected an older man from your voice on the telephone. It must be wonderful to have a nice position like this at your age. *(April hoots.)* Now, Mr. Katz, you're not gonna kick Horse out, are you? I got a letter from him and he said he was really gonna try hard this time. You're gonna give him one more chance, aren't you?

KATZ. No.

MRS. BELLOTTI. *(Contrite.)* What'd he do?

KATZ. He's crazy. He don't make sense. He don't talk sense. He's crazy.

MRS. BELLOTTI. It's the alcohol, that's what it is. I've told him but he gets out, and he gets so keyed up and nervous and anxious he takes a drink and he can't stop. People don't know what he's really like, like I do.

KATZ. He steals things.

MRS. BELLOTTI. You won't let him come —

KATZ. No. You gotta pick up his things. I told you before.

MRS. BELLOTTI. How can I do that? I'll have to take a little bit at a time. His daddy can't help, he had his leg took off; he can't get outta the house; he's on morphine.

KATZ. Take 'em like you got to take 'em, but take 'em.

MRS. BELLOTTI. What'd he do?

KATZ. He's crazy. Last time I let him come back he stole the telephone outta his room. Tried to sell it back to the hotel. Said there was no telephone in his room.

MRS. BELLOTTI. See. He didn't need the money either. He was making money clammin'. We bought him the rake — he saved eighty-five dollars and bought a boat, and then one day he sells the boat to a guy downtown for ten dollars. He said he wanted to sell something. *(She wanders to the lounge by Jamie and the Girl.)*

GIRL. He won't let him come back?

MRS. BELLOTTI. *(Shakes her head.)* And my husband lost his leg. Did you know that? *(Both Jamie and Girl shake their heads.)* He always had trouble with it. He was a diabetic and he's had to watch what he eats for ten years. We thought he was going to be all right; then he got a craving.

JAMIE. Does he drink?

MRS. BELLOTTI. Oh, no, the doctor won't let him touch it. *(Jamie nods.)* But last summer he got a craving for fruit. He ate fruit all summer and he got worse and worse and...

JAMIE. I thought fruit was healthy for you.

MRS. BELLOTTI. Not for a diabetic. With all that sugar. *(Jamie nods.)* But he craved it. And he had to go to the hospital and they took off his leg.

JAMIE. *(Simultaneous with her.)* Took off his leg.

MRS. BELLOTTI. It was either that or — that was the alternative. And he just got home from the hospital a month ago, and if he sees Horse's things come into the house, I don't know what he'll do. He already sent the neighbor girl I got watching him to the store for apple juice. I came home and he'd drunk a gallon of it.

JAMIE. Our dad died of diabetes.

MRS. BELLOTTI. Isn't it a terrible thing?

JACKIE. Come here. *(Jamie goes to her.)*

MRS. BELLOTTI. I gotta get Horse's things. *(After a beat she gets up with a sigh and goes to the desk.)*

JACKIE. What are you tellin' her?

JAMIE. She was telling me about her husband.

JACKIE. I heard what you said. You want me to leave you again? Is that what you want? *(He sulks.)* You just mind your own business. *(To Millie.)* He's a little mixed up.

MILLIE. I'm sure you'll straighten him out.

JACKIE. I hope that's a friendly remark.

JAMIE. She said her husband —

JACKIE. What have you been up to? Let me smell your breath. *(He resists.)* Let me smell your breath. *(He does.)* Are you tryin' to kill yourself with those cigarettes? Is that what you're doing? Where are they?

JAMIE. I just had one I found in the —

JACKIE. I don't want to know where you found it. Where's your angelica stick? I told you to suck on —

JAMIE. It doesn't work.

JACKIE. *(Getting another.)* That's because you're not sucking on it. You're not sucking it; you're chewing it. Suck it. *(He resists.)* Suck it. *(As everyone turns.)* What the hell you looking at? Ain't you ever heard anybody say suck before?

MRS. BELLOTTI. *(Overlapping.)* Could I have Horse's keys? To get his things? *(She gets them.)*

GIRL. It really doesn't make any difference 'cause we all have to move anyway. They're tearing down the whole building, so we all have to move.

MRS. BELLOTTI. It's just so difficult to find a place that'll take him…

GIRL. I know. *(Mrs. Bellotti goes upstairs.)*

BILL. Whadda you know; you don't even know him.

KATZ. He's crazy.

GIRL. Well, anybody named Horse. By his own mother.

APRIL. Guy last week said I reminded him of his mother. *(Laughs.)* I — No, it's too dirty, I'm not gonna tell it.

BILL. I thought you were going to bed.

APRIL. *(Laughing.)* I kicked him out. I said — I wasn't entertaining no mother... *(Laughing.)* No, it's too dirty.

JACKIE. *(To Jamie.)* Now what's wrong with you?

BILL. *(To Girl.)* You been up the whole night, have you?

GIRL. I'm not sleepy any more; I think I had too much tea to sleep. *(Pause.)*

JACKIE. We'll get someone to sign it; you ain't worried about that, are you? *(Pause.)*

BILL. Don't worry about them; they ain't worth it. *(Pause.)*

GIRL. I'm not; I just don't like to see people need things is all. *(Pause.)*

JACKIE. We put the car on the road, we won't stop till we hit Utah. *(Pause.)*

BILL. Don't you think you better go to bed?

GIRL. I will before long; I don't sleep so much. *(Pause.)* You don't have to remind me; I been up twenty-six hours in a row. *(Pause.)* I just don't like to see people...need things is all. *(Pause.)*

JACKIE. What's wrong? We're gonna be all right. *(Pause.)* You don't have to think about it; I always come through, don't I? *(Pause.)* We put the car on the road, we won't stop till we hit Utah. *(Pause.)* That's what you want, isn't it?

BILL. Everybody needs somethin', babe.

JAMIE. We're not going to Utah.

GIRL. I just don't like to think about it.

JACKIE. Whadda you mean?

JAMIE. We're not going.

BILL. Don't you want anything?

JACKIE. Don't talk so loud.

GIRL. Oh...

JAMIE. We're not going to Utah.

GIRL. I want everything.

JACKIE. Just shut up about it. I told you we'd go.

GIRL. For everybody.

JACKIE. They don't have to know our business.

GIRL. I want everyone to have everything. I really hate spring here. Spring is the messiest thing I ever heard of. Dribble, dribble, dribble for three months straight. The radio said it'd be warm today; it used to rain and then it'd be sunny. I mean, immediately. When I was a kid.

BILL. That was when you was a kid?

MR. MORSE. Your move. *(Jamie moves, Mr. Morse jumps him double.)*

GIRL. It almost never rained anyway. But when it did, just the next day all the cactus would bloom all over.

JACKIE. *(Almost a whisper.)* Miss? You know that loan shop? What time do they open, do you think? Would they be open by eight o'clock?

MILLIE. *(Quite loud.)* The pawnshop? I'd imagine a business like that, they would get an early start.

KATZ. *(Regarding the receipt.)* Whose name is that?

JACKIE. The bloodsuckers.

BILL. *(After a glance at the book.)* Martha? What'd you put here?

GIRL. Oh. That's "Lilac Lavender." Only I wasn't sure how to spell Lilac, so I kinda scrawled it. Whadda you think? *(Both turn back without comment.)*

JAMIE. *(Getting up from the game as the long cry of a train whistle echoes through the lobby.)* I'm going to help that lady move her boy's stuff down.

BILL. Which one is that? Lilac?

GIRL. *(Moving to the lobby.)* That's a freighter. I don't think they even stop here.

MORSE. Here! Where are you going?

JAMIE. I'll come back; I'm not finished.

MORSE. You can't get up in the middle of the game. If you leave the game, I win.

JAMIE. *(From the stairs.)* No, you don't.

MORSE. That's the way I play.

GIRL. *(Giving Paul a gentle push.)* Hey, you said you wanted to see Mr. Katz?

PAUL. *(Stirring.)* Come on... *(Back asleep.)*

BILL. *(Phone.)* Four-three-oh-seven. Yeah. Martha?

GIRL. No joke, Bill, I really hate that name.

BILL. That's who she asked for. Don't take your calls down here.

GIRL. *(Going behind the desk.)* O.K., O.K. *(On phone.)* Hello; hi, Veda.

APRIL. *(Over. Going behind the desk.)* You ever hear the one about the —

BILL. I don't want to hear it.

APRIL. What the hell kind of mood are you in?

BILL. I've had enough of your jokes for a morning.

KATZ. Don't sit back here; come on, there's a coffee shop on the corner.

GIRL. *(To Bill.)* Gotta pencil? *(He gives her one.)*

APRIL. That's pretty good, honey, you get room service. I have to stand on the ever-loving corner.

BILL. Just knock it off.

APRIL. I wasn't talking to you, squirt.

BILL. Come on, get out — you aren't supposed to be behind here. This is private back here.

APRIL. You got a problem, don't take it out on me.

GIRL. Would you stop talking when I'm on the — I'll be there. *(Hangs up.)* That's pretty impolite!

BILL. You too, go on, get on out. You aren't supposed to be here.

GIRL. Mr. Katz said I could take calls here if I was down here instead of in my room.

BILL. Well, it's not my problem; I'm off.

MORSE. Where did he go to?

JACKIE. Just never mind.

APRIL. Where you gotta go?

GIRL. Not far; just up to the Haven Motel.

BILL. Far enough without any sleep.

GIRL. Would you stop being a daddy to me. You want to help, you can give me a lift.

BILL. I'm not giving you a lift; you can take a taxi; tell your john to pay for it.

GIRL. Thanks a lot.

BILL. It's not even eight o'clock in the morning; you're going out to turn a trick. You got to be out of your mind.

APRIL. When we gotta be out of here?

GIRL. You're really an ogre.

KATZ. One month, you gotta be out.

JACKIE. Whadda you mean, one month?

MILLIE. That's what's in the notice.

JACKIE. Let me see; where does it say that? You can't kick us out of here without a notice. Give me my mail. Did I get one?

MILLIE. *(Simultaneous.)* I was going to tell you, but it was a little surprising. I thought you could wait and find out for yourself.

GIRL. One month? Where is Bill going to work?

BILL. Just don't worry about me.	MORSE. Good! Serve you all right!
GIRL. Yeah?	JACKIE. Maybe you don't care
BILL. Yeah. You don't worry about me working and I won't worry about you sleeping.	where you go; I happen to have specific plans.
	MORSE. Right. I don't care.

GIRL. Did you know we were going to all be out in the street in that short a time and didn't tell me or anything?

BILL. You're on the street now. Just because I know something doesn't mean I'm at liberty to tell it.

GIRL. You knew! You knew we were going to have to go. You are really an ogre! You're terrible.

BILL. I'll bet you don't even know what an ogre is.

GIRL. I certainly do; I sleep with five or six every day.

BILL. I don't want to hear about what you do.

GIRL. Well, it certainly isn't any of your business. I don't understand you at all —

BILL. — I don't care what you do with your life —

GIRL. One minute you're friendly and nice and the next minute you're —

What do I care where you go. I'll be glad to get rid of the lot of you.

JACKIE. You dummy, you think you're going to stay here?

MORSE. I don't intend to divulge my plans to anyone here. You aren't the only person with plans.

JACKIE. *(April and Katz are cued in now.)* To hell with it. I don't care. They can tear it down. I'm taking my brother and getting the hell out of here anyway.

MORSE. Good. Nobody cares. We don't care!

JACKIE. Tear it to hell!

MORSE. Tear it to hell! RIP IT DOWN! *(He begins to unpack his barbells.)*

JACKIE. I don't care if you tear it down this week. Because I don't intend to hang around here. That's not the way I am. I don't hang around where the damn building's coming down on my head. Fuck it. I got enough sense to get out when the gettin's good. This place would fall down in another six months anyway!

(Suzy's john comes down the stairs walks directly through the lobby and out the front door.)

BILL. — I just wish you were old enough or mature enough to know what you're throwing away. I personally don't care a dang what —

APRIL. *(Cued above with Jackie's "To hell with it.")* If I'm expected to get out of here before my month's rent runs out, I know somebody who's

GIRL. — as bad as my own daddy. Worse. Because he at least didn't care what I did. He didn't even care if I was a hooker as long as I kept him in enough money to buy beer. That's why I left, only you're worse than he is.

BILL. — you do with yourself or how many ogres you entertain in a day.

GIRL. I'll bet you don't even know what an ogre is!

going to get a fat refund on her bill.

KATZ. Nobody is refunding anything. You stay through June. Nobody's paid past the month of June.

APRIL. Don't expect to see my tail... *(Suzy off, begins to wail.)* till the first of June, daddy. Just let me tell you right now. I don't care if the pipes bust and the place is flooded to the third floor. *(She notices Suzy as she appears on the stairs.)*

SUZY. *(Off. Over Katz, April, Bill Girl, Jackie and Mr. Morse. Cued by April's "Don't expect to see my tail...")* You bastard. What do you think you're doing. Come back here! YOU CHICKENSHIT! *(She appears on the stairs wrapped in a towel and nothing else wailing after the john. Bill turns on the radio furiously.)*

SUZY. Come back here, you fuckin' masochist. He beat me! Why didn't you stop him? He locked the door on me! He pushed me out of my door and locked the door on me! Police! Why aren't you doing something? What do we pay you for, you yellow crud ? Yellow crud!

APRIL. What are you doing with the towel, there, Suzy? *(She laughs.)*

SUZY. *(Each sentence makes April laugh more.)* What the hell are you laughing at? I'd like to see what you'd do. You shut up! You shut up! *(Slaps at her with the towel.)* You're

KATZ. Get upstairs. Get on, get out of the lobby. You can't come down here naked.

JACKIE. What the hell are you doing? *(Mr. Morse begins to march up and down swinging the barbells. Katz catches sight of him now.)*

KATZ. *(To Suzy.)* Suzy, get upstairs. I'm gonna call the cops on you. They would as soon run your ass in again as look at you. Get up to your room. Go on or spend another night in the can; make your choice.

MORSE. *(Singing.)* O sole mio; O sole mio; O sole mio — *(Over and over as he marches on.)*

disgusting! I'm calling the cops! I want to make a complaint! Against April Green! And against the management of this hotel! Scum!

PAUL. (*Waking. Cued by "disgusting."*) What the hell is this? What the hell is going on here? This isn't a hotel; this is a goddamned flophouse! This is a flophouse!

SUZY. You're right; that's exactly what it is; it's a goddamned flophouse. This is a flophouse!

JACKIE. Get your ass back up those stairs. If my brother comes down and sees you like that, I'm going to take you apart. Who the hell do you think you are? I hope to hell they kick your ass out into the street!

KATZ. Get up to your room; what the hell is this? Don't listen to April. Come on. Get upstairs. April, you shut up; I've had it with you two.

JACKIE. (*Over; cued by Paul.*) Right! This is a goddamned flophouse. Exactly. A fuckin' flophouse!

(*Jamie carries a box down the stairs dropping it when he sees the naked Suzy. Staring with his mouth open. The box contains hotel soap, towels, washcloths, etc. and things stolen from the neighborhood shops. Nearly everyone on stage laughs as Jamie gapes at Suzy and the lights fade. The music soars over their laughter. Curtain.*)

ACT TWO

Music from the house fades into the radio. Mrs. Oxenham snaps it off. Natural tableau: In the lounge Millie sits reading a newspaper. Mr. Morse and Jamie study a checkerboard. At the desk, Mr. Katz looks at an open receipt book; Paul leans on the counter watching him. Mrs. Oxenham studies a stack of laundry lists. Afternoon.

Jamie, without moving, studying the board, sucks on a stick of herb candy. This is the only thing happening. Rhythmically: suck — pause. Suck — pause. Suck — pause. Suck — pause. Suck — pause. Suck.

PAUL. *(Finally. Belligerently, which is his nature.)* Are you looking for it or are you doing something else? *(Pause. Katz writes something, frowns at book. Mrs. Oxenham turns a page. Jamie sucks, moves.)*

MORSE. Huh! *(He studies the board. Millie looks up at them, smiles to herself, as she does most of the time, looks back to the paper.)*

PAUL. He left about a year ago, or a year and a half.

KATZ. I told you; he wasn't here. He was somewhere else.

PAUL. He was here. Is this the Hotel Baltimore? Is this 63 East Madison Street? Is this Baltimore? You have people who get mail here who don't live here?

KATZ. Ranger. No.

PAUL. Granger. G. Granger.

KATZ. No, nobody like that.

PAUL. Do you remember every —

KATZ. Ask Mrs. Oxenham; I don't know him. *(Paul looks at him. Takes in air, blows it out. Looks over toward Mrs. Oxenham, begins to move down the counter to her. Mr. Morse moves.)*

MRS. OXENHAM. *(Before he reaches her; suddenly busy.)* I don't remember him.

PAUL. *(Rapid exchange here.)* A little quiet guy; he'd be about sixty-eight or seventy; and he wears a little derby…

MRS. OXENHAM. *(Cutting in.)* No, if he was here I'd remember him.

PAUL. — Not "if." He was here — for two years; he wasn't a transient —

MRS. OXENHAM. — I don't know anything about it —

PAUL. — Well, do you keep records? You keep rent receipts? Do I have to tell you what to do?

MRS. OXENHAM. — I can't take time to go through two years of room receipts looking for someone who never lived here.

PAUL. You don't have to go through them. I'll go through them. You don't have to do squat.

MRS. OXENHAM. You don't have to use that —

PAUL. — I'll go through them if you're paralyzed, lady —

MRS. OXENHAM. — We're not going to turn our records over to —

PAUL. — Listen, I been here twelve hours, all I been getting is a shell game here; you people think you're the C.I.A.

MRS. OXENHAM. We're not at your beck and call. We're doing you a favor.

PAUL. I don't see you doing diddle. *(She glares at him, but in a minute, as a martyr, takes down a stack of record books.)*

MORSE. *(Immediately. As Jamie moves.)* You have to take your jumps.

JAMIE. I don't have to.

MRS. OXENHAM. What name was that?

PAUL. *(Beat.)* Granger. Paul Granger. G-r-a-n-g-e-r! *(Beat.)* P-a-u-l.

MRS. OXENHAM. Sit down; if it's in here, I'll call you. *(Beat.)* When was he here?

PAUL. It's been more than a year — like a year and a half. *(He waits a moment as she begins looking. Then turns.)*

MRS. OXENHAM. *(To his back.)* We're not a missing-persons bureau, you know.

PAUL. *(Sits in the lounge, disgusted. Looks around. Focuses on the checker game. Watches them a moment.)* You play chess? *(Morse and Jamie turn to look at him, then back to the board. Paul looks away.)*

MILLIE. I've been sitting here reprimanding myself for being so unobservant. I was realizing that there are very few people living here whom I would remember a year after they left. They come and go with such a turnover…and if he wasn't obtrusive…

PAUL. He wasn't

MILLIE. I was at work by seven-thirty and usually not back before six; where was he employed, do you know?

PAUL. He wasn't. He was retired. *(Millie goes back to her paper. Paul sulks and lights a cigarette, looks over to Mrs. Oxenham. He becomes aware that Jamie is looking at him. Jamie is trying to frame a request for a cigarette.)* Whatta you gawkin' at? *(Jamie snaps back to the game. Sucks. Morse moves. Millie has glanced up and back down. The switchboard buzzes. The Girl enters, sees a message in her mailbox, goes directly to the office.)*

MRS. OXENHAM. Four-three-oh-seven. We don't do that. I don't know anything about it. Who's calling ? *(To Katz.)* It's another antique dealer about the fixtures.

KATZ. Give them the number.

MRS. OXENHAM. Call Newgate Development RA 6-3700. *(Disconnects. Mrs. Bellotti comes in. She tries to gesture, "I'm going upstairs to —" as Mr. Katz looks up and back down — She drops it and starts on up.)*

GIRL. *(Tosses message in wastebasket. To Katz.)* You know what I've decided, puddin'? They're not going to fix the water or the elevator or anything, are they? They're trying to force us to leave. Aren't they?

KATZ. You got a month's notice; that's the legal notice.

GIRL. Yeah, but you don't expect anyone to live here a month with conditions like that.

MRS. OXENHAM. We've got a man workin' on the boiler right now. I called him as soon as I came in.

MORSE. *(Overlapping, cued by "boiler." The exchange starts low and personal and builds.)* You can't move twice.

JAMIE. I'm not.

MORSE. You took your hand off it.

JAMIE. I did not.

MORSE. You moved your hand; take that back.

JAMIE. I did not.

MORSE. You did so, young man!

JAMIE. I was thinking.

MORSE. You're trying to cheat!

JAMIE. You're a liar! *(Morse takes Jamie's checker from the board and throws it to the floor. Glares at him. Millie follows this exchange, looking from one to the other, just before the action. Paul ignores it to the end or nearly [Beat]. Jamie takes a checker of Mr. Morse's and throws it on the floor. They glare [Beat]. Mr. Morse takes a checker and throws it on the floor. Each further move is an affront. They glare. Jamie getting hurt and belligerent, Mr. Morse angry and belligerent — Jamie takes a checker and throws it to the floor [Beat]. Mr. Morse takes the candy stick from Jamie's mouth and throws it to the floor [Beat]. Jamie takes a pencil from Mr. Morse's pocket, breaks it in his hands, throws it on the floor. Mr. Morse stands. Jamie stands. Mr. Morse takes up the board, spilling the checkers, and with difficulty tears it in two along the spine and throws it on the floor. Jamie glares. Takes up the checker box, tears it in two, and throws it to the floor [Beat]. Mr. Morse overturns Jamie's chair. Now they grapple, slapping weakly at each other and making incoherent noises and grunts, two very weak individuals trying to do injury to each other. Injury would be impossible. When they struggle, Millie stands to get away.)*

MR. KATZ. *(As Jamie tears the box.)* Here, that doesn't belong to you; stop it. Both of you; sit down and act right or you can't stay down here. Come on! Both of you!

GIRL. *(Overlapping.)* Jamie. Shame on you. Come on, stop that, what are you doing; you two babies. Shame on you. Stop fighting. What are you doing? *(Girl reaches them as they separate. Mr. Morse, from humiliation, shuffles directly to the only door in sight.)*

KATZ. *(Also coming from behind the office.)* Where are you going? Here, you can't go in there —

GIRL. Mr. Morse, come back and apologize; don't go in — *(To Katz.)* Oh, he isn't going to hurt anything. My God! *(Morse closes door as she reaches him.)*

KATZ. — Get him out of there.

GIRL. Mr. Morse, you can't go in there, that's the broom closet. *(Knocks.)* Mr. Morse? You're sitting in there on the slop sink, aren't you? With all those smelly mops. Mr. Morse, Jamie's sorry.

JAMIE. *(To her, joining her as Katz picks up checkers.)* I am not!

GIRL. *(Grabbing him, putting her hand over his mouth. The contact of a girl confuses and amazes him as much as the situation.)* He's sorry.

MORSE. *(Offstage.)* No, he isn't.

GIRL. *(As Jamie struggles to talk.)* What?

MORSE. *(Offstage.)* He isn't sorry!

GIRL. You hurt him very badly. *(Jamie struggles to protest.)*

MORSE. *(Offstage. After a beat.)* Where?

GIRL. You blacked his eye. *(Jamie gasps at the scope of the lie.)* *(To Jamie.)* Come here. I want to show you something. *(As she gets her purse.)*

JAMIE. What?

GIRL. *(Digging in her purse, getting out the mascara.)* Something fun.

JAMIE. What? *(Girl spits on the mascara.)* No. No.

GIRL. Hold him, Mr. Katz. *(Katz returning to the desk, gestures, "I want nothing to do with any of you." Hating it, protesting, struggling, Jamie nevertheless lets her put the darkening around his eye.)*

JAMIE. No, no, it's — Don't, come on! Don't mark me up.

GIRL. *(Over.)* Mr. Morse, he's in pain! It's terrible; you ought to be ashamed of yourself, Mr. Morse.

JAMIE. *(The second she releases him.)* Let me see. *(She hands him the mirror.*

Whining.) No...He didn't do... *(Mr. Morse opens the door. Girl takes the mirror. Jamie slaps his hand over his eye.)*

GIRL. Go on — show him, Jamie. Show him what a brute he is. Show him what an ogre he is. *(Jamie does, pouting as though it were real.)*

MORSE. Good. Good. *(Jackie enters. Jamie puts his hand back over his eye and goes to the lounge to pout.)*

JACKIE. *(Livid.)* Is anyone here driving a blue Plymouth? Does anyone in this hotel belong to a blue Plaza 1970 —

KATZ. *(Overlapping.)* What do I know, I don't know what kind — what are you coming in here; you're always upsetting people; accusing people.

JACKIE. *(Less excited.)* — I just wanted to know 'cause I got a scratch on my left front fender about two feet long. People have no respect for other people's property. You just got to learn that and live with it. Let me use your pen. *(Suzy with stoic bearing, walks down the stairs in her most conservative clothes. As Katz glances up, her head raises slightly and she walks on evenly.)* Is today a Jewish holiday? What's happening today? I been to three different pawnshops; they're every one closed.

MILLIE. I think it's Memorial Day.

GIRL. It's Memorial Day today.

JACKIE. The whole damn city's closed up like a nun; something's going on. Is the Post Office closed?

GIRL. Oh, sure.

MORSE. Where's the checkerboard?

KATZ. No more checkers. You get too excited.

JACKIE. What happened? What's wrong with your eye? Who put that goop on you? *(Girl is saying Shhhh!)*

JAMIE. He did.

JACKIE. All right, what's going on?

GIRL. Mr. Morse hit him.

MORSE. *(Overlapping some.)* I hit him.

JACKIE. *(To Jamie.)* You starting fights with people now? *(To Morse.)* Why don't you pick on somebody your own size?

MORSE. That boy is a hellion, and I taught him a lesson

GIRL. We were just kidding around.

JACKIE. *(Spitting on a handkerchief.)* Wipe that off your face.

GIRL. Shhhhhh! *(Jamie takes the handkerchief and sits.)*

MORSE. I hope you've all learned your lesson.

GIRL. You don't know your own strength, Mr. Morse. *(To Jackie.)* It was just a joke.

JACKIE. Well, I don't want people joking with Jamie; he's not in good health.

GIRL. We were just goofing.

JACKIE. *(Going to desk.)* Well, I don't want you goofing with him. *(Paul starts to get up. Mrs. Oxenham gives him a stony look and opens the records. Girl sees him.)*

GIRL. *(To Paul.)* You're still here; I thought you'd be gone. Did you get a room? *(Pause.)*

PAUL. I'm trying to get some information.

GIRL. Are you just in town?

PAUL. Yeah.

GIRL. Where from? *(Beat.)* How did you get here? Train? Hitch? Where's he from, Millie?

MILLIE. I'm sure if he wants you to know he'll tell you.

GIRL. Millie sees things, knows things, she sees ghosts and auras and things. And believes in things, like reincarnation and old Chinese religions like yoga —

MILLIE. I certainly do not. And yoga is something one practices, not something one believes in.

GIRL. Well, then you practice it.

MILLIE. I certainly don't practice yoga.

GIRL. Come on, you know what I mean —

MILLIE. I can't remember someone he'd like me to remember, I don't think he'll be much impressed.

GIRL. Who do you want?

PAUL. Are you one of the residents? How long have you been here?

GIRL. Lived here? Seven months. Before that I was everywhere; I'm from Arizona. Where are you from? *(Paul looks around.)* I'll bet I've been there. I'll tell you the places I've been and you tell me if I name it. 'Cause when I left home I went every place, for almost six months. I didn't stop more than three days in any one —

PAUL. *(Getting up, going to the desk.)* Are you looking for it?

MRS. OXENHAM. When I find something I'll tell you.

GIRL. *(Whispered, to Millie.)* Who's he looking for?

MILLIE. Ask him.

GIRL. Who're you looking for?

PAUL. My granddad. *(Sitting back down.)* You didn't know him. He probably left before you got here.

GIRL. Is he Mr. Morse? Mr. Morse, do you have grandchildren? *(Mr. Morse turns to go.)* You don't have to go.

KATZ. Stay out of that closet.

MORSE. *(Has actually swerved to the closet — now the stairs.)* I'm going to my room!

JAMIE. Good. Good riddance.

JACKIE. *(From the desk.)* Just clam up over there.

KATZ. Come on, don't spread that stuff here.

JACKIE. I'm not bothering you. This is official.

KATZ. Go over there.

GIRL. Don't expect Mrs. Oxenham to help you. She's an ogre. She's not human. *(Distracted.)* Boy, this place. *(Looks around.)* I been up thirty-three hours. I'm not trying to find out your business, I just want to have a conversation. O.K., tell me if this is where you're from. Uh. Denver. Amarillo. Wichita. Oklahoma City. Salt Lake City. Fort Worth. Dallas. Houston. New Orleans. Mobile. Birmingham. Memphis. St. Louis — don't look down, I'm watching your eyes to see if you make a move when I say the right one. Kansas City. Omaha. Des Moines. San Francisco. Portland. Seattle. Spokane. Minneapolis. St. Paul. Milwaukee. Chicago. Indianapolis. Cincinnati. Columbus. Cleveland. Pittsburgh. Buffalo. Albany. Utica. Boston. New York. Providence. Atlanta. Tallahassee. *(Paul begins to smile.)* Orlando. Tampa. Jacksonville. Daytona Beach. Palm Beach. Fort Myers. Fort — Fort Lauderdale! Fort Lauderdale!

PAUL. *(Smiling.)* No.

GIRL. Fort Myers.

PAUL. No.

GIRL. You smiled.

PAUL. I'm not from Fort Myers.

GIRL. Then where? St. Louis.

PAUL. No.

GIRL. 'Cause that's when you looked away.

PAUL. You haven't been to those places.

GIRL. I certainly have.

JAMIE. You've been to Salt Lake City?

GIRL. I been to every state in the Union. Some of them three times.

PAUL. That'd cost about —

GIRL. Yeah, I sold cookies. Come on, you're trying to distract me. Los Angeles.

PAUL. No.

GIRL. Bakersfield.

PAUL. No.

MILLIE. Louisville. *(He looks at her — reaches for the paper, she hands it to him.)*

PAUL. Where is it? *(He hands it back to her, she finds the item and returns the paper to Paul.)*

GIRL. *(Overlapping the action. Amazed.)* Is that *right?* I would have *said* that.

JAMIE. Come on.

GIRL. *(To Jamie.)* I would. I've been there. I went from Knoxville to Chattanooga to Nashville to Evansville to Louisville to Cinci — *(She notices something is wrong.)* What? *(Paul hands her the paper. She glances down, then up.)* Your name's Paul? *(Back to the item.)* The third. What's St. Clemens?

PAUL. *(Pause.)* It's a work farm.

GIRL. What'd you get busted for?

PAUL. Selling grass.

GIRL. They give you two years —

PAUL. Shhh!

MILLIE. *(Whisper. At the same time.)* Now, not so —

GIRL. — for selling grass?

PAUL. You're supposed to drink sour-mash whiskey. You're not supposed to be selling grass. I was an example. They like their students drunk, they don't like them —

GIRL. You were in *school* and they gave you —

PAUL. Shh — come on.

GIRL. In college? *(Pause.)* I'm impressed. I didn't even make it past junior year in high school. I hated it.

PAUL. Don't let it bother you. It's just a way to keep the kids off the street.

MILLIE. It doesn't seem to be working, does it?

GIRL. *(As Paul smiles at Millie's joke and she smiles back.)* Boy, I was terrible in high school. I failed every subject except geography. I was pretty good in history but I was a genius in geography. Naturally, I'd be good in something I couldn't possibly use. Actually, I do use it, though. Like when a john is shy or weird or something, I can ask him where he's from and get him talking. I don't think that's what Mrs. Whitmore had in mind when she taught us geography. *(Beat.)* You're looking for your granddad? Did he just disappear? While you were — "working"? Will they look for you?

PAUL. No. Do you mind?

GIRL. Did you just sneak off?

KATZ. *(To Jackie.)* What are you doing? What are you spreading that stuff around?

JACKIE. Come on, man, you're impossible; I'm not bothering you.

KATZ. You are. Bothering me. Go over there; get this stuff —

JACKIE. All right, come on. *(Gathering it up.)* I don't need a hassle. *(Moving.)* Man, I can't get my blood sugar up today. *(Sitting in lounge. Dumping her papers on the table: change-of-address cards, a copy of* Organic Gardening, *etc.)* I got about a dozen things to do here. I walked all over town this morning. We're getting out of here tomorrow.

JAMIE. Yeah?

JACKIE. I go to that insurance place; they give me a receipt for my money; I get that paper in my hand and we're gone. *(Mrs. Bellotti comes down the stairs, carrying a box, and exits.)*

GIRL. *(Almost a whisper.)* She's taking out her son's clothes. She's got a husband with his leg off, and her son's been kicked out of here, and the father has sugar diabetes and hates the son anyway. God. I hear something like that and I just want to lock myself in the bathroom, order a sausage and anchovy pizza, and eat the entire thing. *(Pause.)* I occupied the bathtub on my floor once for three straight hours. You know those assorted boxes of bath salts with eight different scents? I put in all eight. I called the Pizza Shack — they'll deliver any time of the day or night anywhere in the city. I have their number on my wall about that big, like it was one of those numbers you call in case of emergency. I ordered a pizza; I filled up the tub and sat there for three solid hours. There wasn't a single bubble in the tub by the time I got out. It took me the rest of the day to unpucker. Of course… *(Raising her voice, using Jackie's magazine for a megaphone.)* …Now, that's out. There's no more hot water. They're trying to get rid of us.

JACKIE. Come on, don't mess with that. I mean, you can look at it but don't mislay it.

GIRL. What is it?

JACKIE. *(Continuing to fill out the cards; tossing it off.)* That magazine you can't get on a newsstand. You have to order that magazine to come to your home. I gotta look up their offices 'cause I have to send them one of these change-of-address cards. You subscribe to it. You get one a month. It's fantastic. *(Pausing in her work a second.)* You know anything about growing rice?

GIRL. What?

JACKIE. Growing *rice?* It's a water plant, isn't it?

GIRL. I don't know.

JACKIE. 'Cause rice is nature's most perfect food. Because of the balance of its nutrients. That's what this country ought to be growin' instead of all that fuckin' wheat. You know those plants out past Fort McHenry? You know what they do?

GIRL. They're sugar plants, I thought.

JACKIE. Refining. Sugar refining. They take natural sugar and turn it into shit. And then they pollute the atmosphere doing it. You can't get people to care about the environment. Of their own planet. Did you see *Planet of the Apes?*

GIRL. No. I wanted to.

JACKIE. Well, they knew what was happening. *(Back to the magazine.)* You ought to read that. You know the great discoveries? Like the discovery of bacteria; and the discovery of uranium; the discovery of sulphur drugs? Like that?

GIRL. *(Serious, nodding.)* The discovery of penicillin…

JACKIE. Right. Well, the next major discovery — scientists are going to find this out, they're gonna be researching this. These people in this magazine already know it. *(Pause.)* Garlic.

MILLIE. What?

JACKIE. *Garlic.* It's biodegradable. *(Millie and Paul watch without expression; the Girl listens seriously; Jamie is aghast but excited.)* You know DDT is out; DDT is killing us. You know that. *(Pause.)* Garlic juice. Has in it… *(Reaching for the magazine.)* …this is just one aspect; it has about four separate aspects… *(Finding it.)* …it has in it three separate "All-i-um Sul-phates." Three separate killers. Bug killers. Which just happen to be the three separate strongest bug killers known to man. *(Jamie says with her, "known to man.")* There's three different articles about garlic in this one issue.

GIRL. Is it all right to eat it? Because I've eaten it.

JACKIE. Sure, it's good for you. That's the amazing thing. But — for the insecticide, what you do is: you take — this is what we're going to do. We may be the first. On this scale. You take detergent suds, and the juice from Mexican hot peppers, and garlic juice. And you mix those together and it'll kill anything.

MILLIE. I'd think it would.

JACKIE. But it won't hurt the worms. The earthworms. That's what you want, because they're necessary to you.

GIRL. What are they for?

JAMIE. *(As Jackie starts to speak.)* Air.

JACKIE. A — a bunch of things. Different things. Where's your candy? *(Jamie looks at Mr. Katz.)* And…well, look at this. You probably never saw anything like this before. For real. *(She takes a paper from her purse — quite proud.)* That's a deed. A land deed. *(Hands it to the Girl.)* That's for twenty acres. That's where our money went; that's a pretty good investment, considering. That's fifteen dollars an acre. We heard it advertised on the radio.

GIRL. That's fantastic. Where? *(She hands it to Paul.)*

JACKIE. *(Looking over Paul's shoulder.)* It's all in here — we have to find it — "Two miles —" It goes for miles — that's how big it is — "south of Pepin and six miles west of —"

GIRL. Carter. Sure. Utah.

JACKIE. We were driving down from Buffalo, we heard —

GIRL. Are you from Buffalo? I didn't know that.

JACKIE. We was headed down to Florida to work on the crops; we heard this offer — I said to hell with pickin' somebody else's tomatoes; we'll raise our own crops.

GIRL. *(Unsure.)* Sure…

JACKIE. We don't need no house. We're sleeping in a sleeping bag. If it rains, it gets nasty, we sleep in the car. We get sick of that, we move into a motel.

GIRL. How do you know there's a motel? If you've never been there?

JACKIE. Of course there's a motel; the country's gone to shit; there's always a motel.

GIRL. Don't you hate it? I spent the entire morning in a motel listening to some wheeler-dealer buying and selling most of the lumber south of the Mason Dix — *(Suddenly.)* Wait! Wait! Millie! Could I buy a railroad? Could I buy stock in a railroad? If I gave you six hundred dollars, could you go wherever it is and buy stock for me? Or could you take me there? And introduce me to your broker? Do you have a stockbroker?

MILLIE. No — I never had any interest in it; I only invested because there wasn't anything particular that I wanted. I wasn't interested in the stock —

GIRL. — You could go to the annual meetings; you could speak out —

MILLIE. — Oh, I don't know anything about it.

GIRL. You could tell them to shape up. Will you introduce me?

MILLIE. Surely; one day, if you're interested…

GIRL. Not one day. Not today because it's a holiday, but tomorrow.

MILLIE. Well, if you're still interested in it and you —

GIRL. — Come on, say yes.

MILLIE. If I feel like it, if you remind me.

GIRL. You don't live on this planet, Millie, you really don't.

MILLIE. No, I know, I never seemed to connect with the things —

GIRL. — I mean you're so sweet; a person just forgets completely how batty you are.

MILLIE. Fairly batty, I believe.

GIRL. Really, completely crackers sometimes.

MILLIE. — Well, not so bad as that, maybe —

GIRL. — But intelligent and all, you know —

MILLIE. — Oh, I was never completely stupid; just outside, I'm afraid, with no particular interest in peering in. When I realized that so much of people's preoccupation was in worldly houses, I realized that —

GIRL. I like that — worldly houses.

MILLIE. — that I was quite outside. I was one of fourteen, you know. I was the youngest of —

GIRL. Fourteen brothers and sisters?

MILLIE. Oh, I come from an enormous family; it wasn't at all unusual at the time; a huge old Victorian house outside Baton Rouge; an amazing old house, really, with — when you ask about spirits — oh, well, you couldn't keep track of them all. Banging doors, throwing silverware, breaking windows. They were all over the house. There was a black maid — slave girl, I suppose, and a revolutionary soldier and his girl, and a Yankee carpetbagger, and a saucy little imp of a girl who sashayed about very mischievously. She'd been pushed out of a window and was furious about it. Storming through the upstairs, slamming windows shut all over the house. It was quite an active place.

GIRL. Oh, I love it.

MILLIE. And when my aunt died — a wonderful old lady. It had been her husband's house. I must have been only eight or nine. She died and her sisters and brothers — my father even — scrabbled over her silverware and clothes and jewelry. Even the pots and pans. One cook ran off with all the cooking vessels. None of the things meant anything to my aunt, of course; she hardly realized she had them. I remember my father, with a Georgian silver teapot in one hand and an epergne in the other, yelling, "If Ariadne were alive she'd be scandalized!" And I thought, no, she wouldn't, Daddy, she'd be very amused. At all of you.

GIRL. And you're like her.

MILLIE. Not really. I'm very silly; she was quite a marvelous lady. You couldn't be like that today.

GIRL. I think you are. You had a cook? Who ran away with the —

MILLIE. Oh, yes, for some reason she decided to take every kerosene lamp and taper in the house. My uncle had been very frugal about them, so I suppose she thought they were valuable. She ordered a wagon and loaded it full. She was so foolish, that poor woman. Completely mad, of course. A wonderful old battle-ax. Carrying off vast old zinc tubs — four feet across. God knows what use they had, and big old copper vats and pans, skillets, spoons, wooden spoons, even the slop jars. While everyone was upstairs squabbling over the linen. They came down for supper — we had an enormous old-fashioned wood stove in the kitchen; she had managed to dismantle half of that before she gave up. *(Chuckles.)* I still remember all of them sitting around in the dark eating bread and jelly sandwiches. There wasn't even a coffeepot!

PAUL. I don't get it.

MILLIE. *(Hand on his knee, embrace.)* Nor did I, Paul, I didn't get it at all. But I thought it was very amusing. *(Beat.)* Spirits are very peaceful, of course. They don't act up unless there's tension in a household. But oh, my! That night! Did they carry on! You've never heard such caterwauling!

GIRL. Oh! I want to see it! Spirits doing that! Don't you hope it's true? I mean scientifically true? I want them to come up with absolute scientific proof that there are spirits and ghosts and reincarnation. I want everyone to see them and talk to them. Something like that! Some miracle. Something huge! I want some *major miracle* in my lifetime!

JACKIE. Did you know the first two hours after you pick them, green beans lose twenty percent of their vitamin C?

GIRL. How much have you got?

JACKIE. A lot, but you shouldn't eat them. What you should eat is kale.

JAMIE. Kale.

JACKIE. It's a kind of lettuce. And lettuce has opium in it — if you know how to get it out.

JAMIE. *(With her.)* ...to get it out.

MRS. OXENHAM. *(As Mrs. Bellotti comes in and goes upstairs.)* Here's your party. Young man?

PAUL. *(Jumping up — going to the desk.)* Me?

MRS. OXENHAM. This isn't going to tell you anything. It's just a rent receipt.

PAUL. Is that your signature?

MRS. OXENHAM. I can't remember every person who pays rent here two years later.

PAUL. He was very quiet and neat. He wore a derby. He had a very soft voice and he was — shit, don't you ever look at people?

MRS. OXENHAM. That's all I can tell you, I told you it wouldn't do any good.

PAUL. Do you remember if he left a forwarding address?

MRS. OXENHAM. We don't accept forwarding addresses.

PAUL. Grayish hair and —

MRS. OXENHAM. That's all I know; I don't remember him.

PAUL. Would you remember it if he fell dead in the lobby? If he was found in his room —?

MRS. OXENHAM. That didn't happen. *(Phone.)* Front desk. *(Writes down a number, looks in the book, and dials.)*

GIRL. He wore a derby?

PAUL. He was a workman. When he retired he wore a suit and a derby, because he wanted to look like he was retired...

GIRL. What is a derby? Really? *(Pause.)* Are you from a poor family?

PAUL. No.

GIRL. Oh. Were you close? To him? *(Pause.)*

PAUL. He squinted a little...

GIRL. You were, weren't you? Close.

PAUL. He wanted to come live with Mom and Dad, and they wrote him they didn't have room for him. They didn't want him. *(To Millie.)* He sang songs...all the time...under his breath...my sister...

GIRL. What? Your sister?

PAUL. She talked about him all the time...she told me about...what he was...like — like what he was like.

GIRL. She told you? Didn't you — ever meet him?

PAUL. How could I meet him, I was always off in some goddamned school.

GIRL. And you want —

PAUL. *I* want him! *I* have room for him!

GIRL. Well, don't take it out on me.

JACKIE. Where did he work?

PAUL. I called them. They started getting his pension checks back — they don't know where he is...

JACKIE. You finished with that, I don't want to lose that. *(Magazine — Girl hands it to her.)*

GIRL. What did he do?

PAUL. He worked. Mother's family had about a billion dollars' worth of whiskey distilleries — that's why Dad married — Granddad kept right on working. They were all so damn high-society they wouldn't associate with anyone like —

GIRL. You don't talk to the person you're talking to. Did anybody ever tell you that? You talk to yourself. You don't look at people.

PAUL. *(Glowers at her. Finally.)* He was an engineer.

GIRL. Oh, God; every boy in Phoenix Central High was "going into engineering"; that's all they ever talked about was their T squares and slide rules. I never did tell them I didn't know what engineering was; maybe you can tell me. What'd he do? Exactly?

PAUL. *(Glowers.)* He was —

GIRL. — Relax.

PAUL. Huh?

GIRL. Relax. You're all tense. You're just like a — You're all tense. *(Pause.)* What'd he do? *(Pause.)*

PAUL. Who?

GIRL. Your granddad?

PAUL. He was an engineer. For the railroad. He drove the Baltimore and Ohio between —

GIRL. *(On "Ohio" standing, bursting into tears.)* NO! No! Oh! Oh! He drove a train! Oh, I want to meet him! I want to talk to him!

PAUL. Well, you find him; you think of a way and I'll let you talk to him.

GIRL. Somewhere! You don't know. How I feel! You can, too. If he was here, of course you can find him. Stay for Bill; I'll help you. Oxenham isn't any good, she wouldn't look for her own grandfather — and I don't even know the day people; the afternoon people are temporary and, anyway, I got to get some sleep and Bill comes on at twelve.

PAUL. I was here last night.

GIRL. Yes, but you didn't tell us what you were doing — dummy — why didn't you say something?

PAUL. I gotta be somewhere tomorrow.

GIRL. Come on, everyone's gotta be somewhere tomorrow; I want to meet him. Where was his run? Do you know? Did you know him at all?

JACKIE. Come on, don't jiggle the table.

MILLIE. I think — *(Mr. Morse has been coming down the stairs — He works his mouth, waves his arms, but no words come out. Millie stands. Katz goes to him. Mrs. Oxenham stands. The Girl sees him. Jackie does too. Finally, almost reaching the landing.)*

MORSE. Been-been-taken-everything-that-person. I been robbed. I been robbed.

KATZ. What? *(Jackie starts to leave.)*

MORSE. That person.

KATZ. Where you going? You were up there, weren't you?

JACKIE. I got things to attend to.

KATZ. You're not attending to no more business for a minute.

JAMIE. She didn't touch your things. She hasn't been near your things.

KATZ. You just keep out of it.

JACKIE. I helped him out with a problem he had. I don't know what you're talking about. You been picking on me ever since I came here. That's all you know, because you don't like the way I look or the way I dress or something! You don't like the way I live!

MORSE. That's the person. Took my wife's things. That's all I have in this world.

JAMIE. She didn't go up there.

KATZ. All I'm saying is, give it back. Turn it over to him. And all of it and this minute. Everything you took. What's missing, Mr. Morse? What are you missing from your room?

MORSE. What?

KATZ. What's gone, what are you missing?

MORSE. My things! My wedding cuff links and my necklace that belonged to my wife! And my mother!

JACKIE. Yeah, well, I didn't take his fucking mother; he's crazy.

MORSE. And four rings; a gold ring and a sapphire ring and — I don't remember...

JACKIE. *(Overlapping from "sapphire.")* I got things to do — you can search my car and you can search my room — I've got nothing to hide; we got business.

KATZ. *(Grabbing her.)* You're not leaving.

JACKIE. Why me? Why not somebody else? Let me go or I'll kill you, you son of a bitch —

KATZ. *(Struggling with her.)* Give me her purse — *(Girl shakes her head.)* Give me her damn — *(Wrenching it away from her, dumping it on the floor.)* I been listening to you talking about pawnshops.

JACKIE. *(Flailing; but held back by one arm.)* No; get out of my personal things. That belongs to me — those things belong to me. *(As Katz finds a knotted silk man's sock at the bottom of her purse.)* That ain't his. Stop it!

MORSE. Give me that! Give me my things! *(Katz hands it to him.)*

KATZ. That right there could get you ten years!

JACKIE. *I got dreams goddamn it! What's he got? (Katz lets go of her. Morse goes to the stairs. She sags into a chair.)* What's he got?

MORSE. *(Deeply shaken.)* I'm going to report this incident.

KATZ. You're going up to your room. You got your stuff — is that all of it?

JACKIE. *(Weakly.)* You robbed me.

MORSE. I'm calling the police.

JAMIE. I'll beat you up!

KATZ. Your phone's out of order. It's your own damn fault to let people in your room.

MORSE. *(Going up and off; mumbling.)* I have my rights.

KATZ. You got no rights here. *(To Jackie.)* I want you and your brother both out of here tonight.

JACKIE. I'm paid up here till —

KATZ. I'll refund your rent money — out tonight, or I turn you in myself.

GIRL. Not from Mr. Morse. He doesn't have anything. He never hurt anybody.

JACKIE. You ripped off one of your scores, you told me so.

GIRL. He could afford it.

JACKIE. Just because you have protection. *(Returning pen.)* I don't want you thinking I'm taking your fuckin' ink pen. *(At desk.)*

GIRL. I wasn't going to tell you, but you got nothing.

JACKIE. I got what I need.

GIRL. That land you got won't grow nothing. I know that place. I may not know much but I know that —

JACKIE. What are you talking about? You're a liar — you don't know anything about it. That's farmland.

GIRL. — because I been there. On the Rio Grande Zephyr. It's nothing but a desert — a salt desert, it don't even grow cactus. Six miles west of Carter, two miles south of Pepin — it's desert for a hundred miles.

JACKIE. It's farmland! That's farmland! I got brochures. I got pictures.

GIRL. Even I know better than to buy land from the radio. You can't get farmland for that price nowhere. You ought to be ashamed of yourself, robbing Mr. Morse.

JACKIE. *(Snatching up the deed putting it in her purse.)* I know what I'm doing for my brother and... *(Goes about collecting her things — she knows instinctively that it is true.)* You may not know anything about growing...we know what we're doing. *(She blindly collects her papers stuffing them into her bag. Pause.)*

JAMIE. That's not fair…

JACKIE. Be still.

GIRL. Or maybe…maybe I'm wrong. Maybe I have it mixed up. I don't want to hurt anybody.

JACKIE. Ain't nobody been hurt by you or…

JAMIE. Anybody. *(He is about to burst into tears.)* You're —

JACKIE. *(Crying out.)* Shut up! *(Looks around, sits, falls into a chair.)* Boy…everything I try… *(Pause.)* I liked you, too, Well. We live and learn. *(Getting up, taking her purse and bag.)*

GIRL. Oh, Jesus.

JACKIE. Come on. We're gonna go eat. *(Jamie goes out.)* We were getting out of here tomorrow, a few hours one way or the — *(The energy drains from her, her mind scattered, she stands blindly holding back tears.)*

GIRL. Jackie? *(Jackie starts and runs out, the Girl runs after her.)* Maybe it was a lie. I was just mad. I haven't had any sleep. Forget I said it. Please. *(Mrs. Bellotti immediately comes down the stairs and follows them out, carrying another box. Millie has moved to the shadows of the stairway. Paul stands in the center of the lobby.)*

MILLIE. Your grandfather is alive, Paul. *(The lights begin to fade. He looks for her, sees her.)*

PAUL. Where is he?

MILLIE. Oh, I have no idea. I don't know him. I never met him. I only know that he isn't dead.

PAUL. How do you know?

MILLIE. I don't know how I know. I never know how I know; I just know he isn't dead. *(Millie and Paul freeze. The lights are very dim. Katz and Mrs. Oxenham prepare and leave. Bill enters and turns on the radio. Millie moves upstairs. Paul stares after her as the music from the radio spreads to the house and the lights dim out.)*

ACT THREE

Midnight. On stage, Bill and Mr. Morse. Bill is at the switchboard. Mr.
Morse sits in the lounge, not at ease. Bill opens a bag from a deli and takes
out a sweet roll. He takes a sip of coffee from a paper container. He glances
at a note left on the board, plugs in the board while still standing, glancing
at the clock. Rings. Sips coffee.

BILL. It's twelve *(Glance at clock.)* oh-six. You getting up? Good morning —
Billy Jean, Lilac Lavender, Martha. No, no talk, come down if you want
to gab. *(As April appears, descending the stairs, wearing a long diaphanous*
gown.) April's down here.
APRIL. *(To herself.)* Down, down, down...
BILL. No, I got work to do. *(Disconnects, smiling at the phone. Then to April.)*
Look at you, done up fit to kill.
APRIL. That seems to be the consensus. Evening, Mr. Morse, baby.
BILL. One of those nights, huh?
APRIL. Bill, tonight wasn't even in the book. You see that john just walked
out of here?
BILL. Didn't pay any attention to him.
APRIL. Just the least bit flaky.
BILL. Yeah? What's the problem?
APRIL. If my clientele represents a cross section of American manhood, the
country's in trouble.
BILL. I'd think it would be.
APRIL. I don't need it from you this morning. I called Martha's pizza palace
and ordered a pizza, that's how bad it is.
BILL. That bad, huh? You get to bed?
APRIL. *(She laughs.)* No, Bill, what can I tell you? It was one of those nights.
The room got a workout. I turned fifteen on the floor, twenty in the tub,
and fifteen across the top of the dresser. I'm not lying. Definitely flaky.
Usually I can count on one in five getting a little experimental.
BILL. Not today, huh?
APRIL. Today we drew a full house. *(Laughs.)* Guy says, "What's that?" I say,
"That's the tub, that's where I keep the alligator, better stay back: You
ain't got nothing you can afford to lose." Says, "I'd kinda like to make it
in the tub." I say, "Honey, look you ever see one of these? It's a bed. It's
kinda kinky but let me show you how it works." End up, we make it in —

BILL. *(Said with her.)* In the tub.

APRIL. Right. Tell him all we got is cold water, it's gonna do you no good; nothing would do. *(Laughs.)* He gets in, sits down, I turn on the water and nearly scalded his balls off.

BILL. I got it fixed.

APRIL. Yeaaah! Spanking red from the butt down. Loved it. Stayed in for twenty minutes. Very groovy experience for him. If I knew he was coming, I'd have dug out the rubber duck.

BILL. Anything to get somebody to like you.

APRIL. Like me? Pay me. They know me from the wallpaper. *(To Mr. Morse.)* Don't they, darlin'?

MR. MORSE. It's too hot.

APRIL. You noticed that, did you?

MR. MORSE. It's no good for my health. You got to have circulation of air. This hotel is overheated. They're trying to make us all sick.

APRIL. See that. There's always a logical explanation for everything.

GIRL. *(Entering in a terry robe and slippers.)* Morning, Bill. Morning, honey.

BILL. You get any sleep?

GIRL. Did I? I fainted. Besides, with Oxenham guarding the gates, there wasn't any point. She is absolutely no help at all. Where's Paul? That guy?

BILL. No messages.

GIRL. You seen him since you been on? That guy who fell asleep in the lobby last night.

BILL. Went out; left his bag.

GIRL. *(Shaking herself awake.)* Oh, golly! Brufff! Oh, it's getting warm. Cross your fingers. Maybe it's finally spring.

BILL. Supposed to get up to seventy today.

APRIL. Two more weeks and everything will stink.

GIRL. *(Taking a bit of his roll.)* Anyway, we got a project.

BILL. You do, huh? Come on, that's breakfast.

GIRL. Not *me.* We do. *(She goes to the files.)*

BILL. Don't pull that crap — what are you doing?

GIRL. Didn't your mother ever tell you; the first warm day you start the cleaning. *(Occupied with pulling out boxes of files.)*

BILL. *(Over.)* No joke, that stuff's dirty. Wear some clothes when you come down here.

GIRL. Come on, I told Paul you'd help him or he would have given up, so you got to help too.

BILL. Oxenham will have your hide; you know that.

GIRL. I'll put them back. I figure there are all those boxes in the basement. I can go through those too.

BILL. What boxes?

GIRL. Don't you even explore your own place of business?

BILL. *(Buzzer rings.)* I just work here. There's rats down there; you can't go down — come on. *(As she dumps a pile of boxes.)* What are you doing? What do you want with those?

GIRL. Answer your phone.

BILL. *(Into the phone.)* Hold it.

GIRL. That fellow who was here —

APRIL. Freak.

GIRL. That freak who was here is looking for his "long-lost granddad." Everyone has been about as helpful as a stick. And we're going to find some trace of the old man. Something to go on.

BILL. *(Phone.)* Yeah? *(Dials.)* Don't pull those things out here.

GIRL. Don't you like mysteries? Don't you want to help someone? Besides, you're going to anyway, because I volunteered you. The man may be lost; he may have amnesia; he was a trainman, Bill. He drove the B and O for twenty-six years. And he's in there.

BILL. *(Phone.)* They don't answer. *(Disconnects.)* I don't know where the hell you get your energy. How long did you sleep?

GIRL. Long. Six hours or more. April, where were you for the action? You missed the excitement.

APRIL. I saw plenty of action; you're right, I missed the excitement.

GIRL. Did you hear about the — Did you tell them, Mr. Morse?

APRIL. Mr. M. is none too spry tonight.

GIRL. Where are they? Jackie and Jamie? Did they leave?

BILL. Who's that?

APRIL. Flotsam and Jetsam?

BILL. Note here says three-nineteen's checking out. Car's not out front.

APRIL. Don't tell me that heap actually moves.

GIRL. It better move, they've been eighty-sixed.

BILL. *(Mock disappointment.)* Awww, that's too bad.

GIRL. I gotta have something. You want a cup of tea?

BILL. I could stand a cup of tea. There any water in there?

GIRL. Yeah, it's fine. April?

APRIL. Huh? Yeah, sure. What?

GIRL. Tea. Mr. Morse?

APRIL. Like a cup of tea, Mr. Morse?

MORSE. Too hot.

GIRL. This will take forever.

JAMIE. *(Entering.)* Has Jackie been here?

BILL. Don't know; I just got on. *(Sotto voce to April.)* Is he Flotsam or is he —

APRIL. He's a sweetie, aren't you, baby? We thought you were gone. Is who here?

JAMIE. Is Jackie back yet?

APRIL. Ain't seen — her. Where's she supposed to be?

JAMIE. *(Looking at the Girl.)* She went to get gas for the car.

GIRL. Morning, Jamie. Are you speaking to me? *(Beat.)*

JAMIE. Morning.

GIRL. You look sleepy; you sleepy? *(He is — shakes his head no.)* What time did you get up?

JAMIE. Six.

APRIL. You had a nap?

GIRL. Six this morning?

JAMIE. Every morning.

APRIL. You helping her carry things down?

JAMIE. She took her stuff — I have to take my own, though. That's the way we do it.

GIRL. *(Back to files.)* This is going to be a snap.

APRIL. What time did she go out for gas? *(Beat.)*

JAMIE. 'Bout six.

APRIL. This evening. Well, see, she's probably looking for natural gas.

JAMIE. No lead.

APRIL. *(To Bill.)* No way. *(Phone buzzes.)*

BILL. Four-three-oh-seven.

APRIL. *(To Jamie.)* Honey, I don't really think it's necessary to drag down a lot of things till she gets here.

JAMIE. *(He looks to the front door and hardly takes his eyes off it.)* This is it.

BILL. *(Holding receiver.)* Billy Jean? Billy Jean?

GIRL. "Billy Jean"? That's three weeks ago. I can't, I'm in the middle — ask who it is — he won't tell you.

APRIL. Here! *(Rushes to the phone.)* Hello, this is Miss Billy Jean's "girl"; she's in the tub; could I ask who's calling her, please? *(Pause.)* Umm hmmm. I'll tell her. It's Mr. Last-month-all-night-at-the-Statler-Hilton, madam, shall I toss him in?

GIRL. Oh, God. What do you call it when a guy has really terrible breath?

APRIL. Par for the run.

GIRL. Well, this guy has a terminal case of par for the run. *(Gives herself completely to phone.)* Hi. You're back. Of course I do, silly, Penthouse B.

APRIL. *(Poking Bill.)* Penthouse B.

GIRL. It's great to talk to you; only I'm freezing. I will not, you could get electrocuted.

BILL. For what?

APRIL. Talking on the phone in the tub.

GIRL. Well, that's a lot better, only I can't. Mom's in town; isn't it a drag? You did? Was that all you liked? That wasn't my fault if I got a little carried away. Listen, could I send over a great friend? *(April laughs.)* O.K., then just call Veda. But you call me back when you're in town again, you hear? I won't promise anything; not with you. Bye, bye. *(Hangs up.)* Jesus. Can you imagine the drag? Dinner and eight hours in the feathers and he thinks he's Rockefella giving you fifty dollars.

BILL. I don't like you taking those calls down here.

GIRL. You gave it to me. *(Back to books.)* I mean, if a person is interested in making any money, the man ought to realize. The money's in turnover, not in lay there.

SUZY. *(Comes clicking down the stairs carrying four small suitcases setting them down. She is dressed in a skintight very short pink suit.)* That's just the first load. Don't anybody get up. I got it arranged so I can do it all myself.

BILL. That's a pretty snappy outfit, Suzy.

SUZY. *(Going.)* Don't you just love it? *(Gone.)*

APRIL. I kinda like that pink jobby she had on last night. Would you look at that luggage? That girl has got to be the cheapest whore in town.

GIRL. I got it! I got one. See? *(Pokes Bill.)* I'll bet I haven't been here five minutes. Oxenham could have told him that; he didn't ask any leading questions.

BILL. What have you got?

GIRL. I know when he left. I got them renting his room out. *(To other files.)* Now what? I don't know what half of this stuff is. Letters. Terrific —

BILL. Come on.

GIRL. What if he wrote to change his address or send things? Or any of a thousand reasons. That's where you'd find a return address —

BILL. *(Overlap.)* Put those rent books back in there —

GIRL. — When I'm finished. Why don't you let me cover the board and you go out and get us a hamburger before they close.

BILL. April ordered a pizza.

APRIL. Yeah, ought to be here any minute.

GIRL. Thank God; you're a sister of mercy. What's this? Wrong year. See, I know when he left. I only have to look at the one month or a little after. What's in the broom closet; there's dozens of boxes in there; they're probably years old, aren't they?

BILL. I haven't been in there.

JAMIE. Excuse me…

GIRL. *(Looks up — slows down some.)* Me? What, Jamie…?

JAMIE. I don't know your name…

GIRL. I know — I'm working on it. What's wrong, honey?

JAMIE. Did you really go there? *(Pause.)* We heard that the Mormons was good farmers…

GIRL. I imagine they are. They've irrigated all the — Jamie, there aren't any Mormons *near* where your land is; there's nothing near there. I mean, I didn't get out, but it's just white sand — it's salt and soda, it looks like. Cactus can't even grow there.

JAMIE. If we brought water, we could…

GIRL. Jamie, you irrigate that land, you'd have twenty acres of Bromo-Seltzer.

SUZY. *(With two more pieces of unmatched luggage and a box tied with an extension cord.)* Listen, I'll be right back down. I got a surprise.

BILL. What's happening? Are you checking out?

SUZY. *(Dumps it.)* Yes, love; do up my bill. Take it out of — here — take it out of that. Don't anybody leave the lobby; you gotta promise me. *(She is gone.)*

APRIL. You gotta give it to her; the girl really knows what looks good on her.

GIRL. God, this is going to be depressing.

APRIL. What's that?

GIRL. No, I won't read them. God, they're depressing. All filed away. Nobody will ever answer them.

BILL. Just look at the envelope; you don't have to read them.

GIRL. I know, but I can't help it. Half of this is from the Welfare Department — from everywhere. I sat down over in the park and this perfectly normal-looking woman sat down. Well dressed, sixty years old — and she started talking to me…Jesus. It really gets me that a normal person never opens her mouth. It's only the crazies that'll talk to you.

APRIL. What's her story?

GIRL. Oh…she feeds dogs. Stray dogs. She goes around to all the butcher shops, and for three hours every day she feeds the poor stray dogs — I mean, it's probably a good thing to do; but you got to be crazy even to

do anything good. She says isn't it wonderful to be able to have something like that. Says she considers herself lucky because there's so many
dogs in Baltimore.

APRIL. I consider myself *un*lucky because there's so many dogs in Baltimore.

GIRL. I think she was trying to convert me.

BILL. Come on, you're getting filthy there. Look at that.

APRIL. I always say if a lady —

GIRL. *(As Paul enters.)* Where have you been? Where'd you go?

PAUL. I went to eat.

GIRL. Did you bring anything back, I'm starving. April, where's that pizza?
Never mind — look; come here and look; my God, I'm not going to do
this by myself.

PAUL. *(To the desk.)* What is it?

GIRL. Just follow this. Room two-oh-three — that's your granddad's receipt.
That's for December 14 — that's probably the one Oxenham showed
you — they go back forever — but — look at this. December 21 I didn't
find anything — nothing for his room at all. Then. December 28. J.
Smith. Room two-oh-three. So he left between the fourteenth and twenty-
first of December. Probably on the twenty-first, when his week was up.

PAUL. Doesn't really matter…

GIRL. It's a fact. A first fact. If we're going to call like the Salvation Army or
flophouses or hospitals, we've got a specific date. You can't expect them
to look through six months of records. Also, I have a cop friend on the
pussy posse, but I don't think I should go to them first thing — on
account of your experience. We don't want them getting curious.

PAUL. That doesn't tell you anything.

GIRL. It certainly does! You came here knowing nothing; you've got to narrow it down. *(The sound of a train.)* Listen! Son of a bitch. What time is it?

BILL. *(Glances at clock.)* Twelve — [whatever]

GIRL. An hour and a half late. Jesus. And that's good. And they're conscien-
tious. The engineers — it's not their fault; it's everyone else doesn't give
a — Still, it's better than yesterday, they sailed through at five-thirty;
they might as well just cancel the whole run; tell people to take the
planes. I really have no use for airplanes; I'd be just as happy if everyone
fell into the sea like what's his name.

PAUL. Icarus.

GIRL. No, it was Gary Cooper or Cary Grant; I get them all mixed up. The
Continental came through this afternoon on time — I sent the front
office a telegram of congratulations — I honestly did. Anyway, besides

this, phone calls; they keep a record of every outgoing call; we could find people in town he called. He must have known someone. Nobody's so shy they don't know someone. I don't care what kind of hat he wore.

SUZY. *(Flushed, coming down the stairs with two bottles of champagne and a shopping bag.)* All right, here it is. This is it; it's cold too; I've had it in the fridge all afternoon. Bill, open this up, we're having a toast. I called the cab already, kids, so we just got a minute, but that ain't cheating us out of a little party.

APRIL. Open it, Bill.

JAMIE. Are you going too?

SUZY. I sure am, honey. I don't need to have a place falling down around me before I take action. I got paper cups and everything. Mr. Morse, you're going to have a drink, honey, aren't you? It's nice and cold.

APRIL. He'll love it.

BILL. It's morning for me. I'm not on your schedule.

SUZY. That's the best time in the world to drink it; champagne doesn't have a time to drink it. Come on. I just wish we had some nuts. I didn't have time to think of everything.

JAMIE. I got some. In my bag.

SUZY. That's all right, honey, they're yours, we don't — *(She is pouring.)*

JAMIE. No, I got lots of them. *(He takes two large jars from his bag.)*

SUZY. Don't anybody drink till we have a toast.

APRIL. Where the hell did you get those?

JAMIE. We always have them; we got a whole case of them.

APRIL. Jesus Christ, they're soy beans.

JAMIE. They're great for you. And they're good.

GIRL. I want something, if I'm going to be drinking champagne; I've not had a bite.

SUZY. Hold your cup, honey. This is the real stuff. *(Next is Paul.)* Take a cup.

PAUL. No, thanks, I'm not — *(To Bill.)* I got a bag in —

SUZY. *(Overlapping.)* Yes, come on; we may be a flophouse, but we know class: see, I remember. Only nobody else, 'cause there ain't that much; if anybody comes in, we're just drinking ginger ale.

BILL. *(Raising his glass.)* Uh…uh…To Suzy!

SUZY. *(Immensely pleased.)* No! Not to me! Come on, to this place! To…

APRIL. To us!

ALL. To us! *(They drink the toast and make appropriately enthusiastic responses.)*

SUZY. This is the real stuff.

APRIL. These things are good.

GIRL. They are, they're great.

SUZY. You can't eat soy beans with champagne! Well, that's sweet, honey — isn't he cute — where's the dy — his sister?

APRIL. She went for "gas." At six o'clock. This afternoon. She'll be right back.

SUZY. Oh. *(Beat.)* Hey, these are real good. What'd you say they was?

JAMIE. Barbecue-flavor soy beans. With sea salt and tomato powder.

APRIL. I think it's the sea salt that does it.

SUZY. O.K. One more round. There's plenty more. While it lasts. *(Pouring around.)* This is California champagne. This isn't that New York State stuff. One of my johns told me the difference. New York wines are made with a whole different kind of grape. It's all in the grape.

GIRL. I didn't know champagne was made out of grapes. I thought —

APRIL. What'd you think it was made out of, soy beans?

SUZY. *(Overlapping a bit.)* Sure it is; California grapes are the same grapes they use in the French champagne. The Frenchies brought them over and planted them in California. In New York they got the wrong grape!

APRIL. Cheers, everybody.

SUZY. *(Overlapping.)* I love champagne because you got to share it with people; sittin' around drinking champagne all by yourself without an event would be like jerkin' off.

APRIL. Well, we got a first-class event here.

GIRL. I'll tell you one thing I'm not going to do; I'm not going to move from here.

APRIL. I'm with you. We'll throw ourselves in front of the wrecking ball.

GIRL. Besides, I have a friend who knows law and I hate to blow it on the one month's notice, but it's three months'. And then we don't have to move.

PAUL. *(To Bill.)* They all got friends into something.

GIRL. Baltimore used to be one of the most beautiful cities in America.

APRIL. Every city in America used to be one of the most beautiful cities in America.

GIRL. And this used to be a beautiful place. They got no business tearing it down. April and me and Mr. Morse and Millie. And Jamie.

SUZY. That's a delegation with balls.

GIRL. Where's Millie?

BILL. Millie went to bed. Said she was gonna try to sleep.

SUZY. She ought to be having some of this.

BILL. They might not get it torn down. They got a committee now to try to save it.

SUZY. Yeah, they also got antique people calling every ten minutes making bids on the door knobs. My money's on the vultures every time.

APRIL. This is fantastic stuff, Suzy. You're a dedicated woman.

GIRL. Who would we go to to make a protest?

SUZY. Only… *(With pride.)* …I got to tell you. I'm not moving into another hotel. I got an apartment. On the twelfth floor. It's got five rooms. There's a doorman; there's only one other girl sharing it with me.

APRIL. Wait; this is very familiar —

SUZY. — She's a sweetheart. She's read everything ever printed. Even newspapers.

APRIL. A wife-in-law.

SUZY. — Well, there's nothing in the arrangement that calls for that tone of voice. And I can have a pet if I want one. And I do. I've longed for a pet. I love animals.

APRIL. People who keep animals in the house are sick. Pets and pimps.

SUZY. I would be very good to an animal.

APRIL. I don't care, it's still sick.

SUZY. I have great love for animals.

GIRL. What kind of an animal?

SUZY. All kinds. All animals. Puppies and kittens and little calves and ponies, and all of them.

APRIL. And a cuddly little woolly black pimp.

SUZY. All non-human animals. And fish. I don't like tropical fish.

APRIL. My husband used to keep fish.

GIRL. I didn't know you were married.

APRIL. I didn't either. *(To Suzy.)* Who is it?

BILL. What's a wife-in-law?

GIRL. *(Overlapping.)* Come on, Bill, how long have you worked here?

APRIL. *(Overlapping.)* Ask Suzy about wife-in-law arrangements. She's the authority —

SUZY. *(Overlapping.)* It's nothing like that. She *asked* me, I'll be the wife, honey. I'm nobody's second fiddle. You don't have to worry about me. She's just there to keep house as far as we're concerned — she'll be the in-law. She can't turn two hundred a day.

APRIL. Who is he? Are you going back with Eddie?

SUZY. I certainly am not. Who do you think I am? I may have a soft spot in my heart but I don't want —

APRIL. *(Overlapping.)* You got a soft spot in your head.

SUZY. — This man is not like that. Eddie was a pimp; this man is a man.

APRIL. Who's the boy friend this time?

SUZY. Not this time. This is my first *real friend.* Eddie was a pimp.

APRIL. You're telling me; a pimp fink.

SUZY. This man is a man!

APRIL. Yeah, what does he do?

SUZY. He does nothing! And he does it *gorgeously!*

BILL. How'd you get talked into another arrangement like that?

APRIL. They don't talk, they croon.

SUZY. Tell me you don't need someone; maybe you don't, but I do; I need love!

APRIL. All you have to say to a hooker is cottage small by the waterfall and they fold up.

SUZY. You know I don't appreciate that word.

APRIL. Whadda you call it?

SUZY. I am not a that-word; I am a friendly person and it gets me in trouble.

APRIL. — You're a professional trampoline.

SUZY. That is why I'm leaving! Derision! Derision! Because I'm attacked with derision every time I try to do something wonderful. Driven into the arms of a common pimp! *(April hoots.)*

GIRL. We're just thinking about you, Suzy.

APRIL. *(Overlapping.)* You've been down this road.

BILL. *(Overlapping.)* How's this one any better than Eddie?

SUZY. Just don't worry about it. Billy's never beat up one of his wives...ever!

APRIL. Jesus God, she's going with Billy Goldhole.

SUZY. That is not his name. And to call him by that name is to show your ignorance. And if you say he's beat up on anybody, I don't believe it.

CAB DRIVER. *(Entering.)* Somebody here order a taxi?

APRIL. Go on, I don't want to have anything to do with you.

SUZY. Yes. Here! This here. *(She starts to pick up some of the luggage.)*

CAB DRIVER. I'm not a moving van, lady. What is this?

SUZY. This stuff here; you can't take it quick enough.

CAB DRIVER. I'm double-parked out there. I can't take all that. Where you going to? With this crap?

SUZY. Don't sweat it, mister. I'm taking my share. I'll pay double the meter.

SUZY. I'm leaving this hole. Hole. Hole. Move it.

CAB DRIVER. I said I'm double-parked out there, lady. I'm not in the —

SUZY. You're double-parked. Tell me about it. The whole fuckin' country is double-parked. I hope they tear down the place with all *(Picking up almost all the luggage as she rants.)* you in it. Goody-two-shoes included. I'm just sorry I gave you a little party. You don't know enough to appreciate it.

CAB DRIVER. Come on, lady, shake it.

SUZY. Shove it. *(They exit.)*

GIRL. She's got to be the worst judge of character in Baltimore.

APRIL. She's gotta be the worst character in Baltimore.

BILL. She drew the cops here four times in one night once.

APRIL. Whadda you say, Mr. Morse? Unstable woman, huh?

MR. MORSE. *(Who has not been following, still holds his untasted cup.)* Very good. Thank you.

GIRL. I wonder if the apartment has eleven-foot ceilings.

APRIL. It's got an eleven-inch licorice lollipop is what it's got.

SUZY. *(Bursting back into the lobby, bawling. Super-emotional, hugs them in turn while speaking and is gone with the last word.)* I'm sorry. I know you love me. I can't leave like that. Mr. Morse. We been like a family, haven't we? My family. Baby. I'm not that horrible. I can't be mad. Bill. I'll always remember this. *(Gone. A few seconds of stupefied, gawking silence.)*

PAUL. I got a bag back there.

BILL. Yeah. *(Handing it to him.)*

GIRL. Hey. Paul. You're supposed to be doing this with me. You're supposed to be helping.

PAUL. No, that's O.K. You don't have to do that.

GIRL. Did you find him? While you were out?

PAUL. *(Overlapping.)* Of course I didn't find him; he's gone. That doesn't tell you anything.

GIRL. Well, we knew he was gone; the thing we're trying to do is find him.

PAUL. He could be anywhere.

GIRL. He could be *some*where.

PAUL. It's not your problem. It was a bad idea. Thanks.

GIRL. You got room for him, I thought. Hey. *Talk,* for God's sake. What are you doing?

PAUL. I'm trying to go, do you mind?

GIRL. How can you be so interested in something —

PAUL. — Would you get off my back? What's your problem? I didn't ask for you to help me. I didn't ask you.

APRIL. She volunteered. You got some gripe, write to her; she collects stamps.

GIRL. Oh, I do not.

PAUL. Look, you're probably being very nice; but thanks, anyway, O.K.? Granddad isn't here. They don't know where he is. Nobody here knows where he is. It's all the same.

GIRL. Not yet; but I can find him. Nobody vanishes.

PAUL. It's just as well, probably. I got things to do.

GIRL. — It just isn't as easy as you thought. You been bitching Oxenham for being no help. Let us help.

PAUL. *I* wanted to find him. He'd move out of a place like this the first chance he got; he wasn't a derelict. You don't know him. *(Millie begins to come down the stairs.)*

GIRL. I said I wanted to know him.

APRIL. Hey, Millie.

MILLIE. *(Vaguely.)* Oh...hello, then...

PAUL. *(Mumbled.)* Well, I'm sorry...

BILL. Thought you were sleeping. *(She raises a hand as if to say, That isn't important.)*

GIRL. Millie, tell him not to give up. Tell him we can find him or he's gonna just give up.

MILLIE. Oh, that's too bad.

APRIL. Ought to be easy enough to find. Ten-foot white-haired giant. Chops down cherry trees; doesn't lie about it.

GIRL. Come on, April; he was a trainman.

PAUL. Thanks, anyway, I'm sorry I got you involved. I'm not calling the Salvation — *(Begins to go.)*

GIRL. I *like* getting involved. Paul? You know what armor is? I had a scientologist tell me this. You're tied in knots all through your — Are you going to keep on looking for him? *(Silence — Paul glares at her.)*

APRIL. Knock once for yes and —

PAUL. It's not your business one way or the other, is it? *(To them quietly.)* Thanks very much, anyway. Thanks for your interest.

GIRL. *(Over "thanks very.")* You don't care about him. What if he's in — *(He goes.)* — some home for the — You! Boy, you're a —

APRIL. Creep.

GIRL. Creep. Well, I don't know if he doesn't really care or if we scared him off.

BILL. You can't help people who don't want it.

GIRL. I think he probably has trouble making friends.

APRIL. I think he has trouble making water. *(Pause. To Millie.)* Have a drink of Suzy's champagne. Help you sleep.

MILLIE. *(Taking a cup.)* Oh, I doubt that.

GIRL. Well, damn piss hell poot.

BILL. Just watch your language back here, O.K.?

APRIL. *(Pouring.)* Come on...

GIRL. *(Dialing the phone.)* No, it makes me...

APRIL. Bill?

BILL. Don't get me drunk here, now.

APRIL. Jamie? Come on. We won't tell her. *(Jamie comes to get the drink and goes back to the lounge.)*

GIRL. *(On the phone.)* Penthouse B. Is he in the dining room? Well, tell him Billy Jean — No, don't bother; I couldn't bear it. No message. *(Hangs up.)* I could just kill Paul Granger. That's why nothing gets done; why everything falls down. Nobody's got the conviction to act on their passions.

APRIL. Go kill him then.

GIRL. I mean, it's his idea to find him. I don't think it matters what someone believes in. I just think it's really chicken not to believe in anything!

BILL. *(Pouring another.)* Come on, join us.

GIRL. No, I'm going to take a bath while there's hot water. I'm just filthy.

BILL. Come on, drink to Suzy.

GIRL. *(Taking the cup — to Millie.)* Suzy left us.

MILLIE. Again?

APRIL. Exactly. God help her.

GIRL. *(Drinks.)* I hate that. You like that, Jamie?

JAMIE. It's O.K.

MILLIE. Well. I've got no business down here.

APRIL. Drinking champagne, huh?

GIRL. I'm going up too. *(She starts upstairs; Bill starts to pick up the books. Preoccupied.)* Don't you put those away; I'm not finished with those. *(Bill looks off after her, aching.)*

APRIL. *(Snaps her fingers lightly at him. One. Two. Three. Four.)* Hey. Hey.

BILL. Come on, April; knock it off. *(He sits at the switchboard.)*

APRIL. Bill, baby, you know what your trouble is? You've got Paul Grangeritis. You've not got the conviction of your passions.

JAMIE. April? What time is it?

APRIL. It's a quarter after — *(Looks at Bill.)*

BILL. *(A glance at the clock.)* Twelve-thirty. Nearly.

APRIL. She probably got stopped on account of the license.

BILL. *(Under his breath.)* Sure she did. *(To Millie who is retiring.)* Millie, you want a wake-up call?

MILLIE. *(Almost laughing.)* Oh — no point in — unless you just feel like talking. Good night, everyone.

MR. MORSE. Paul Granger is an old fool!

MILLIE. Did you know him, Mr. Morse? Oh, God...I felt one of us should... remember him.

MR. MORSE. He's an old fool.

APRIL. *(Turning on the radio.)* You tell 'em, baby.

BILL. Try to sleep this time.

MILLIE. *(Going off.)* Well, if it happens…

APRIL. *(To Jamie as the song comes on the radio.)* Come on, Jamie. Off your butt. Come on; dance with me. This may be your shining hour.

JAMIE. No, come on.

BILL. She's just teasing you.

APRIL. Hell I am.

JAMIE. I don't feel like it.

APRIL. You eaten anything today? *(He nods.)* What? Some health-nut crap?

JAMIE. Bacon and eggs and a hamburger.

APRIL. What kind of health food is that?

JAMIE. There's no health-food place close enough.

APRIL. Come on; you're so shy, if someone doesn't put a light under your tail, you're not going to have passions to need convictions for. *(Jamie walks uncertainly to April. A pizza delivery boy enters.)*

DELIVERY BOY. Somebody order a pizza here?

BILL. April?

APRIL. *(Without looking at him; taking the check.)* Take it up to the second-floor john.

BILL. Second floor, turn right. The door at the end of the hall. *(Delivery boy goes.)*

JAMIE. I don't know how.

APRIL. Nobody's knows how. What does it matter; the important thing is to move. Come on; all your blood's in your tail.

BILL. It's twelve-thirty; he's been up all day; he doesn't want to dance.

APRIL. Sure he does.

JAMIE. Tell me how.

APRIL. Come on, they're gonna tear up the dance floor in a minute; the bull-dozers are barking at the door. Turn it up, Bill, or I'll break your arm. *(He turns it up a little.)* Turn it up! *(More. April and Jamie latch arms go one way then back. She joins in singing with the radio and as the lights fade and they turn back circling the other way, he joins in as well. Bill stares off, then smiles at them. Mr. Morse sips the drink and watches them. The sound from the radio moves into the house. Curtain.)*

END OF PLAY

SERENADING LOUIE

To Rob Thirkield

We will serenade our Louie
While life and voice shall last
Then we'll pass and be forgotten with the rest.

The Whiffenpoof Song

Michael Storm, Tanya Berezin, Edward J. Moore, and Trish Hawkins
in the Circle Repertory Company production of Serenading Louie.
Photo ©1976 by Gerry Goldstein.

INTRODUCTION

I think this started in Chicago, before I came to New York. By the late 1950s I had realized that I would never have the money and probably not the inclination to finish school; and probably didn't need to if I was going to be the great painter or the great graphic designer of my dreams — my heroes were Matisse and Saul Bass. I had just turned twenty. I was working in the small, close-knit art department of a large, rather pedestrian, ad agency (and later in several three- and four-man art-service firms, a couple of them damn good) doing work menial enough and simple or repetitive enough to be quite forgotten as I eavesdropped from over in my corner. At the large agency I was ten to twenty years younger than the other men in the art department. (There was one cheery woman who was alternately ignored and cruelly satirized. Unless she was really feeling her oats she just bounced around with a smile, not saying much.) So this was mainly a bunch of guys in a room (separated into cubicles that we talked over and through, think one big room) bull-shitting and bragging and harassing each other and bitching the clients and the chicken-livered account executives (a good ad agency succeeds or fails on the nerve, balls, imagination of the account executives), behaving generally rather nakedly. It was my first contact with working, free-associating, socializing, older, white-collar men. I was blown away. By their competitive nature, their hostility, by their closeness, by their candor. By their bitterness and cynicism:

Time: 9 A.M.
Place: A pedestrian advertising agency.
Woman: *(Cheerily.)* Good morning, Bob.
Bob: *(Stops in the middle of taking off his coat.)* Oh, God, will this day never end. *(He meant it.)*

Another image from Chicago: I had moved to Glenn Ellyn, a suburb, and was commuting. I went to my train, remembered I was supposed to be somewhere else that night and quickly detrained (conductors really use that word). Coming toward me were two men in their mid-thirties, only lightly drunk, their arms around each other, clutching each other, one was or maybe both were sobbing. They were saying loudly, "I really love you, man," "And I love you." "But I mean I really *love* you!" "I know, I believe it 'cause I really love *you!*" Their passion was so startlingly intense that I half expected them to rip each other's clothes off there on the platform. Instead they embraced, the way men do, arms-length, holding each other by the biceps, shaking each other, staring into the other's teary eyes. And split—one to track seven, one to track eight — each to his own suburban home.

By the time I began *Serenading Louie* I had met hundreds of straight men in their thirties; business partners, stage directors, producers, actors, lawyers. I had seen them with their wives and lovers. I had heard the husbands trash their wives and the wives nearly castrate their husbands. I had seen friends and relatives through bitter separations. I had had lunch with a friend and his girlfriend and dinner the same night with him and his wife. I had seen a very bright man who could only converse with his equally intelligent wife in funny accents and a man who was so in love with his wife after twelve years of marriage that it was chilling. I'd had God knows how many affairs myself. I began writing notes for a play about two married couples who were quite close, probably some of them had gone to school together. I told Marshall W. Mason what I was thinking. He said, Tennessee Williams already did that; it's called *Period of Adjustment*. Great. I didn't work on the play again for two years. I knew what I was thinking about was quite different from Williams' play, but all the air went out of me in an instant. Marshall says he's since learned to say nothing while a writer is working on a new piece except, "That sounds great, I can't wait to read it." I carried the "Louie" notebook with me everywhere. It wasn't a play, it was scenes, it was one-line sketches. I went to Europe with the La Mama Troupe, my roommate most nights was an actor who talked endlessly about his marriage. I couldn't write a thing. I had enough material for two plays but it wouldn't come together. I threw it aside and wrote *Lemon Sky*. I went to the country home (in the middle of winter, in the middle of a snowstorm) of a married couple who fought with each other and me and their kids the entire snowed-in weekend. I got home (a miracle, the roads were solid ice, a trip that should take an hour and a half took five) Sunday night about ten o'clock, angry with them and the world. I dragged my typewriter into the middle of the living room, sat on the floor beside a small portable record player, put on Judy Collins' "Who Knows Where the Time Goes," played it over and over at top volume and, bawling like a child, singing along loudly, flew through the notebook. I had had the whole play, some of it for years, without knowing it. Scenes that were fifty pages apart became one, pages fell into juxtaposition. One of my problems had been that I had fought for a year to save them from the tragic ending, but really there was no way out of it. At four in the morning my landlord, who lived directly below, knocked on the door and said, "We keep expecting you to stop yelling but it's just been going on and on." I turned the volume down and whispered the lyrics along with Judy. By noon the next day I had the first draft of *Serenading Louie*. I had been working on it for three years.

Now, that all sounds fairly easy, but actually the play has gone through more revisions than anything I've written. I may like best the first three-hour-plus draft, with long, tortured asides to the audience, that was done at the Washington (D.C.) Theatre Club. Davey Marlin Jones directed it there. Teenagers, recognizing their elders, broke from the audience and fled up the aisle crying. At the end of the play's first performance at least fifteen people lined up at the water fountain with tranquilizers in their hands. Davey thought that was great. I wasn't so sure. I told him it wasn't really my intention to ruin people's evening. But the play was unwieldy and badly focused. I cut most of the long speeches to the audience. In another draft I took out all the asides to the audience. I decided that it was too easy for a character to say what he was really thinking only to the audience, even though it was sometimes very funny. What if the character said that aloud, and the other three had to deal with it? But what had been written originally as an aside didn't sound right delivered within the scene. In this edition, I've gone back to the original impulse, much of the asides are restored.

Still, I think of this play as a broken thing, inchoate and recalcitrant. It is probably in its most coherent form here. Someone said you never finish a thing, you abandon it. That is more true of this play than anything I've attempted. And still I weep for these characters' pain. I couldn't save them but I love them.

ORIGINAL PRODUCTION

Serenading Louie was first presented at the Washington Theater Club in Washington, D.C., on April 1, 1970. The cast was as follows:

MARY	Anne Lynn
CARL	Arlen Dean Snyder
GABBY	Jane Singer
ALEX	Robert Darnell

Directed by Davey Marlin-Jones
Setting and Costumes by James Parker
Light and Design by William Eggleston
Production Stage Manager Robert H. Leonard

Serenading Louie was presented by The Circle Repertory Company in New York City, on May 5, 1976. The cast was as follows:

MARY	Tanya Berezin
CARL	Edward J. Moore
GABBY	Trish Hawkins
ALEX	Michael Storm

Directed by Marshal W. Mason
Setting by John Lee Beatty
Costumes by Jennifer Von Mayrhauser
Lighting by Dennis Parichy
Production Stage Manager Dave Clow

Serenading Louie was presented by The Second Stage in New York City, on January 17, 1984. The cast was as follows:

MARY	Lindsay Crouse
CARL	Jimmie Ray Weeks
GABBY	Dianne Wiest
ALEX	Peter Weller

Directed by John Tillinger
Setting by Loren Sherman
Costumes by Clifford Capone
Lighting by Richard Nelson
Production Stage Manager Kate Hancock

CHARACTERS

CARL Ex-quarterback, maybe a martini overweight, warm, introspective.

MARY His wife, ex-homecoming queen, from conservative and wealthy family; breeding everywhere.

ALEX Fast becoming a public hero; boyish, entertaining, shrewd.

GABRIELLE The only one not a graduate of Northwestern, she's from Stevens; not dithery, her situation is dithery.

All are around thirty-four.

Serenading Louie

ACT ONE

The present. Early evening.

The living room of a suburban home, north of Chicago.
A door to a kitchen, through which is the garage, at least one set of French doors leading to an outside area, a window seat, and a door to the master bedroom. Stairs up to the child's room. Spacious and expensive, modern or traditional, American antique furniture eighteenth or early nineteenth century and good. There is a rather fierce decorative Balinese shadow puppet on one wall. This one set, which should look like a home, not a unit set, will serve as the home of first one couple, then the other, with no alterations between.

Lighting from actual source, or the illusion of such. The divisions between scenes in the first act should be marked with an abrupt blackout. At the end of the scene, blackness, followed by lights up full in as short a time as possible — no more than, say, ten seconds.

SCENE 1

(After midnight. The silent TV plays the last few bars of the National Anthem then shows only snow, the only light in the room. Gabrielle opens the bedroom door, standing in the light of the door, in her nightgown, holding a pillow in her arms.)

GABRIELLE Alex? Are you here? Alex?

ALEX. Yes.

GABRIELLE. Were you asleep?

ALEX. No, that's all right. *(Turns off TV. The only light comes from the bedroom door.)*

GABRIELLE. Honey…?

ALEX. Oh, God.

GABRIELLE. What's wrong?

ALEX. When you get into that tone of voice and say honey like that, I know we're up for the night.

GABRIELLE. No, we aren't...I... *(Pause.)*

ALEX. What, Gabby? *(Pause.)* What, I'm sorry.

GABRIELLE. Nothing. What can I say?...Nothing... *(Goes back to the bedroom, closing the door, effecting a blackout.)*

ALEX. I said I'm sorry. *(He opens the door, stands there.)*

GABRIELLE. *(Off.)* No, nothing.

ALEX. Gabby? *(Pause.)* Gabby, baby, I'm sorry, what? *(Pause.)* Gabby? *(He goes into the bedroom, closing the door, blackout.)*

SCENE 2

(Nearly evening. The only light is on the desk.)

CARL *(Coming from the kitchen as he closes the outside door, he calls from off-stage.)* Sweetheart? *(He enters.)* Honey?...Mary...?*(He yells up the stairs.)* Hey, baby? *(He goes to the patio door, yells out.)* Mary? *(He shuts the door, turns, and sees the light — he goes to the desk, picks up a note, and sits as he reads it. He lets the note float from this hand back to the desk, shuts his eyes a moment, reaches to the desk lamp, and turns it off. Blackout.)*

SCENE 3

(Gabrielle, a.k.a. Gabby, is asleep in a chair, a book in her lap. She awakens as Alex comes in the front door.)

GABRIELLE. Hello baby; I didn't realize... *(Alex looks to the living room; seeing her, he shows the barest recognition. He leaves his topcoat in the foyer closet, and as she talks he comes to the sofa, bringing his briefcase.)* Have you read this? It isn't...well, I don't know what it isn't. Like a drink? What kind of day? *(A pause. Alex crosses to the desk to pick up the mail.)* I was in town and going to stop by or call, and then just got too tired. Claris wanted to call it a day too. She's really...oh, I don't want to say anything. I suppose we all are, but she really is. More and more. You know I went back to bed and slept till almost ten-thirty. I thought pot wasn't supposed to give you a hangover. Maybe I'm just getting something. You slept terribly, perspiring all...I think I enjoyed last night; you seemed to.

Carl's fun, isn't he? Of course Mary's great. I kept thinking *(Enjoying this.)* that my head was going to...leave my...you know, with pot I've decided that it changes the focus of my eyes. I see things at a distance more clearly. Or something. I don't know, it's very funny. *(She leaves for the kitchen.)*

ALEX. *(Aside to the audience.)* Any moment now you'll hear a woman talking to the roast.

GABRIELLE. *(From the kitchen, to Alex.)* I heard a joke. There was this...no, I won't, I'll call Mary and get it straight. I always mess them up. *(Alex goes to the foyer closet, gets his cigarettes from his coat pocket, comes back, picks up his briefcase, and sits at a chair with a lamp beside. He opens his briefcase. Noises are heard from the kitchen — the oven door, etc.)* I think I've *(Reenters, crossing to the sofa.)* got a really good roast for a change. It's getting cool, isn't it? *(She drifts to the window where she sits after a moment, looking out.)* I used to love the autumn so much. Oh God, I *(Thinking of an amusing story, laughing a little to herself.)* remember one time on the way...you know, it had frosted and I had a little purse — it must have been the first grade, and I picked up this leaf. This bright red leaf because it looked...there was a frost...a thick rime covering it — and I put it in my purse to give to the teacher to tack up on the bulletin board because it was...I thought it was so lovely. *(She laughs, quite to herself. Smiles. Looks out the window.)* Up through Thanksgiving I love it. Brisk...crisp. Bitey. Astringent. The Farrenstein's sugar maple looks like it's on fire — did you see it? *(She thinks about something, laughs to herself...a "humph" sound, twice. Perhaps she thinks about a Halloween experience; perhaps she says a very dear, "Oh," as in "Oh, dear, how silly of us," and then looks outside again, smiling. A sigh.)* I want to remember to ask Alison when it is you cut back delphiniums...she's incredibly knowledgeable on...I've probably already... *(She starts to go somewhere, has a new impulse, turns.)* I don't think kids now...oh, maybe they do...I don't think they enjoy Halloween as much as we did. Why don't we get a jack-o'-lantern? I'd love that. I'll make some pies...that isn't silly, is it? *(She ducks into the kitchen again, speaks from offstage.)* Aren't you cute...Very good. Actually I think you could use a little...no, that's *(The oven door closes; she comes back.)* lookin' pretty good, huh! *(She sits at the desk, looks to Alex. She smiles, watching him concentrate on his work. She tilts her head to the side. Count twelve before he looks up.)*

ALEX. *(Rather like, "What, darling, I'm sorry, but I'm busy.")* What is it?

GABRIELLE. Nothing, I just like to watch you working.

ALEX. *(Lighting a cigarette.)* Humph. *(He looks back to his work.)*

GABRIELLE. *(Moving toward the phone.)* I should call Alison and ask her. I think she said October or the first of November...I should remember, mother... *(Seeing a note by the phone.)* Oh, Mrs. Porter called and said...what is it? Look at page fourteen of the *Sun-Times*...did you see that? *Sun-Times,* page...

ALEX. Yeah, it was nothing.

GABRIELLE. *(Crossing to the sofa.)* Is that some explosively scandalous disclosure for tomorrow? I thought we were finished with all that. *(Pause. Alex continues without acknowledgment.)* I know better than to ask if I've done something, don't I? *(Alex looks up. Beat.)* Or haven't done something. *(Alex goes back to his work.)* It isn't going to be one of those "silent" nights, is it? Working all night silently and then going to work and calling me five times to talk about nothing as though you hadn't been silent? I don't much like those nights, but I rather enjoy the phone calls. Or aren't we supposed to talk about it? *(Beat.)* Would that impede your spontaneity? *(Beat, as he doesn't react.)* It wouldn't. *(Alex looks at her directly. She holds his gaze. Count five. He shakes his head, looks back to his papers.)* It doesn't... *(Suddenly she thinks of the roast.)* Did I? No, I did. *(She moves to the sofa, picks up her book.)* Actually, I'm enjoying this. I mean it's nothing...you know. *(She sets the book on her lap, opens it, settles down, begins to read. Alex clears his throat. She looks up smiling and back. He stacks some papers, lays them aside. Rather dramatically he stubs out his cigarette. Looking to her, he shakes his head. She continues to read.)*

ALEX. *(Going to the bedroom.)* I guess I should know by now, shouldn't I?

GABRIELLE. What's that honey? *(She looks up, not certain where he has gone. Calling toward the bedroom.)* Baby? What'd you say, hon'? *(She listens.)* Honey? *(After a second, getting up, crossing to hall, calling.)* Alex?

ALEX. *(Off.)* What, for God's sake?

GABRIELLE. Nothing. I wondered...where...

ALEX. *(Off.)* I'm going to lie down.

GABRIELLE. Really? Honey, you...

ALEX. *(Off.)* What?

GABRIELLE. Nothing, only you spend...and dinner's just...

ALEX. *(Off.)* All right, I won't lie down; it doesn't *(Returning, he crosses to the desk.)* matter to me, I'll work, it doesn't matter. *(He turns on the lamp, sits, and reopens his briefcase, looking through his papers.)*

GABRIELLE. It's just that when you're home you spend every waking hour asleep. Of course, you're never home.

ALEX. I'm not asleep, Gabrielle.

GABRIELLE. Well, awake then; it's worse if anything. I know your eyelids like the back of my hand. If I lie down beside you, you get up. You look in pain if I sit on the side of the bed to talk to you anymore. Oh, I'm sorry, you must be exhausted...don't work...if you're tired, of course you should lie down.

ALEX. I'm not tired.

GABRIELLE. Would you like a drink? Before dinner? Alex? Would you like...

ALEX. *(Making a notation, interrupting, preoccupied.)* No, thank you, hon'. *(Pause. She goes into the kitchen. Alex looks up to the door. There are noises in the kitchen. Alex lights a cigarette. Watching, thinking. He looks at the floor. She reenters. Alex goes back to staring through the papers, smoking. She walks over to him, behind his chair.)*

GABRIELLE. Is that a speech? Are you...

ALEX. No, I just never seem to get to this.

GABRIELLE. What's that?

ALEX. Nothing, it's nothing.

GABRIELLE. I'm looking very fondly toward you going back to trial cases. The cold-blooded murders I can understand — all that dirty politics and under-the-table graft and deals is all so...Dinner's on the brink. You hungry?

ALEX. I'm not very, actually. *(He continues to work. She smiles, walks to the window, looks out.)*

GABRIELLE. It's getting dark earlier and earlier. Pretty soon... *(She turns on the living room light. She smiles to Alex. Then a thought crosses her mind and she frowns.)* Do we know a man with white hair? We don't know many older people, do we? A very...well, not quite distinguished-looking man, but nearly, I think he's...following me.

ALEX. Where?

GABRIELLE. Well...I know, isn't it? But in town I thought I saw him... then, when I came out of the Safeway. He was in a car watching me... but really *watching* me. And across the street from the florist. I ran to the car; then he followed me in his car and drove on by when I turned in the drive. I suppose I imagined it? I mean, what could he want, right? During the hearings I would have been really frightened, but now that it's all over — well, I get so jumpy at every little thing lately. I feel so inse...Oh, it's silly, isn't it? *(Pause.)* I don't know how to react to these moods you get into lately. *(Pause.)* I... *(Pause.)* Well, there isn't someone else, is there, Alex? *(Alex turns to her.)* Doesn't that sound silly, but I can't

come up with…It's driving me nuts, and that's all I can come up with.
I won't care…honestly…well, maybe I'll care, but I won't do anything;
I just wanted to ask, it's been on my mind.

ALEX. No, Gabby. There isn't. I really, well — *(He goes back to his work, quite irritated.)*

GABRIELLE. I didn't know, I thought maybe…I…I have your report memorized almost. The summation I think I could actually quote verbatim. I thought it was brilliant. Ponderholtz must be spitting nails…I've been so…Oh, I'll be quiet. I know. I'm being silly…so many things…I'm sorry. I guess I'm just nervous tonight. It's silly. I was with Mary yesterday. For some reason, she decided to be confiding. I don't know why me. I suppose she thought…Poor Mary. She's having an affair. Did you know that? I don't know if you know him. He's very good-looking. We saw them on the street; they have three kids…girls too. His wife's very attractive…I couldn't imagine. Apparently they're in love. Of course they both have the children. It just makes me nervous. I wish she hadn't told me. I hate secrets. *(Alex stares at her. A pause.)* Did you know anything about it?

ALEX. I thought it was possible.

GABRIELLE. Does Carl know?

ALEX. How would I know? *(Pause. Gabrielle crosses to the window seat.)*

GABRIELLE. I wouldn't do that to Carl. He scares me sometimes. He's so…trusting…He's too…something. I wouldn't want to…what do you think?

ALEX. *(Not unkind.)* I think you're overreacting.

GABRIELLE. So what's new? *(Sits.)* They finally sold that summer cabin up on Lake Elizabeth.

ALEX. Good, they hadn't been there in years.

GABRIELLE. Well, Lake Elizabeth isn't what it used to be.

ALEX. What is?

GABRIELLE. *(Looking down into the window. A laugh.)* Oh, there's a little fly…a drunk fly here. Turning fall, isn't it, old boy! He can't *(She passes a fanning hand at it.)* even fly off. *(She is struck by a remembered line of something.)* Oh, what is…? "Flat upon your bellies — where the…" What…how does…? "Where the fuzzy flies are crawling…buzzing… crawling…By the webby window lie. Watch the…Read me…" Or "young lovers by the…" *(She thinks for a moment.)* I can't, I can't…I've no idea. Silly, anyway. How's it coming? *(Alex continues to work. After a second she looks outside, then back.)* Alison's sister is…well, I don't think you know her. *(Pause.)* Alex? *(No answer. More urgently.)* Alex? *(After a second.)* I don't want to — *(Gabrielle smiles and looks down, out the window, a hand to her face. She begins to cry. Alex, without looking at her, puts his work aside, stubs out the cigarette, and gets up, walking briskly to the closet. Frantically Gabrielle wipes her cheeks, running after him.)* I'm sorry honey, I can't imagine! Alex? It's just…I'm sorry, Alex. Come on. *(Alex has taken his coat from the closet, throws it on.)* Alex, where…Baby, I don't know what's wrong… *(Laughing.)* I think I must be…Baby, please don't go! Alex! *(Alex slams the door on her last word, and with the sound the lights go out: Blackout.)*

SCENE 4

(Early evening. Carl is standing in the middle of the room. Mary enters from the bedroom, carrying her shoes. She is getting dressed, will put on the shoes, belt, scarf, etc. during the scene.)

MARY. Gabby scares me. I don't know if she scares me or if she's freaking out and imagining it: Someone keeps following her.

CARL. Man or woman?

MARY. Oh, she's a very sweet girl. You should indulge her sometimes. She's scared.

CARL. I just asked if it was a man or woman. *(Carl crosses to Mary to zip her dress.)*

MARY. A man but not like that. Oldish, very distinguished, she thought. Very unlike a rapist. *(Carl has slipped his arm around her.)* Is your watch right? I've got to split. Hat, gloves, purse, shoes, what?

CARL. Keys, list…

MARY. What list?

CARL. Did you have a list?

MARY. No list.

CARL. Umbrella?

MARY. It wouldn't dare. Purse, scarf, shoes, gloves, keys, no list… *(Carl crosses to the closet and gets Mary's coat.)*

CARL. I thought it was a party for someone's birth…

MARY. *(Crosses to the desk.)* Right! Right…present! Thank God, that's all I'd need. *(Mary takes it from the desk, putting it into her purse. Carl follows to the desk.)* Present. Keys in purse. Pencil for bridge scores…Anyone else we'd make it during the week, but Sue works. If you'd let me know you weren't going in today. Now, you're not going to forget to pick up Ellie at five-forty. She hates walking home carrying her ballet slippers.

CARL. Check.

MARY. She loves the class; she just doesn't like the school. Take her night bag, drop her at Bunny's, I've got her PJ's and all her paraphernalia already in it.

CARL. I know, I know.

MARY. And you'll remember to turn off the oven when the bell rings.

CARL. *(In a thicker mood than she.)* I'll not forget.

MARY. Chicken pot pie; it's no good burned. You're going to forget, aren't you?

CARL. *(Smiling.)* No, no, what's to forget. The bell rings, turn off the oven.

MARY. There's bologna and cheese in the fridge if you forget. It should be time by now.

CARL. You're going to pick up Sue?

MARY. Sue and Alice; I'm late, you're right. *(Mary crosses to the front door.)*

CARL. *(Frowning, reluctantly.)* Honey, I'd like to... *(Carl halts, looking at her. She looks at him. All movement and sound are arrested for a count of fifteen.)*

MARY. *(A rapid, overlapping exchange now.)* What, doll?

CARL. Talk, you know.

MARY. I know...we will. Nothing's wrong is there? *(Mary crosses to the living room.)*

CARL. No, no.

MARY. With that Atlanta business?

CARL. No, no.

MARY. *(Still lightly.)* What is it?

CARL. No, no, it's nothing.

MARY. We're running all over, we're never home together. I know...

CARL. It's nothing. Mary, I just get...edgy...it'll pass.

MARY. *(She crosses to Carl, maneuvering him to the sofa.)* I know, baby, It'll pass. *(She sits, smiling.)* Sit a second.

CARL. It's O.K., no, it'll...

MARY. Sit a second. *(She pulls him down to sit beside her, relaxes.)*

CARL. No, I never know when I'm going to be here; even Ellie, with her new schedule...

MARY. Oh, but she loves it...

CARL. No, no. I think it's great. She's a little lady...a little goddess.

MARY. I don't think Ellie would respond well to being worshipped. I know I wouldn't.

CARL. Sure you do.

MARY. Do you like the shadow puppet?

CARL. Yeah. He's cute; it's cute.

MARY. A little fierce, but I thought he was amusing. He's about a thousand years old...well, old in any case, they said. He's parchment.

CARL. They had puppet shows back then? And we think we're so advanced.

MARY. I wouldn't think they'd be much like ours. I mean it's not Punch and Judy. I think it's more closely related to religious stories, like for children, but not just...

CARL. Bible school.

MARY. Well, it wouldn't be "Bible." Their equivalent..."Bhagavad-Gita Illustrated" or whatever. *Bible school?* Did you do that?

CARL. *(Laughing.)* No, I don't think I managed...that was summertime; would have interfered with softball practice, but Sunday School...I went to that every Sunday, bright and early. Well, nine o'clock.

MARY. I can't imagine. What did you do?

CARL. What did...

MARY. What was it like? Did you like it?

CARL. Oh, yeah...I liked...Well, there wasn't any question of not liking...it was this thing you did. We, ah...what was it...? We all had these...our own...like pulp-paper quarterlies — thin little magazines that we were taught from — with orange and black illustrations of young Jesus, aged eleven, in the temple astonishing the...

MARY. Whoever. Right...

CARL. And we were taught by the judge's daughter or his son or some such, and they were seventeen, probably, and knew all the Psalms by heart. Especially the twenty-third. "Valley of the shadow of death, I will fear no evil for Thou art with me. Thy rod and Thy staff, they comfort me..." *(He sighs. Mary is polite attention personified.)* Oh, God...and uh...when it was someone's birthday...their ninth or tenth, we sang: "Ebert's had a birthday, we're so glad. Let us see how many he has had." *(Mary, charmed, has been laughing at this.)*

MARY. Oh, that's wonderful. *Ebert?*

CARL. Well, I just picked Ebert at random, there were some pretty incredible names. We had a boy named Dillard and twin girls called Ima Daisy and Ura Pansy...

MARY. Ura Pansy...no...nobody would saddle a kid with...

CARL. Swear to God. Ima Daisy and Ura Pansy Maggard. That kinda ruins it, doesn't it?

MARY. How can you remember that? How do you remember that tune?

CARL. How do you forget it? I learned it before "Happy Birthday to You." And Ebert had brought pennies and he dropped them into his round cardboard Quaker Oats box with that very severe Quaker in this flat hat...and the pennies hit the bottom and bounced like dropping on a drum. Or it might have been — that's funny — a milk bottle with tin foil over the cap — I remember them both — and in that case they jingled around in the glass. *(Beat.)* I can hear them both. Anyway, as Ebert...

MARY. *(Laughing.)* Ebert.

CARL. Well, or Dillard. We sang, "How old are you?" and Dillard dropped his pennies and we all counted. One. Two. Three. Four. Five. Up to eight or nine, or sometimes very dramatically, "Ten!" and we all...you know, the boys...watched those nine years go into the bottle and longed to be twenty-one and have a draft card...

MARY. I can't imagine.

CARL. Or at least sixteen and have our driver's license, and my Aunt Grace used to say, "Don't wish your life away." Then when the teacher, the mayor's daughter, or sheriff's son, had a birthday, he played too and...

MARY. Of course.

CARL. ...and that was an Event that lasted forever because he had to drop eighteen drumming pennies into that —

MARY. Or the other...the milk bottle.

CARL. Right. And it seemed to last half the Sunday School period.

MARY. I'm sure.

CARL. That was an Event...kids came from the other classrooms to watch. Everything was an Event then. The smallest thing that happened was an Event.

MARY. Of course.

CARL. And we don't have those anymore. Why is that? What's happened? *(He slides from his mood, back closer to his first one.)*

MARY. *(Still quizzical.)* What?

CARL. I don't know. That wars and deaths, birthdays, Easter, even Christmas. Nothing gets to me like that now. *(A slight pause.)* Things go by and nothing reaches us, does it? Nothing's an Event anymore.

MARY. Ummm. *(Pause. She jingles the keys.)*

CARL. *(More or less coming out of it for her benefit.)* You've got to go.

MARY. Oh, I know. *(Getting up.)* Now, I'm not going to tell you about the pie again — if it burns, there's bologna and cheese.

CARL. Turn off the oven; pick up Ellie at five-forty. Take her overnight bag…Drop her at Bunny's.

MARY. You'll be all right. Can we go out tomorrow night? Would you like that? I think I would. Just us?

CARL. Great. Saturday night…

MARY. Dinner and maybe a movie…I'd like that…we can call Betty to stay with Ellen. O.K? I'd love that.

CARL. It's a deal.

MARY. O.K., now, I've got to run. If the girls call, tell them I've left. *(She kisses him on the top of the head.)* O.K.?

CARL. O.K. Right.

MARY. *(Opening the door.)* Bye-bye, sweetheart.

CARL. Bye-bye. *(Mary leaves. Carl crosses to the sofa, his smile fades, he looks down to the floor with a worried look; after a count of ten, he looks up to the audience with a sense of urgency. The buzzer sounds in the kitchen, offstage. Carl turns his head to the sound. Blackout.)*

SCENE 5

(Early evening. Alex holds a large clipping from the newspaper. The silent TV has a football game on. Carl enters from the kitchen with a tray of sandwiches and beer.)

ALEX. Hey, Bozo, who's the war hero, one of your buddies?

CARL. Isn't Mary something else? I'll bet I haven't mentioned that guy more than five times. She recognized him and cut that out so I'd see it. I told you about him, the guy with the camera; sent Mary a picture of me reading one of her letters — sitting on the can. The way they razzed me about her, I had to go into the latrine — the only place I could read my mail in peace.

ALEX. *(Regarding the TV.)* Who's playing?

CARL. It's nothing. It's a rerun of an old Super Bowl game. *(Carl turns off the TV.)* Saw your mug on the news again today. You really kicked against the pricks.

ALEX. Yeah, they wanted an interview…a summary of my committee summation…apparently unable to sum it up themselves…wait till Monday.

CARL. I thought it was over.

ALEX. *(Gets sandwich.)* Wait till Monday, completely different thing.

CARL. What are you into now?

ALEX. Watch Monday.

CARL. Tell me.

ALEX. Better not right now. Wait till it's official.

CARL. No, better tell me now. I have to be in Cincinnati Monday. I have to see some people about an office building.

ALEX. Carl, you're going to be the youngest dead millionaire I know...

CARL. Have you ever heard me say I liked it? Running around like this? I don't go more than I have to — it's not my money; it's the bank's money, the investors' money.

ALEX. What's in Cincinnati?

CARL. It's nothing — an office building, in Oakwood. You know, suburban doctors' offices, dentists — that kind of thing. Half finished.

ALEX. They're run out of financing?

CARL. Money is what they're run out of. Tell me about your thing Monday.

ALEX. They have papers in Cincinnati.

CARL. Oh, great, you bastard, you're going to start giving me hints. I'd know if I'd been following it. I read up on you when I can...Christ, my hands are dry. Goddamn humidifier. Mary waters the plants three times a day. *(Crosses to the thermostat.)*

ALEX. *(He bites something in the sandwich, reacts.)* Jesus, wow.

CARL. What is it? Bite your tongue?

ALEX. *(Pointing to his mouth.)* Tooth. Damn. *(He manages to swallow, breathe, and then throws his sandwich back on his plate.)* I never seem to make it to the damn dentist.

CARL. Looks like you'd better. What is it, tender?

ALEX. Tender hell, it's gone. Oh, Jesus. "For the want of a nail the shoe was lost" — right? Sometimes I can't believe it...everywhere I look it's falling apart. I'm winding up the hearings last week...on my feet...I feel like I'm sweating...I think, Lord, I'm really worked up...I look down and my ink pen's leaking all down the front of my shirt...inside my jacket. Fourteen cameras on me. I'm ripping Ponderholtz's defense apart...brilliantly.

CARL. I'll bet.

ALEX. All I'm thinking is it's soaked through to my skin; I'm standing there like Napoleon. I start leaving fingerprints all over the table.

CARL. Nobody saw it?

ALEX. How do I know? No, just me. Had to wait till recess to change my shirt. Had to take a shower. Elastic on my shorts was blue. Aww, it's always something — my grandfather's pen, too. Beautiful old Waterman…you couldn't buy one like it. I had it in school…holds about a gallon of ink — all down my — oh, Jesus, Carl, I keep feeling my real life will begin any day now. This can't be it. This is just temporary. A dry run. I have a whole agenda of tabled activities. I've got two temporary fillings I've had for a year and a half. They're wearing away a little bit everyday. I can feel it with my tongue. My mother keeps calling me collect — to tell me to write her more often. I have my girl send her clippings — she writes me to get a haircut; you look too thin; I bet you eat nothing but sandwiches. Everything is tabled till next meeting.

CARL. Waiting for someday when the taxes go down and you get the mortgage paid off.

ALEX. I have to discuss this total upheaval with Gabby; I've known for a week and a half.

CARL. That's the Monday thing. What total upheaval?

ALEX. Did I say that? Forget I said it.

CARL. I'm going to figure it out and I'm going to kick your ass.

ALEX. Trouble is, the other day I had a flash of objectivity and made the mistake of asking myself what I wanted to do with my life. You're better off to go at it blind. You take it all in, and it all begins to look…

CARL. And it all falls apart — I know the feeling.

ALEX. Never do that — ask what it's all about. Never do that. *(He gets a sandwich.)* What do you want to do with it? I'll tell you exactly what I'd like to do with it.

CARL. Don't eat that if you're going to get a toothache.

ALEX. No, it's stopped. My thirty-fourth birthday I stood in the yard and looked down the block. This came as quite a revelation to me. I said, Alexander, you are not going to alter the course of the planet in any way. You aren't going to be President, or change the course of law, or eliminate injustice or graft to any tangible extent because you can bellow about corruption from the steeple of the First Presbyterian Church, but all the guys down the block are burning leaves. What they're *doing* with their *lives* is *burning leaves.*

CARL. How do you know?

ALEX. Know what?

CARL. That that's what they're doing. They may be writing to their mother more often and going to their dentist, telling the wife about Monday's upheaval.

ALEX. Carl, where's it getting them? What are they *doing?* They're *burning leaves.*

CARL. All right and burning leaves. It's important to them to have leaves burned. You like a sloppy lawn. Don't knock them for cleaning up.

ALEX. Paying bills, fighting with Gabby, pains in my leg, firing the secretary, heartburn. That's just not what it's all about. I begin to see the sense of following the call of Maxey Gene Connell and flying to Ibiza. *(Aside.)* Law buddy of mine...Phi Beta Kappa...valedictorian, Ph.D. in chemistry on the side. Tending artichokes and wild strawberries on the sunny hill of an island off Spain. Now it's going to take a great deal of talking to convince me he's got the wrong idea.

CARL. As big a hypochondriac as you are? Where would you find a dentist.

ALEX. No, it's stopped, it's fine.

CARL. Alex, life is a ballbreaker, it really is. Twenty percent of the people in the country are on dope, twenty percent of France is wiped out on wine twenty-four hours a day. It's too much for them. They can't take it. They can't take life, man. I don't blame them. It's a mess. When I was a kid, I had it all worked out. The whole point was to be happy. I was going to write a book..."The Principle of Life" I was going to call it.

ALEX. Modestly.

CARL. Well, goddamn it, I wasn't wrong! Of course I didn't have any principles except you should go to church on Sunday and be kind to dumb animals. And work sounded like play; I didn't know it was work.

ALEX. You were also single, which doesn't hurt.

CARL. No, that's different, that's the only good thing in all of it. I just thought it would be all very simple. "Building," "developing" were terrific words. I didn't think it'd take business managers and advisors and accountants and lawyers and investors, and every time you wanted to do something as simple as plant a tree you couldn't get a hold of a landscaper's accountant's secretary. I didn't know you had to get ahead; hell, I thought you could just lope along.

ALEX. You've managed to get pretty well ahead.

CARL. In the beginning it was fun; hell, it was a ball game. But people aren't prepared if you just want to play fair. It amazes me. The whole country's profiteering and pickpocketing each other; it's a daisy chain. That's what business amounts to. We're all telling each other every minute how important all the things we believe in are, how the world would collapse if we let up for a minute believing all the things we believe and doing all the things we do and, hell, nobody believes it. We all know it's a shell

game. It strains all our faculties keeping all the lies straight and juggling
all the rationalizations and pretending we don't notice everyone struggling with it, and you tell me you're not contented with your lot. Jesus
Christ, Alex, it's a lousy lot...nobody's content with it. Hell, I know
what it is; of course that's what it is!
ALEX. What what is?
CARL. Monday. Your Monday thing. Th—   lease it.

to expect me home for dinner, I say, honey don't expect me till late. So
she doesn't expect me till six or seven. I get home at ten, she's crawling
the walls, I say, honey, don't *expect!* If we'd have to sell the house...or

CARL. Probably should have.
ALEX. You think I don't believe that? I know men who for a fact have got
    their wives pregnant just because they were becoming exhausted with...
CARL. *(Overlapping a good deal.)* Don't start again, what do I know about it?
ALEX. Maybe that's why a girl wants it. So she'll get pregnant. I mean,
    finally. Maybe that's why they're so compulsive, without even being
    aware of being compulsive. We might be dealing with some psychologi-
    cal or biological truth here. Maybe they can't even help it.
CARL. Maybe you're just undersexed.
ALEX. No, I'm not under...
CARL. Wait. It isn't that, is it?
ALEX. What? Undersexed?
CARL. Did someone die? *(Pause.)*
ALEX. When?
CARL. You're not talking about Old Man Hayes? Representative Hayes,
    dying six days after being reelected to something like his fiftieth term in
    the House; keeled over flat on Michigan Avenue. The Governor has to
    appoint a replacement to fill Hayes's term. Is that an *(Crossing to the fire*
    place.) appointment or do we have a special election?
ALEX. No, no, no, no. It's a special election. But the Governor does hand
    pick the nominee.
CARL. So, call it an appointment.
ALEX. Call it an appointment. *(A long pause. Carl looks a little troubled, con-*
    fused.) And?
CARL. No, I think it's fine for the Governor and the Mayor and the Commis-
    sioner of Transportation. It's so logical and glamorous and popular. It's th

obvious move. Hell, why wouldn't Gabby go along with it if that's what you want. Is it?

ALEX. I said I'd consider it.

CARL. Oh, sure. *(Troubled pause.)* I know you really do have very definite feelings under all the...It's just not what I expected.

ALEX. Well, listen. I'll be going. I want to thank you for the toothache.

CARL. No, wait a minute. Is that what you want? Politics?

ALEX. I said I'd think about it.

CARL. You wouldn't have to sell your house or rent it. You'll only be gone for two years. *(Alex reacts.)* Oh, hell. You get to Washington, you'll never come back. You'll be president.

ALEX. If I knew you were going to be so happy for me...

CARL. You're a natural...

ALEX. I can't discuss it now...

CARL. O.K., O.K....of course not. You know damn well if you want it, I want you to have it. What's with Gabby now? Why isn't that working? What's antagonizing things?

ALEX. I don't want to discuss it; it's fine...

CARL. You look happy enough to me — when I see you, the two of you...you're the perfect couple.

ALEX. I'm happy. I'm O.K. I feel great! I don't know why! Of course we look happy to you. We go out and she's fine. We have a ball. We get home and she changes completely. Her voice changes, the way she walks changes, she stops laughing, or she starts laughing seductively.

CARL. *(Aside.)* He's off again.

ALEX. It's like she has a little movie of the evening up in her head and we've come to the X-rated scene. You should see the array of nightgowns she's got. She must think I've got a fetish. Or maybe she has. Why should it only be men who have fetishes? Outside with you and Mary she's fine. She comes home with just me and she changes completely. I love her too...out. I could fuck her under the table. We get home and she practically turns to oatmeal on the threshold. She loses every bone in her body. I have to hold her up. Her kisses all turn to tongue. Like she was trying to get me hot. Hell, I was hot already. If I don't bang her in the pachysandra, she's going to turn me off by the time I can get my pants unzipped.

CARL. Your problem is you don't like big sloppy kisses. Other guys I could name live for big sloppy kisses. Some people think big and sloppy is the only way to kiss. Every book you read, "She melted into his arms with her mouth moist and open…"

ALEX. I don't know what books you've been reading lately.

CARL. You're making a big issue out of what is basically a matter of taste. I'd say offhand that you didn't love her, but I don't want to hear it.

ALEX. No, not that. Well. Less and less. You don't love someone all the time. You love them for moments. A while now and a while after a while. And with Gabby the times are getting fewer and — all right — you like to get me going. Prove my lack of convictions. Get me going. I'm sorry to be such a drag-ass, kvetching about my problems when your business is in such good shape, your married life is on such solid rock, so idyllic — and so…

CARL. I didn't say that. Don't start in on me now.

ALEX. The one good island in a shit-soup of disillusions.

CARL. Come on.

ALEX. Carl, you're completely transparent. Never play poker, Carl; you're going to lose your shirt.

CARL. We're not at your hearings, Alex; you're not on the House floor. Don't cross-examine me.

ALEX. Then what is it? You're turning all wooly and introspective. Morbidly thumbing over your…

CARL. I haven't felt well.

ALEX. You're a physical horse, Carl. Mentally, the species is somewhat different lately.

CARL. I've had headaches for the past…

ALEX. I don't know how you can tell a hangover from a headache in the condition you're usually in.

CARL. Alex, I'm not interested in being the subject of one of your tirades.

ALEX. Hell's bells and goddamn, Carl; you know she's cheating on you, don't you?

CARL. You son of a bitch!

ALEX. Don't you? *(A long pause.)*

CARL. Does everybody know?

ALEX. I don't think so. Gabby told me.

CARL. She isn't a whore…I think she really loves him…it isn't like that.

ALEX. Did she tell you?

CARL. No, she doesn't know I know. I don't imagine. I saw them once. Well, I knew before that. I mean, it's something you know. There uh…"there needs no ghost," you know? "Come from the grave to tell me this…"

ALEX. Yeah, yeah, I know, got it.

CARL. He has a family too. Three girls.

ALEX. You know who he is?

CARL. Oh, sure…no, skip it. This isn't any good. It's no big deal. It's a comedy…it's a farce; it's not to be serious about.

ALEX. But you know who he is?

CARL. Yes. He's my CPA. See? His firm does the accounts for my office. Now, no more. I don't think about it. It's all the same to me.

ALEX. Mary is a powerhouse, Carl, you've got to keep ahead of her…Hell, you know that. You used to be ahead of things.

CARL. At least you didn't say I got to keep on top of her.

ALEX. What are you doing? Joking? What are you doing?

CARL. Alex, I see it like I see everything else — like I'm up in the air and it's down on the ground happening to someone else. It doesn't affect me. Nothing, now…shut up about it. Please.

ALEX. O.K.

CARL. I am doing nothing. To my surprise. Nothing. Waiting.

ALEX. Floating.

CARL. Waiting. It'll burn out. My God, we've been married nine years; it's normal. It's no big deal. I envy your energy that you can be concerned. It isn't Mary; Alex, I'm sorry. I can't get involved with anything. What did you call me, "wooly"?

ALEX. No, no.

CARL. "Wooly" is perfectly fair. But I'm sorry, even as you're going on about Gabby and you, I keep thinking — I mean, I love you very much — but if it came to the worst, you'd split up and she'd get the house and alimony and you'd get Washington and the car. And besides, I know it won't come to that. I can't imagine you taking old silent Hayes's seat in the House because I can't imagine anything. I come home and I read what you've been saying and watch the roundup of the day's news events and all that's happening in the world and it seems like a lot is, but I don't follow it. I watch and hope along that something will involve me. Touch me. Grab me. Piss me off. Something. Involve. It's the same thing as with Mary. I can't galvanize any concern. Nothing anyone says is real — how am I supposed to relate to it? Involve. I have an office manager who boils over…gets worked up over…I remember, when I was…You'll remember…everyone remembers…I don't know when it was…twelve years ago or more…I was a kid. No, I was only about twelve or so, so it was longer ago than that. Somewhere in Colorado or Ohio or Wyoming or somewhere in the *world* a little girl was playing in her backyard or near a mine shaft or somewhere, and the ground caved in or she got too close to the well, but she fell down, way down — forty or seventy feet or so into a hole. I don't know where it was, but this little girl was in this hole in the ground. She was about three years old or five or something like that. And they couldn't reach her, and firemen came and men with various kinds of gear — and they were afraid of caving in the sides of the hole, and they tried to dig her...reach her...dig her out. They could hear her and knew she was alive. And everyone all over the country stayed around their radios and prayed for her. And telegrammed the parent's hope and messages of compassion and love and hope for this little girl. It was like a war, it was like a kidnapping or like that. A whole country — the whole world — people ten thousand miles away — were alarmed and concerned for this one...one...one girl. Little girl. This little kid. *(A long pause.)*

ALEX. And what? *(Beat.)* What happened?

CARL. *(Looking at Alex.)* Huh? You don't remember that? I thought everyone would remem...No, I didn't mean it like...It isn't a story or something. It happened. That wasn't what I meant...I remember she died before they could reach her, but that wasn't why I...I didn't tell it to be sad. I just think of that time as a time when people were involved. Those events where the whole world goes into suspension and holds its breath at once, and for a little while comes together in something they realize is in some way, more important — significant — than anything else at that moment. Some crisis. Some danger. *(A wondering, brief pause.)* We've gotten much too civilized for our own good, Alex. And I wonder...at times...what...the pagans...the primitive people...how they felt after a public sacrifice. There's a need, some need, somewhere, for that important...contribution. So many people feel compelled to sacrifice themselves in one way or another, excuse or another, cause or another. Themselves or something very dear. Or expose it to danger. *(He sits.)* I try to understand her. Mary. I try to understand that she needs for some reason to expose our marriage to danger. That she needs the danger more than she needs whoever it is...more than she wants anything with Donald. Not sacrifice it if possible, but expose it to danger, herself, our marriage, Ellen. But then probably I just want to think that because I don't like believing that she loves someone else more than she does... It's usually the man's place to have the affair, isn't it? I thought that was our downfall. *(Beat.)*

ALEX. From the last statistics I read I understand it takes two.

CARL. Maybe I'm just naive about that. Ironic thing, of course, being she's safe really, because I can't for the life of me seem to get involved in being betrayed. Even by someone I love so...well, you know. Because like everything else for the last two years or so it just doesn't seem worthwhile Al. Alex. Alexander. It happens to someone else. Of course you're tied up into things, various concerns, you're...

ALEX. Oh, hell, yes. I have concerns out the ass. The government, birth control, the aged, the starving, the homeless and the shiftless, the useless...

CARL. Yeah. Well, I see it and I try to say all the things I feel, express my concerns, but deep down I'm not fooling myself because I know that really...honestly...at bottom...I don't care. I don't care. I envy you that you can, but I just don't care. I don't care. Care. C-A-R-E.

ALEX. I know how to spell it. I see it on el posters.

CARL. When's the last time you were on the el train?

ALEX. A lot. Really, I go. All the time. Never mind. Skip it.

CARL. They make love in the afternoon, for God's sake. When they can get away. We never did that, even before we got married. When I was getting my degree. She was a morning repeater. But not afternoons. She never liked to. Does Gabby? *(Carl gets a drink.)*

ALEX. Oh, come on, Carl.

CARL. No, no lie, does she? Gabby? if you don't mind...

ALEX. You can't learn it by the books. Your experience is not my experience, my experience isn't yours. It isn't even Gabby's experience! Sure. Sometimes. Given Gabby. We have. She loves it!

CARL. *(Suddenly.)* Cathy Fiscus. Was the little girl's name. Little Cathy Fiscus.

ALEX. *(Looks to him, smiles. A pause.)* In the afternoons, yeah, sure. Afterwards...should we go out...among people...Saturday afternoon, Sunday. I feel...well, like I've had it. Castrated. Shot. And I don't mean it funny or clever — spent. Oh God, now you'll go to work or get on the phone, someone'll ask you what you did you'll say, oh...spent the whole goddamned weekend hearing this story about a castrating female or about this guy who felt castrated...but try to see what I mean, past all this, what really is...for me...or for you...or Gabby. I mean walking with her, if we've made love in the afternoon, and go out, sometimes I get really mad at her for having robbed me of something. It's like I'm "safe" now. I feel like I'm this temporary eunuch in her...power. It's nothing strong, and it's only in the back of my mind, fizzing away back there where it's worse...But I get furious with her. I'd just like to be reassured that I wasn't the world's only man who felt cut, gelded — after sleeping with his own wife. Ravaged...I'd like just once, dear God take me back to the good old eras past, just once like to ravage her! I wish to hell it was Gabby who was...You don't know how easy you have it.

CARL. Sure, right.

ALEX. You'll never have that delicious feeling of being in service.

CARL. You know I don't agree with any of your...I always feel very proud...

ALEX. Hell, you don't know how good you've got it. Mary plays around with your accountant and you stay home...

CARL. Come on...

ALEX. ...Crocheting a goddamned afghan or something. *(Carl slugs Alex quite hard — and immediately, with a cry, grabs hold of Alex's shoulders — holding him tightly.)*

CARL. Alex, Alex. I do! I do! I try to understand and see what's going on, and I see it all go by sometimes like a movie. But I try to understand why she needs this or how it happened and because I rattle on about it I think it doesn't move me any more than anything else...Alex, why does she have to do it? *(Alex, taken completely off stride, is trying to answer, trying to comfort, but neither is possible. Shouting.)* WHAT'S SHE TRYING TO DO? I DON'T KNOW WHAT TO SAY. I DON'T KNOW HOW TO FEEL, ALEX. I DON'T KNOW HOW TO FEEL. I WANT IT BACK — LIKE IT WAS. IT WAS GOOD THEN. *(Flooding. Alex, over, can mumble, "What, Carl, what?")* IT WAS GOOD THEN, GOD-DAMN IT, WHEN I WAS OVER THERE — OVERSEAS — AND WE WROTE LETTERS TO EACH OTHER; IT WAS GOOD THEN, IT WAS GOOD THEN. IT WAS GOOD! IT WAS! *(Blackout.)*

END OF ACT ONE

ACT TWO

Night. The room is brilliantly lit around the bar area. Mary and Alex are talking to Gabrielle, quite spirited, laughing; lines tumble over each other. They sometimes include the audience.

ALEX. And we're jammed-packed into someone's god-awful claptrap of a...

MARY. Eddie Bender's god-awful Pontiac...

ALEX. Eddie Bender's Pontiac. All bellowing these sing-along songs at the top of our lungs, we're sliding all over the road, we've got about six dozen oranges in a shopping bag...

MARY. *(Completely over.)* Oh, God, yes, I'd forgotten all about the oranges...

ALEX. ...down around our feet with two ounces of Vodka shot into each...

MARY. Yes, because the faculty frowned on us passing the flask at games.

GABRIELLE. Oh, God, oh, how...

ALEX. Right, right...

MARY. They didn't mind us drinking, they frowned on us passing the flask.

ALEX. We get to the game to see Carl who was like the most important quarterback in the history of the Big Ten.

GABRIELLE. *(Completely over.)* I know. I know.

MARY. *(Over.)* He really was, you know.

ALEX. And by the half we didn't even know who we were playing.

GABRIELLE. Who spiked the oranges?

MARY. Who knows?

ALEX. One of the premed bunch, with a syringe.

MARY. I'll bet he went far.

ALEX. And for some reason Bender almost never drove his own car and you have...

MARY. I don't think he even had a license.

ALEX. *(Without stopping.)* ...no idea who's driving or who's sitting on your lap, but her hair's in your face and mouth and all the windows are open and there's a wind flying through the car...

MARY. Bitter cold — November.

ALEX. ...an everything smells of leaf smoke and wool sweaters and the oranges and leather...

MARY. Old Spice aftershave and cigarettes and we're all bundled up in blankets and quilts... *(Carl enters, his collar turned up.)* Hello, darling. You get Betty home all right?

CARL. Yeah.

MARY. It's getting cold, isn't it?

CARL. *(Putting the keys in a bowl.)* Warm in the car.

ALEX. And Bozo always took bass. He wasn't bass, but he took the counter stuff...

MARY. Because he couldn't carry a...

ALEX. Hey, Bozo! *(Singing.)* "You throw a silver dollar down upon the ground and it'll roll — because..." Come on! "And it'll roll...because..." Come on, that was your part... *(Carl has just come into the room, still with his coat on, as he will remain through the scene. His arms are slack, rather troubled, not at all in their tempo.)*

CARL. I don't...

ALEX. You flubbed your part. You took bass.

CARL. I don't remember, not on that one...

MARY. You remember that, honey, sure you do.

ALEX. Sure you do.

ALEX AND MARY. "A woman never knows what a good man she's got, until she turns him...down, down, down, down" — you mean to tell me you honestly don't remember...?

MARY. Everybody knows that.

ALEX. That one?

CARL. *(Crossing to the steps to Ellie's room, troubled, unheard.)* Ah, guys, would you mind terribly...

ALEX. I think he only re-   MARY. Everyone excepting
membered the...   Carl was bombed.

GABRIELLE. Well, he had to play.

MARY. Speaking of pleasantly high, how come you haven't any grass this week? Where do you get it, anyway?

ALEX. I'll never tell.

GABRIELLE. He won't even tell me.

MARY. One of your future constituents has a backyard plot. Well, that will never do. Why don't I mix up something strong for a cold night.

CARL. *(Crossing to the dining room.)* Sure.

MARY. Something quasi-exotic like a sidecar. And we'll toast our new congressman.

ALEX. I haven't said I'd take it; I'm thinking. We're thinking aren't we, darlin'?

GABRIELLE. *(To Alex.)* Hadn't we better go soon? It's incredibly late.

MARY. No, it isn't bad. On a cold night like this and after that movie I think a sidecar sounds conservative.

CARL. *(To Alex.)* I was probably worrying about the game and not singing any...

ALEX. You worry? Are you kidding? He didn't have a nerve in his body.

MARY. Did you remember to pay Betty?

CARL. Yeah.

MARY. I hope she isn't coming down with something. Ellen catches anything communicable within twenty miles. She looked dreadful.

CARL. *(Crossing into the entry, he gets a mask.)* She said she had a toothache.

MARY. Oh, God. Has she seen a dentist? *(Alex groans.)* That's the most horrible pain.

GABRIELLE. None for me, love.

MARY. Sure you will.

ALEX. Come on, a nightcap.

GABRIELLE. I'm half asleep already.

MARY. *(To Gabrielle.)* You didn't know the Northwestern campus did you? I keep forgetting.

ALEX. It used to be beautiful. Really lovely.

MARY. Before the landfill.

GABRIELLE. I can't say I like it now.

MARY. Oh, it's a crime, but it used to be marvelous. Carl, would you stop playing with that — what is that you're playing with?

CARL. You guys see this? *(Picking up the mask of a bull.)* I got it at the — *(Holding the mask to his face.)* Moooooooooo!

GABRIELLE. No. No. Carl! Oh, that's terrible.

CARL. You don't like it?

GABRIELLE. Oh, God.

CARL. I liked it. They're plastic. They had incredible masks this year.

MARY. Remember when plastic was going to save the world?

GABRIELLE. No, I love it, no, it's great, but not a cow! Why a cow?

CARL. That's not a cow. That's a bull!

MARY. Carl was a bull and Ellen was a calf; he took her trick-or-treating around the...

GABRIELLE. Oh, how great...

ALEX. You should have asked Gabby to come along...

GABRIELLE. Yes, I'd have loved it.

CARL. I was a smash in all the living rooms on the North Shore.

MARY. *(She gives Carl a drink.)* Darling, you were smashed in all the living rooms on the North Shore.

CARL. That too, that too...

MARY. They cleaned up. Didn't you see the dish of knosh in the hall?

CARL. That's me. I'm Taurus. The Bull. It's a bull.

MARY. *(Pouring and passing drinks.)* Darling, you're Scorpio, you're not Taurus. I'm Taurus.

CARL. Really?

MARY. You know that; your moon's in Taurus.

CARL. *(He gives the mask to Mary.)* Well, you should have it then. Here.

ALEX. Or you could wear it on your moon.

CARL. That'd be a neat trick.

MARY. *(Dryly.)* Wouldn't it. *(They sip their drinks.)*

GABRIELLE. Ummmm. Lemon juice, brandy, and…triple sec?

MARY. Cointreau.

GABRIELLE. Ummmm. Cointreau.

CARL. The other one, the other song I remember. "The Poor Lambs," the "Whiffenpoof Song." That "Baa, Baa, Baa…"

ALEX. *(Overlap.)* Oh, God, yes.

MARY. Yes, yes — that's my favorite.

GABRIELLE. *(Sings.)* Gentlemen songsters… *(Others haltingly join in.)* My God, we even sang that one at Stevens. Where's that from, that's Yale or Harvard.

MARY. It's got to be an Eli…

CARL AND ALEX. *(Sing.)* We are poor little lambs…

GABRIELLE. It invariably made me cry…

Who have lost our way*

MARY. I love it.

CARL. All the boys around the piano in about twelve-part harmony.

ALEX. Baa, baa, baa.

ALEX. Very serious. Camping it up — till we got drunk enough — then really serious.

ALL. *(Sing.)* Gentlemen songsters…

MARY. *(Over.)* Oh, but we loved it.

GABRIELLE. Oh, I did too.

ALEX. You should have seen this nut at school. I'll bet they were sorry they let him in. Nobody needs a quarterback that bad. I mean he was a legend.

CARL. No, I…

* *See special note on copyright page.*

100 LANFORD WILSON

ALEX. He was, he was a legend. Like Paul Bunyan or something. He used to live way the hell out in the boondocks. Out of town about a mile from…

MARY. Two miles.

ALEX. Way the hell out, halfway to Skokie.

CARL. It kept me in shape.

ALEX. *(Energetically.)* Finally he got a car Jun…what was it, Junior year?

CARL. Sophomore. By Junior I was rooming with you and Carson; we were…

ALEX. Anyway, Freshman and Sophomore years he's out at wherever the hell it was, and he trots into town, jogs into town in sweatpants.

MARY. Destroying all the girls right and left.

ALEX. Like hell; he looked deranged.

MARY. Yeah, with his dong flopping around in those sack pants.

ALEX. You wouldn't know him. He looked wild. He wasn't a pussy cat like he is now…

CARL. I wasn't any different.

ALEX. *(Without pause.)* You…He looked deranged. And he runs — sprints into town and this is legend — he's busting toward town and this car pulls alongside of him…

MARY. Oh, God.

ALEX. Driving along, Carl doesn't slow down and the guy asks if he can give Carl a lift into town, into the field, and Carl says "No thanks, I'm in a hurry!"

MARY. *(Over Alex.)* Hurry! *(All laugh.)*

CARL. Well, I was; I wasn't even thinking.

ALEX. I mean he was a character! Senior year he nearly wrecked our academic career. Carson and I used to sneak into the room at about four A.M. trying not to wake up Bozo here or turn on any lights and we'd go sprawling over a clothesline this guy's strung across the room. Waist high. But not as a joke. For real. To hang clothes on. I spent half the year on the floor tangled up in his goddamned wet jerseys and sweat socks. Look at him, you know it's true. *(Carl is grinning. He follows the conversation but stands; the others are seated, a bit off from them.)*

CARL. I never knew what time you were…

ALEX. *(To Mary.)* Well, I don't have to tell you what it was like.

CARL. No, she controlled me pretty…

MARY. It was different, though. I only dated him a couple of times before he decided the army needed him for two years. It was incredible. I didn't know what to think. He used to come to me with shoe polish on his cuffs, smelling like a bootblack — and he'd always had a couple of drinks to steel his nerve. No, the post-grad days were — he was the returning star and I was the returning homecoming queen. All very lauded over, though they couldn't see allowing us to live in the fraternity house.

GABRIELLE. With his wife, I guess not.

MARY. Not wife...

ALEX. Concubine.

MARY. Paramour. Total scandal. And of course Mom, who's more conservative than...well, you know...was ready to disinherit me.

GABRIELLE. Oh, God, no. All that Wedgewood. *(Carl crosses to the bar, makes himself another drink.)*

MARY. Exactly, almost an ultimatum — the carpets or Carl. No, the wife came afterwards. Everyone was greatly relieved. *(Aside.)* This is when people still pretended to be moral, you understand. They celebrated for days.

ALEX. We celebrated for nights.

MARY. We really had a neat little house.

CARL. It was cozy. It was cozy.

MARY. It was small. And with drainpipes that made disconcerting digestive noises all night and a fireplace you could have built a closet in. But not a fire, unfortunately.

GABRIELLE. Of course.

MARY. *(Aside.)* And we did not "have" to get married.

CARL. Not at all, not at all. Ellen was two years yet.

MARY. I just held out as long as I could.

CARL. Yeah? Yeah? I thought you just finally saw the light. Then we bought a little travel agency...

MARY. Mom's wedding present.

ALEX. And then a little motel, and then a little shopping center...

GABRIELLE. *(Aside.)* And than a little subdivision.

CARL. It was something else living with this chick. I'd never seen anything so clean. Not just the house, but I used to come home, walk in the door, and the place smelled of...not perfume...but powder — nothing smells that clean. Used to blow my mind.

MARY. It was very special. Carl was thinner, firmer then. Hard as a wall. And really agile, for his weight, and eager. We made love after he studied till midnight. And then...sleeping so close and warm, we used to wake up just as it got light out...

CARL. *(Gently.)* Summertime; summer term.

MARY. ...and go at it all over again. I'd fall back asleep, curled up against his chest with his sweaty-wet face at my ear murmuring, "Marry me, Mary, marry me, Mary, marry me..." *(Aside, distantly musing.)* I don't actually think...that I loved him then. But I love him then now.

ALEX. I ran into Carson about a month ago.

MARY. That was their roommate.

ALEX. We had dinner. He's living in Philadelphia. He has four kids. He weighs three hundred pounds. Spent the whole goddamned evening trying to sell me life insurance.

MARY. Well, Alex, with four kids...

ALEX. The team could have used you when you went back too.

CARL. Naw, naw, they could have had a good team that year.

ALEX. Yeah, except for Hanesfield as wide receiver. Guy had hands of margarine. And if you think Burns...

CARL. Yeah, well, maybe they could have used a...

MARY. What's wrong, darling?

GABRIELLE. What? Nothing.

ALEX. Yeah, yeah, yeah, yeah.

MARY. Silly.

CARL. They asked! They tried to get me coaching or something. I couldn't cut it. I used to go out and pass a few with them.

GABRIELLE. It sounds lovely. I just...Oh, God, I'm terrible tonight I'm just no good at all. Do you get nervous?

ALEX. Hell, you couldn't...

MARY. God. Yes.

CARL. Anyway, I was getting pretty slow, by then. *(The men improvise.)*

GABRIELLE. ...I mean all the time...

MARY. I know *just* what you mean. How come?

GABRIELLE. Oh, it's just me. I'm incredibly tired lately; I haven't energy for anything. I should take vitamins or something. Eat something.

MARY. Spinach.

GABRIELLE. Ummmmm.

MARY. Or oysters.

GABRIELLE. Ugh! Thanks, not. I'd prefer being tired.

MARY. That's right, you're the one.

ALEX. How come, doll?

GABRIELLE. Oh, who knows? I thought the movie was depressing. I can't bear the city anymore.

ALEX. You mean after the shops close.

MARY. Well, Washington won't be much improvement.

GABRIELLE. No, there's just too much going on. There's…

MARY. Don't let those faggots get to you.

GABRIELLE. It isn't just that. There're just too many people in the world.

ALEX. You're just upset about the demonstration.

GABRIELLE. That was not a demonstration. That was a carousal.

MARY. Demonstration of lifestyle, maybe.

GABRIELLE. I couldn't make out *what* they thought they were doing.

ALEX. I tried to tell you; you weren't interested.

GABRIELLE. No, and I'm still not; I don't care.

MARY. Nor do they.

GABRIELLE. You try to just drive into town for a perfectly simple evening —

ALEX. At a skin flick?

GABRIELLE. In any case.

MARY. Decidedly disappointing, by the way.

ALEX. For the girls maybe.

MARY. I never felt so overdressed in my life!

GABRIELLE. In any case, to be held up by students — or I don't even know if they were students — swarming all over the street in beards and glitter and eight-hundred-dollar Loden coats.

ALEX. They didn't do a thing, they did no damage — they held up traffic.

GABRIELLE. And to aggravate matters, I thought you were going to get out of the car and join them, you almost…

ALEX. They were only having fun; they didn't threaten you, Gabby.

GABRIELLE. The reincarnation of Siegfried himself — they did, they knew it made the people in the cars uptight.

ALEX. *(To Gabrielle.)* Well, now whose fault is that, is that their…?

GABRIELLE. It just didn't seem like the most propitious time to announce a political career.

ALEX. If it were a question of announcing it, I can't think of…

MARY. They weren't so bad.

GABRIELLE. *(Over.)* Oh, I know, I'm wrong. I'm wrong. It's perfectly all right for them to do as they please — after all, what is it I'm so anxious to protect, who am I kidding? It's just...*(Aside.)* Forgive me, O.K.? I don't want to see it. If it's all the same to everybody.

MARY. They're difficult not to see.

GABRIELLE. I know all the arguments, it's all I ever hear; O.K., change it all; I want it to change too — my God, if we're going to be in Washington next year, I'd better have some convictions.

MARY. Not necessarily, from what I hear...

GABRIELLE. Only I want to wake up one morning and everything will have been magically accomplished overnight. I'm just not the revolutionary type.

MARY. Me either.

GABRIELLE. I'll go about as far as to sign a petition. *(She sits.)*

MARY. I won't even do that. I do nothing. Oh, God, I feel myself more and more becoming an emotional recluse like Mom. Mom walks through her apartment trailing a literal cloud of Jungle Gardenia and two little lilac poodles — Fou Fou and Poo Choo or something — who are continuously high on perfume vapor. And that's her entire life — somehow managing to be elegant, tottering about the apartment trailing the vapors and the two spaced-out poodles, with a cigarette and a glass of white wine in her one hand and a polishing rag in her other. Looking for blurs on her furniture. Fingerprints. She's unbelievable. Ellen, of course, loves her, loves visiting.

GABRIELLE. Real furniture, though.

MARY. Oh, God, beautiful. *(Aside.)* Period Newport, museums are creaming; and about a dozen real Kazaks, a blockfront John Townshend chest-on-chest you could die from. And that sustains her. Without interests or friends. I just think the old girl knows something I don't.

ALEX. Or doesn't know something that you...

MARY. No, I don't believe that anymore.

GABRIELLE. *(Under.)* Alex, you wanted to call the service.

MARY. *(Continues, as Alex goes to the phone.)* I'm getting so mean and small and insular — oh, well, it's unimportant, I suppose we all are...

ALEX. *(At the phone.)* What, what?

MARY. Oh, I just have no patience with people — anyone in the least different from us. And I don't mean importantly or socially, I mean in the prettiest possible sense. Example: I drink coffee black, have all my life — I'm really getting deeply intolerant of people putting cream and sugar in their...I sit there watching them measure and dribble and stir and clink and drip their spoon and smile — I really just have no patience with them at all. You put together a dinner party for eight which should be perfectly simple, and Rosie tells you Marvin doesn't eat lamb or Sandy breaks out from chocolate — then leave! Go away. I don't want to know you. I am utterly unconcerned with the person who likes okra.

ALEX. What you're saying is you're this very selfish, very spoiled little girl.

MARY. Oh, come on; well, yes, of course, but you know you feel the same.

ALEX. No, I really don't think so.

MARY. I have a private theory that we're all like that. We all. Our generation. The older generation is…

GABRIELLE. Older.

MARY. Older. And the younger…well, those I don't understand at all. I think I might admire them tremendously, but…

ALEX. Absolutely.

MARY. I'm quite sure — no, not absolutely, I *think*. But I'm quite sure I don't understand them at all. They're so bright and so damn dull all at once. See, I think of the kids and I feel like Mom; I think of Mom and I feel like the kids.

ALEX. Oh, no, Mary, no…

MARY. *(Putting her cigarette out.)* Why are you always so pigheaded? I'm trying to teach you something.

ALEX. It's just a question of do you want to align yourself with the past or with the future.

MARY. Tell me about the future, and I'll let you know.

ALEX. I'll tell you about the past. The kids today know this. We were silly to quit swinging from the fruitladen trees and start growing wheat. But wheat makes cake and cake is good and that's rationalization.

MARY. I think you sound like a shoo-in for the under-eighteen vote. Which reminds me, you need a haircut; I've been meaning to tell you all night.

ALEX. That's all Gabby says to me. Mom too.

GABRIELLE. I don't think your mother would vote for him.

MARY. I don't think Mom knows women have the right.

ALEX. Of course I'd like to have got out of the car and gone with those kids.

MARY. *(All overlapping a bit here.)* …I don't see Alex as the firebrand of social…

GABRIELLE. *(Over.)* Alex.

ALEX. It's what I feel. With their awareness of what the hell is happening on this planet — I'd give anything to be seventeen now. Eighteen.

GABRIELLE. I wouldn't, thanks.

MARY. Oh, well, Alex, love, darling! That's a whole different thing altogether. *(To Gabrielle.)* I wouldn't either. I had acne and no breasts at all. Let me pour another round and we'll *(She rises, collects the glasses.)* toast Ponce de León and Alex can lead us in a prayer for world harmony.

ALEX. Carl had better do that; I'm a bit out of the praying habit.

GABRIELLE. None for me, darling.

MARY. Right, darling, with your Sunday School experiences.

CARL. Hmm?

MARY. Carl is three sheets to the wind.

CARL. *(To Mary.)* Am I?

MARY. You are. Blistered.

CARL. I never know. No one can tell except Mary. I stopped arguing when I passed out mid-sentence once. Do I what? *(They laugh.)* I'm a good drunk. *(They laugh.)*

MARY. Superlative, darling!

ALEX. Pray.

MARY. *(She crosses to the dining room, getting more drinks.)* Pray.

CARL. Pray? Ah...yes.

ALEX. Seriously.

CARL. No, I do, I do.

ALEX. When?

CARL. Every night. Before I go to sleep. Part of my sleep ritual.

ALEX. Every blessed...

CARL. Every night, yes; nearly every night.

ALEX. What do you say, "Now I lay me down to sleep"?

CARL. Uh. Yes. *(Beat.)* I'd as soon not discuss it.

ALEX. At least not drunk.

GABRIELLE. Especially not...

CARL. I'm not what you'd call terribly religious. I've only been terribly religious once. I mean, like everybody else who sits up for the last late show — I jump up to turn off the sermonette...

ALEX. Yeah, before the rabbi from the Cicero precinct can tell me I'm not saved.

CARL. *(Including the audience.)* But when I was thirteen, Mom had an operation. I don't think it was serious but operations scare the hell out of me anyway. And this was for...well, I won't guess, minor in any case. And I became the most zealously religious little boy in town. I prayed and cried and bartered with God — I promised to quit smoking — I'd been smoking already about three years by then — and to never again masturbate. And never swear if He would spare Mom's life.

GABRIELLE. Oh God.

CARL. And when she recovered…quite easily…I was positive it was a direct result of my prayers.

GABRIELLE. Absolutely.

CARL. Dreamed of being canonized — *(Aside.)* we were Baptist, remember —

MARY. Nevertheless.

CARL. I only broke my promise gradually, so I wouldn't notice.

ALEX. Or so God wouldn't notice.

CARL. I didn't actually buy a pack of cigarettes for over a year. By then I had managed to convince myself that she would have recovered anyway. *(He crosses to the sofa, gets a glass. Then he crosses to the desk, looking for a cigarette.)* It's very odd. About prayer. I don't quit because I've got all this time invested in it. When the sky suddenly splits wide open one day and angels sing — you look and say — thank God, I kept up my praying. *(He crosses to the dining room. Beat. He continues, not too seriously, but down.)* But I don't think…a paradox here. I don't think I ever quite forgave Mom for causing me to make a solemn promise I wasn't strong enough to keep. *(Checking for cigarettes.)* Seventeen? No…No, no, no, no. *(Carl finds a cigarette, handing one to Alex.)*

ALEX. *(Rubbing his leg.)* No, I'm trying to stop.

CARL. *(Looking for matches.)* Yeah?

MARY. *(She gives a drink to Alex, Carl, then sits.)* Congratulations.

ALEX. Thank you. All of the twelve hours so far. I'll probably just gain weight. Oh, well, it occurred to me I've been intending to quit for the past five years. No joke. For five years, every week I think I'll save some money and buy a carton of cigarettes; then I think, well, hell, I'm giving them up, I'll have quit before I could smoke them all anyway. *(Carl looks at his watch.)*

GABRIELLE. Darling, it's one-thirty.

ALEX. *(Standing, pressing his hand to his leg.)* Yeah, well… *(Mary and Gabrielle cross to the hall closet.)*

CARL. Your legs?

ALEX. Huh? Oh, yeah.

CARL. Need exercise.

ALEX. No, no. I don't know what it is. Maybe it's just smoking. *(Picking up his coat.)* Well. *(Carl follows.)*

GABRIELLE. *(Getting up, taking her coat, a very smart, quite new fur.)* Oh, yes. Call tomorrow.

MARY. I'm so glad you got that coat.

GABRIELLE. I'll need it this winter if this is any indication.

ALEX. *(Lines overlap from here to their exit.)* Carl, don't forget the game.

CARL. No, I can't watch the team they have now lose.

ALEX. You'll change your mind. *(They are near the door.)*

GABRIELLE. Oh, Alex. Oh, look, it's trick or treat.

MARY. Isn't it ghastly?

CARL. I told you we cleaned up.

MARY. It's all stuck together in one lump.

GABRIELLE. Oh, no, I haven't seen candy corn since I was about twelve.

MARY. It's precious to Ellie. She wanted it in her room, but I convinced her to "share" it with us so she doesn't gorge herself. *(Opening the door.)* Brrrrr. It's cold. It's Christmas soon.

ALEX. Oh, don't mention it.

GABRIELLE. Oh, I love it.

ALEX. She's had her Christmas.

MARY. Of course, with Ellen; I love it too.

GABRIELLE. She's just at that age.

ALEX. Yeah, and Carl would make a great Santa Claus.

CARL. Oh, yeah. *(He wonders back into the living room, still in his topcoat with the collar turned up. He sits on the sofa.)* Ho, ho, ho!

MARY. I love Christmas out here. And all the carolers; it's beautiful.

ALEX. So does she.

GABRIELLE. I do. *(Singing.)* "God rest ye merry gentlemen: *(Mary joins her.)*

GABRIELLE AND MARY.	ALEX. *(Over.)* Ring-a-ding
Let nothing you dismay.	
Remember Christ our Savior	
was born on Christmas	
Day."	

MARY. With their bells ringing.

GABRIELLE. *(Overlapping.)* And they're all bundled up, freezing.

ALEX. She loves anything. *(They say good night. Mary shuts the door after them.)*

MARY. Brrrr. Jesus. *(She crosses to the living room, collects some glasses. Carl pours the last drink from the pitcher into his glass. Mary collects the remaining glasses and pitcher.)* Poisonous movie, didn't you think?

CARL. Pretty bad.

MARY. I'll check on Ellie. Will you be up? *(No reaction from Carl.)* Don't bother I'll be right down. *(Mary exits into the kitchen with the tray.)*

CARL. *(Alone onstage, he sings quietly.)* "To save us all from Satan's power when we have gone astray..." *(Beat. Aside.)* Yes, it's...very difficult.

MARY. *(Coming from the kitchen.)* Don't you think you can take your coat off? They've gone.

CARL. Huh? No, I didn't...

MARY. I'm kidding. *(She kisses him on the cheek, then turns out one lamp.)* Good night love; don't drink any more.

CARL. *(Putting his glass down.)* No, no. *(Mary exits up the stairs.)* All of which is not the subject. Prayer, praying. Not the question. The question is why, with all the others, am I up watching the friggin' last late show in the first place! Watching the last late show; hearing you slip out of your dress and your slip. And brush against the carpet walking across to the closet. Listening to your breathing — after you're asleep. No, hell; it's all got to break! *(Carl takes his glass, looks around, turns off another lamp — leaving the stage still quite light. He takes the glass into the dark kitchen. As he exits, a noise is heard at the front door. A key, stomping, etc. Alex enters, followed by Gabrielle. Gabrielle is somewhat more tired. Alex is somewhat more irritable.)*

ALEX. Wheew! God. The house smells like someone had pissed in the fireplace.

GABRIELLE. Alex! My God.

ALEX. About a week ago. *(They are putting their coats away.)*

GABRIELLE. Really, that's not necessary. What'd...you used to do that?

ALEX. I don't know now if I really did it or just wanted to do it a lot.

GABRIELLE. *(Crossing to the bedroom.)* Where's the bed? — I'm exhausted.

ALEX. *(Tensely.)* Wait a second! *(Pause.)* Did you leave the light on?

GABRIELLE. Huh? Yes, remember?

ALEX. *(Crossing to the living room.)* How come?

GABRIELLE. Oh, I don't know. I feel safer. Foil a burglar today. *(She lies on the sofa.)*

ALEX. Well, that's pretty...

GABRIELLE. I feel terrible. God, I hated that movie.

ALEX. All right. Enough. I've heard enough about that movie. I guess it wasn't a very good idea.

GABRIELLE. Wonderful idea. Terrible movie. Will you think less of me if I don't bathe?

ALEX. No, I might have to sleep on the sofa.

GABRIELLE. Be my guest. Carl was really belting them down at dinner, wasn't he?

ALEX. Yes, well he does that, you know.

GABRIELLE. (*Crossing around the sofa, taking off her dress.*) Are you coming to sleep? You must be dropping.

ALEX. I'm not all that tired, actually.

GABRIELLE. There's a switch.

ALEX. If I turn in early, you aren't obliged to go to bed too.

GABRIELLE. If I didn't want to, I wouldn't. (*She sits on the back of the sofa.*) You want to tuck me in?

ALEX. Yeah, I'll be in. (*She slips her arms around his neck and kisses him.*)

GABRIELLE. Don't get tense, I'm too tired!

ALEX. Tense? What the…what are you talking about?

GABRIELLE. (*Crossing to the bedroom.*) O.K., darling. If I fall asleep, I love you. (*She goes into the bedroom.*)

ALEX. Should I take that as a sign? (*He crosses to the hall. In a German accent.*) Vos dis passing mine bedtroom door bare-asses naked, huh?

GABRIELLE. (*Off.*) It's cold enough for flannel

ALEX. Der es un old-fashioned fräulein, ya? Dis all goosepimply? (*Aside.*) Dis all goosepimply in der.

GABRIELLE. (*Off.*) Yes, And it's not fräulein, it's frau. Good night, love. Brrrr. (*The lights go out.*)

ALEX. Lieblich dassn't vont turked in?

GABRIELLE. (*Off.*) No. Go away. And quit talking like that.

ALEX. (*Straight.*) That's pretty good — car to bed in sixty seconds flat.

GABRIELLE. (*Off.*) I'm falling apart. I don't feel well at all.

ALEX. You sick?

GABRIELLE. (*Off.*) Just tired.

ALEX. You want anything?

GABRIELLE. (*Off.*) No, I'm fine.

ALEX. The radio won't bother you, will it?

GABRIELLE. (*Off.*) Not a chance.

ALEX. Good night.

GABRIELLE. (*Off.*) Night, I love you.

ALEX. I love you.

GABRIELLE. (*Off.*) I love you.

ALEX. (*Mimic.*) Go away, close the door already; turn on the radio. Get out.

GABRIELLE. (*Off.*) There's an idea.

ALEX. Good night, love. (*Alex closes the door. He turns entry light off, he crosses to the living room, goes to the radio, turns it on low — finds a lively station, goes to the desk, looks through a drawer and finds a black-stemmed, white-bowled pipe and a small pouch of tobacco. He packs the pipe, and lights it.*

Then he sits down at the desk, he looks to the door, and lifts the phone qui-
etly. He dials very slowly. Eleven numbers. He listens and looks to his watch.
He sets the phone back in its cradle, wanders to the living room area, and
sits in his chair. He turns off the lamp. The audience can still see Alex. Carl
comes in from the kitchen, still in his coat. He hangs his coat in the closet,
looks around the room…empties an ashtray — something he does not do well
or often. He crosses to dining room and sits. There is a noise off in the bed-
room. The bed jolts. Gabrielle is getting out of bed.)

GABRIELLE. Ah, ah… *(Alex quickly knocks out the pipe and tucks it into his*
  pocket. He turns on the lamp beside the chair. He gets a few steps toward the
  door as Gabrielle opens it. She crosses to the foyer, gasping.) Ah — oh, oh…

ALEX. *(He turns the radio off, crosses to Gabrielle.)* What's wrong? Darling?

GABRIELLE. Are there…

ALEX. What? You O.K.baby?

GABRIELLE. Are there any…oh, no…I'm…

ALEX. *(Laughing teasingly. He turns the light on.)* Hey, what's up? You were
  dreaming. Sweetie? You were asleep.

GABRIELLE. Oh, sweet Jesus.

ALEX. You O.K.?

GABRIELLE. *(She crosses to the bedroom.)* Yeah, Oh, wow; don't wake me up.

ALEX. No.

GABRIELLE. What are you…?

ALEX. I'll be right in. I'm just trying to relax.

GABRIELLE. How long have I been asleep?

ALEX. About five minutes.

GABRIELLE. *(Groaning.)* That's not possible…

ALEX. Go sleep. You want me to come?

GABRIELLE. I'm O.K. Mmmmm. *(She kisses him. She leaves through the door.)*

ALEX. *(Crossing to the door.)* Door shut?

GABRIELLE. Yes, darling, please.

ALEX. Good night. *(Alex shuts the door, unconsciously wiping his mouth with*
  the back of his hand. He looks at his watch, goes to the desk and sits. Alex
  quietly dials the number, listens. Carl sits on his end of the sofa. Re the phone.)
  Goddamn.

CARL. Who are you calling?

ALEX. A girl.

CARL. Age?

ALEX. Seventeen.

CARL. Relationship?

ALEX. I'm not sure.

CARL. You've had her?

ALEX. No, I take her places.

CARL. The ball game, the movies, the museum, the zoo.

ALEX. The botanical gardens once.

CARL. She studies botany.

ALEX. At the University of Chicago.

CARL. And you're in love with her.

ALEX. Something like that.

CARL. Where is she?

ALEX. I was just wondering.

CARL. *(Glancing at his watch.)* It's nearly two.

ALEX. Yeah, I know. Well. *(He hangs up the phone.)*

CARL. No, no, no, this has got to break wide open.

ALEX. Do I love her? Yes. I think so. But unfortunately I suspect that love is only a neurosis that people have agreed everyone should have together. No different from acrophobia. It isn't a natural process. Like breathing, or eating or sex. It's tacked on.

CARL. Swimming isn't natural either, but nobody puts it down.

ALEX. As long as you don't grease up and try to cross channels with it.

CARL. What the hell are you doing with this teenager, anyway?

ALEX. Debbie. It isn't like that.

CARL. It sounds pretty damn sick if you want to...

ALEX. Carl, the other guy's business always sounds sick.

CARL. Well, what do you do? Nothing? What are you...like her uncle?

ALEX. O.K. Fine. Exactly. And she's like my respiratory system. Buddy, I'd as soon not...

CARL. Yeah, fine by me, only I'd think...

ALEX. Carl, it's like I was never young. I must have been purblind and deaf. I didn't see things. You and I drank and had fun and sang, but I didn't see things. This girl knows things I don't even know yet. She knows how to leave herself alone. She has no allegiance, no priorities — everything is valuable to her — equally. As it comes.

CARL. And that's right?

ALEX. I think it might be.

CARL. Oh God, Alex. Don't you want a family? Don't you want to have kids?

ALEX. Jesus! You always ask me that. Every time...

CARL. Yeah, well what do you always answer?

ALEX. 'Cause what I wanted was…

CARL. 'Cause what I wanted most used to be a boy — a son. I would have had fifteen of Ellen to get a boy and loved them every one. No lie — I almost blamed Mary for having a girl. Now, of course, I wouldn't trade her. Funny thing, blame. *(He laughs.)* Hell, it's still one hell of a kick that Donald's had three girls in a row…

ALEX. The CPA, right?

CARL. I hit on an answer. Ellen. Brought us together. Remarkably. Wonderfully.

ALEX. I'd think she would.

CARL. But it wouldn't work now. Not really.

ALEX. Another kid?

CARL. No, not that. I was thinking something else.

ALEX. I thought you were talking about having a…

CARL. No, I was thinking people can be brought together by tragedy. If something happened to Ellen…

ALEX. Carl, nothing's going to happen to…

CARL. But if something did…I always wondered what very, very primitive people…There's something…in…it's a fantasy. All in the air. It's all a house of cards. One fantasy…lie — balanced on two others. I love them, too.

ALEX. Too damn much.

MARY. *(She enters from Ellie's room and speaks to a very preoccupied Carl.)* I'm sorry, darling. I got embroiled in a drunken question-and-answer session. She went back to sleep. Ellen takes more and more after you — she lacks all coherence. What do you make of Alex's career?

CARL. Has he decided?

MARY. Impending then. I can't decide if he isn't just seeing himself carrying a charger, advancing into battle — in which case…

CARL. Honey, you don't carry a charger into battle — the charger is the horse.

MARY. I thought you carried a charger — like a lance. Well, that makes sense. Right then. Charging in *à cheval* — with plumes.

CARL. He might fool us. *(Alex crosses to the desk, sits.)*

MARY. If he's not political, he'll be eaten alive, and if he is political, then I've no interest in him. Why the hell doesn't he just quit and go to work for the Civil Liberties Union if he has such an overpowering social conscience? I know Gabby's confused…

CARL. I'd think so. *(As Mary starts to go.)* You know I had to make a lot of quick telephone confirmations and I knocked them off this afternoon in about ten minutes flat.

MARY. Good.

CARL. And without even skipping a beat I called Donald and asked him how about knocking it off with my wife. *(Freeze. A long pause. Alex dials a number, looks at his watch.)*

MARY. And what did he say?

CARL. I wasn't even sure I could call him; I didn't actually know I was going to till I hung up.

MARY. Whatever gave you the idea there was anything to knock off?

CARL. No, we won't do that...

MARY. Won't do what?

CARL. Pretend. We won't pretend. Of course I'd know. I've known for months. Every Wednesday.

MARY. You're being awfully circuitous for someone with a degree...

CARL. No, Mary...

MARY. I go into town. I've been seeing Mom almost every week...she's no Spring...

CARL. I'm not talking about your mother.

MARY. Well, then I haven't...

CARL. No, Mary, don't, Mary. I go by the apartment at the Commodore every Wednesday afternoon to check and see if he's showed up. To watch the blinds turn. You turn them up and he turns them down. I told you I'd been spending lunch hours around the Hancock Building and you never even heard me. Doubtless your mind was somewhere else; we know how one-tracked you get. We won't pretend.

MARY. When was that?

CARL. Months ago...three months at least; I don't know when.

MARY. Well, why on earth didn't you say something?

CARL. I didn't know... *(Alex hangs up. Carl looks to him and back.)* ...what to say. And I kept thinking it'd break off; you'd give it up.

MARY. When did...

CARL. I did try. I wrote it out once at work, what I'd say.

MARY. My God, you poor darling...

CARL. Oh, come on now.

MARY. No, Carl, if...

CARL. Mary, goddamn it, I do not intend to discuss this rationally! I'll be damned if I will. You said what did he say. He said sure, O.K., fine, and rather briefly, and I hung up. And thought. Quite a lot. I thought I'm twice again his size. I am. I'm about twice the man's size. I could beat the shit out of the guy and you. And that might make me feel a little better.

I'd tell Ellen Mommy fell down the stairs. *(Beat.)* I just assumed, whatever he felt about you, that you managed to be in love and that it'd pass...

MARY. Oh, God, Carl, couldn't I have seen him just because...

CARL. No, I don't like "seen." That's too easy. Say "fucked," say —

MARY. All right, then, just because I got off on it? Without dragging romance through it? Because I dug him?

CARL. O.K., it was hot stuff — better than —

MARY. My responsibility to you hasn't altered in the least.

CARL. Yeah, yeah and Ellen, I know, I know, I know, with all this great guilt we should be even closer now; hell, I guess I should thank him, huh? You must think you married someone else, 'cause I don't work that way. The only thing you can tell me is that it never happened. And how in hell are you going to make it never have happened, huh? How am I going to believe that? None of it happened. The bowl didn't crack, the wheel wasn't bent, the bough didn't break, the cradle didn't fall. You tell me how you're going to tell me that.

MARY. I can't. I wouldn't want to.

CARL. Then goddamn it, Mary, at least you tell me you love, the son-of-a-bitch.

MARY. I don't. *(Brief pause.)*

ALEX. Jesus, God, you add it all up and I don't understand any of it! The farthest star is several billion light years away on the edge of the universe — beyond which is nothing. Einstein tells us. Not even cold empty space. Nothing. Tricky. Now what is that supposed to mean to me? I have to assume that the Earth and her people might at any moment jump its track and catapult us cold and wet — frosty — into a neighboring solar system — and how stupid, preoccupied, and foolish we'll look. Some embarrassingly superior being will frown questioningly and say, "What do you make of all these facts you present me with?" And we'll say, well, we're working on it. Give us another week. "You mean there are people who are hungry and cold and ten percent of your population controls ninety percent of your food and blankets?" Well, we're working on it. But, we're not. We'll do anything except admit that what we've got here is not just a simple problem of distribution. But recently I read a report from the good old government — why I want to be a part of that, I'll never know — that said we (meaning man) have discovered (meaning America, probably), have discovered just about all there is to know. The mind of man has encompassed most all knowledge, and from now on —

however far that may be — we will just be in the process of refinement. That's our future. Sandpapering. Where is the man who wrote that living? When is he living? How would that asshole address himself to the complexity of the human being? To, for instance, that horrible moment when I feel I, myself, just might, one of these deranged and silvery mornings, become that monster you read about who slays his family and himself or fifteen strangers holed up in a tower somewhere...come foaming into the breakfast table with your tie awry and your hair uncombed. *(Gabrielle enters, dressed in a neat suit. She hangs her coat in the closet, stands and watches Alex.)* Moments all the worse because they are recurrent at the most unguarded times when that prospect, however hideous, is very real. In the middle of culminating a particularly successful business deal or relaxing on the beach in the clean salt air, you still feel it way down deep in your nature somewhere. "Well, tonight, God help me, I may just run completely amok with a meat cleaver." *(Alex finishes in a position — arm over his head or some arrested gesture — then turns to see Gabrielle.)*

GABRIELLE. *(Evenly.)* Who's Debbie Watkins?

ALEX. *(The gesture remains arrested. Pause.)* I don't know.

GABRIELLE. I think if you'd have said almost anything else I'd have thought it was a lie. *(A long pause.)*

ALEX. Your...mysterious...man caught up with you.

GABRIELLE. Umm. Her father. I was shown what I was told was a rather unflattering photograph of her.

ALEX. A girl. Student. She goes to the University of Chicago.

GABRIELLE. Well I wish we could bring her out here so I could tear the bitch...

ALEX. Gabby. I have never...believe me; I've never...

GABRIELLE. Touched her! Had her! Told her of my love! Pawed her in the back seat of the car! Caressed her hair? What? What the hell are you doing with a girl that age?

ALEX. *(The line is lost under her.)* There were none of the ordinary...

GABRIELLE. *(As Alex starts to say something.)* Honey! Seventeen? Innocent and fragile. Some little candy-licking, anarchist, amoral teenybopper? Taking her to all...all our places? Oh, I know how innocent it is; you don't have to tell me. Do you advise them on protest procedures? Aren't you on the wrong side of the...aren't you at all curious where she's been for the last four days? She wouldn't bother getting in touch with you because she doesn't even know what fantasies fly around in your mind, does she? Right, Carl — fantasies on fantasies. When I think of the PAIN! Her dad — who is a singularly repellent man…I wonder she isn't in a convent — has yanked her out of the University of Chicago and off to her mother in Honolulu. *(Hard beat.)* So it's over! Aloha! Is there someone else? IN DESPERATION I asked you. No, no, of course not. I'm just temporarily off you — off sex and the world — I have important decisions to make about our lives. Off sex. What, do you run into the bathroom with a wet towel and — I don't know how these things are done alone, in private — whispering her name — Debbie, Debbie, Debbie, over and over… *(Alex takes a step or two toward her.)* You touch me and I swear…

ALEX. *(After a pause. Rationally.)* My relationship with Debbie…

GABRIELLE. You didn't have one. Excuse me, lie, I want to hear it. I'm only sorry to intrude into your bleeding heart with my tirade.

ALEX. You know me pretty…

GABRIELLE. Well enough to know now nothing I've said has meant a thing. You're pounding all over with your loss — planning a way to get to Honolulu…

ALEX. No, not that…

GABRIELLE. You're damned right. She wouldn't know what you were doing there. Would she?

ALEX. I don't flatter myself she'd have allowed me to make a pass at her… She has…friends…she didn't pretend to be innocent…her father doesn't know her at all.

GABRIELLE. I don't mean she's a virgin; nobody's a virgin anymore. I mean she doesn't know anything about how people work. She didn't know she was getting your rocks off for…

ALEX. Maybe she did. I feel she…knew what she was doing.

GABRIELLE. Tell me how it works. Alex; is it vicarious gratification… voyeurism? I'm slow.

ALEX. All right, you hate this kind of scene, you…

GABRIELLE. I love it! Are you kidding! I love it. I'm sick of questioning myself. No more. Pleading. I'm sorry, but my knees are sore. Apologizing. Don't wait up. By God, I was damn near sitting home looming tapestries! Blind! Blind! Blind!

ALEX. *(After a pause. Calm.)* I knew when you mentioned him who he was… and I've never met the man. I don't know why he followed you.

GABRIELLE. *(Musing.)* I told him at first you'd have no way of meeting a girl that age.

ALEX. I had to go to the botanical gardens to see if —

GABRIELLE. I'm aware now.

ALEX. She wants to study botany. She was there; showed me around.

GABRIELLE. And you returned the...

ALEX. *(Lost, after a pause.)* Oh, dear.

GABRIELLE. *(Crossing to the window seat. Furious again at nothing.)* Botany. She. Must. Be. *Agog.* In Hawaii!

ALEX. *(Low, miles away.)* I'm sure she is.

GABRIELLE. Humm. I thought when the sex started slacking off and constant attention waned we had reached a marvelously settled plateau. I felt married. Jesus! What a swinger! And I suppose that's where you were always able to get pot too, isn't it?

ALEX. Yes.

GABRIELLE. I'd think a man of the world would know better than to fall for his connection.

ALEX. Well, if I have fallen for her — and I see no reason why I shouldn't call it that...

MARY. Only a neurosis we've all agreed to have together, like acrophobia, didn't you say?

ALEX. It's all very easy to have perfect vision of the other fellow's failings. Carl says you never felt for...

MARY. *(To Alex.)* In the way he means — last ditch desperation — he's probably right. That isn't love, it's self-sacrifice — feeding your life into someone else's veins — whoever can bear to accept it anyway?

CARL. You didn't think of Ellen or me or...

MARY. Don't ask questions. I'll only answer...my defenses are always down when they should be up and up when they should be down. Do I love Carl? I ache for him. I worry, I pray I won't hurt him; I'll spend my life trying to convince him that I do, rather than hurt him. Isn't that enough?

CARL. You love me?

MARY. Yes.

CARL. Because you're my life.

MARY. I know.

CARL. I never have loved anyone else.

MARY. I know.

CARL. All my life.

MARY. I know.

CARL. Before I knew you.

MARY. I know, darling.

CARL. All my life! Since I was a kid. I was a hero in school and all I wanted, Mary. Everything! Nothing meant anything, nothing was of value to me! In myself! A home, any accomplishment, achievement, position! Morality! Respect! Nothing was of value if I couldn't lay it at a woman's feet some day as a sacrifice, a pledge! The value of everything was in what it meant to you! Now, you better tell me I've built my life on solid rock. It was never a game.

MARY. I know.

CARL. Don't answer me, help me, marry me, Mary. Marry me, Mary; marry me, Mary. Tell me, I vow. Say, I vow.

MARY. Anything, what?

CARL. Say I marry you, to have and to hold, to honor and obey, to love and to cherish, forsaking all others, till death do us part. Tell me we can have it back the way it was.

MARY. I couldn't do that, Carl. *(Pause.)* Carl... *(Pause.)*

CARL. I think the lady had better come into my chamber. *(Beat.)* O.K., Mary?

MARY. Well don't ask, silly. *(She goes into the bedroom, he follows, closing the door behind him.)*

ALEX. *(After a beat.)* I'm beat. Gabrielle, I wonder if I can say it. In my mind. Not always, but often enough, I've had an image of myself with someone. Some ideal. It hasn't been anyone specific — not Debbie really and not you — some girl, image, who moved exactly as I wanted — corresponded with my every move exactly, which I guess is pretty easy in a fantasy. And anything that strengthened our marriage — any real commitment I've resisted. Because I couldn't allow myself to become tied. I've said yes, when everything in my mind said no, resist, it isn't your dream. It isn't your life. Not yet. I know what you must have felt, fighting against something like that. But I've had it. I can't take it. I can't keep lying. It's wearing me out. I've felt constricted, checked at every corner. Maybe I'm someone who shouldn't have been married, not when we were. Maybe it's been binding me just when I had to have my options open, but I can't imagine not having you with me now. Everything is popping for us; maybe it's right that this happened. There's got to be a way we can give each other what we need and take advantage of what's happening here. Maybe we can take this opportunity, go to Washington, start clean, understand each other, giving each other some room. I don't want to stay out here in this wilderness. And we'll try to help...the people who need us. *(Off, in the bedroom, there is a loud pistol shot.)* I think we can do something. Gabby? Maybe we can do that. Can we do that? Finally?

GABRIELLE. You really are a shit.

ALEX. I'm a shit, I'm a shit; I said it, I don't care. I don't want to lose you and I want us to work together. I happen to think we can do something great. We can fly if we only do it.

GABRIELLE. Well, there's time enough, Alex. Who could think now?

ALEX. You know there isn't. There's no time. The nomination has to be made. It's ours if we say yes.

GABRIELLE. Then no, Alex. I mean yes, for you; it's what you want and I'm glad for you, but it isn't what I want. Not a bit of it. Not at all. I want a home, and children, and love…

ALEX. We can have all that and still —

GABRIELLE. And I don't want to help anyone. I'd — in the first place — never be able to convince myself I wasn't helping someone to make myself feel noble, and I'd feel better making myself feel noble honestly. *(The phone rings.)*

ALEX. Oh, Jesus.

GABRIELLE. The service will get it.

ALEX. *(Answering the phone.)* Hello. *(Carl enters, cradling the telephone at his ear, fumbling with a pistol in his hand.)*

CARL. Al? Alex? Hey, meathead! This you?

ALEX. Christ. It's Carl.

CARL. Hell, I didn't recognize your voice. *(This is all very rapid and almost without pause to listen.)* Baby, I tell you. I am the prize hamburger! Well, what do you think? Listen, we talked it over; we sat down like two human beings for a change and…well of course! Hell, she didn't feel anything about that guy…man, I mean the guy's half my size!

ALEX. What did I tell you…?

CARL. *(Laughing.)* Yeah, yeah, yeah; right, right, right… Hell, he must know himself 'cause Mary can't fake it! Alex, it's great! Now listen… *(Carl holds the phone away for a second, gasping for breath. A look of intense pain is on his face.)*

ALEX. Carl?

CARL. *(The happy look is forced back as he speaks again.)* Now, listen, you're going to understand this — you know that place up at Lake Elizabeth? Well, we're going to drive up there, the three of us tonight. And…

ALEX. I thought…

CARL. No. We're leaving right now, Buddy…I just want to *(He is breaking down, but he keeps trying.)* tell you and thank you for listening to all my…

ALEX. No.

CARL. I know! What it must have been! Yeah! *(The laughter becomes blubbering, almost incoherent. Carl is still trying to speak jovially.)* Alex, Alex, she's got a hold of my elbow, boy. We're leaving right this minute. I just wanted you to know so you wouldn't worry. All right, boy? Huh?

ALEX. Sure.

CARL. *(Breaking down completely.)* Listen, you take care of yourself, you hear? Old Buddy? Huh? Old Buddy?

ALEX. Sure. You O.K.?

CARL. I'm O.K. I'm O.K. You be good, Buddy! *(Still nodding, crying, Carl drops the phone, goes up the stairs.)*

ALEX. Hey Bozo? *(After a moment Alex hangs up. Gabrielle goes into the bedroom.)* Gabby did you tell me Carl and Mary sold that house on the lake? *(Alex stands frozen. Grabbing up his coat, he runs out.)* Oh God! Oh God *(Gabrielle comes from the bedroom with an overnight case. She stands in the middle of the foyer. Alex offstage. Pounding on the back door. Ringing the back bell.)* Carl? Bozo? *(Sounds of a window being broken in the kitchen. Alex runs in.)* Mary? Carl? *(Gunshot offstage.)* Ellen? Carl? *(Gunshot offstage. Gabrielle takes a cloth coat from the front closet and goes out the front door. Alex turns toward the sound of her leaving.)*

END OF PLAY

THE MOUND BUILDERS

For Roy London

Trish Hawkins, Tanya Berezin, and Rob Thirkield
in the Circle Repertory Company production of The Mound Builders.
Photograph © 1984 by Ken Howard.

INTRODUCTION

Note: If you are unfamiliar with this play, it would be better to treat this introduction as an afterword. I don't want to spoil the story; it's one of the few real stories I've written.

John Lahr wanted to talk about *The Hot L Baltimore.* He had learned something about comedy from the show. We were at the opening night party for *Hot L,* up over the shoe store. Now, if I could tell a Lahr anything about funny I should have been rapt. I should have been flabbergasted. But no, all I wanted to talk about was this flash, this moment, that had occurred to me a week before and I was certain it was that nugget you prospect and hope for, the one you know you can beat or mold or somehow forge into a play. Actually there were two moments that had come to me unbidden — or bidden to hell and back but you still don't know from where. The first flash, the moment, was this: There are two women, they are in a large screened-in porch that is furnished as a living room. It is late at night. One is sitting on a sofa, she has a drink. The other is pregnant, lying on the floor, doing sit-ups. A child, waking from a nightmare, screams from upstairs. The woman sets her drink down, says, "That's all right, darling, safe from harm," and unhurriedly heads upstairs to her daughter. The other quits exercising, pleasantly exhausted. She turns off the lights and heads to bed. Gradually, as our eyes adjust to the darkness, we see through the screen to the moon reflected across a large lake surrounded by tall trees. There is a wall of night noises, crickets, owls, all the noisy night bugs of the buggy Midwest. The scene is not bucolic, it is somehow menacing. Then there is a noise. The loud crack of (maybe) a stick breaking. And every bug and owl shuts up to listen. Total silence. Something large and threatening is — Out There. The image, the flash, runs in my mind for only a few seconds. The other moment is cheerier. We are in the kitchen of the house. A wife says, "What do you know about the Mound Builders?" The husband replies, "It's this Motel out on the highway." Then he says, no, of course, all around them are these hills, mounds, the unexplained ruins of some ancient Indian culture. And the wife says, Well, why is somebody *tinkering* with them? He looks up alarmed. (Deep organ chords, denoting something sinister.) She goes on to say the talk in town is that someone has been digging around the mounds at night.

I realize all that sounds fairly tame, but what it meant to me was There is Something Outside That's Gonna Get You. There's a monster out there. I knew also that the something outside, the monster, was really something inside. I knew that the play was about work, achievement, and a threat to livelihood, that at the burning heart of the theme was: Why do we strive to achieve? To build, to make our mark? Why are we Mound Builders?

I had known immediately that the people in the house were visitors, renters, outsiders, new to this place, working just for the summer. (It turned out they had been coming there for many summers.) I thought they were probably land speculators or developers or even starting a real estate office. Something to do with the land. The characters would be intelligent and probably wily. The young woman who is pregnant, the wife of the younger speculator, should be a doctor, a gynecologist. I thought the women were just along for the ride, for the vacation. Wives and a sister, so I could explore a man's relationship to his daughter, his wife, and his sister, and their relationship to him.

I had all that during the first four or five months of working on the play. It was sailing along; it was richer, with more complicated relationships than I had ever written before. But it was developing in the damnedest way. It was scenes, completely unrelated to one another. Scenes with beginnings, middles, and ends. Complete fragments, if that means anything. I had the scene with Dan and Delia ("You must answer to get help" — Marshall gave names to all the scenes rather than numbers), the scene with all four of the women. The "spelling-bee" scene. The fishing scene, and the scene afterward, with Dan and his wife ("the fish and the moon"), the scene with the son of the landlord and the young wife ("pitch and putt"). I knew the people so well. But they didn't seem like land speculators. They pointedly refused to talk about their work and the damn play was *about* work. I had over half of the play, scenes from the beginning, middle, maybe even toward the end. And I knew I had nothing. And if this isn't a collage, like *Rimers,* and I didn't want it to be, then why were the scenes so — what? Fragmented.

I was reading about the Mound Builders at the same time, realizing that my characters lives somehow reflected that culture. The reading was fascinating. I had been completely wrong. I learned we know perfectly well what the mounds are. Some early mounds were burials of important tribesmen. The later ones, from a different people who moved into the area, the Mound Builders, are artificial hills on which they erected the civic and religious buildings of their cities. And yes, the Mound Builders had *cities!* Cahokia, near St. Louis, was larger and more populous than Paris or London at the time. They had a strict and complicated social structure and were ruled over by a God-King. I learned that it would be unlikely that the mounds were being desecrated (there goes that scene): All the mounds have been catalogued and either dug or scheduled to be dug. There is a great wealth of information gained from the digs, but, compared to the fabled digs of Egypt, very little of material worth. The North American archeologists are dogged and valued but they are not famous; their work is just not that glamorous or romantic. Most of the recent discoveries have been serendipitous: A bulldozer might uncover a site by accident, in preparation for, say, laying the foundations of a mall. Or a lake bed. All work is stopped, and the contractor tears his hair as the archeologists move in on a salvage operation. Almost all operations are of a salvage nature now.

I was going crazy. I thought maybe these scenes were memories. Maybe someone is narrating this play. Not a narrator, but dictating it to his secretary, reporting on the past summer. A common (and lousy) way of connecting disparate scenes. But who are these people? Why are they down there in southern Illinois? Why are they interested in the mounds? What are they *doing*? It hit me like an unwelcome bolt from the blue. You know perfectly well who these people are and why they're down here. Why they are interested in the Mounds. *These people are archeologists!* I was devastated. I knew nothing about archeology. I had at least six months of research ahead of me before I could go on.

The play was scheduled to go into rehearsal in about a month. I had told Marshall to have a back-up play ready (and not to tell me about it) if I couldn't finish in time. The bastard actually had one: Ed Moore's *The Sea Horse*, one of the most beautiful and successful plays Circle Rep ever produced. And one of the most perfect productions. It moved to another theater and ran for months.

In the meantime, I was reading. Mostly unpublished doctoral dissertations. I was making notes on the jargon. (Body paint or any paint, is not just paint, it's "pigmentation"—why oh why oh why does every field have to make itself impenetrable? The world would be such a more interesting place and so much more accessible without all their damn classy argot.) I would read a hundred pages and only glean the fact that parakeets once were as common in the Midwest as the sparrow is now. O.K., make a note. But gradually the play was coming together. It was the history, told by the leader of the wrecked dig, of last summer. It was not in fragments, it was in *shards*. It was not a lousy way of telling a story, it was logical, it was organic. The story was told the way an archeologist discovers things—in pieces, bits: What is it and why is it *there*? I was talking to archeologists. I was invited on digs with students from the University of Illinois. It was coming along. Only it hadn't taken six months, it had taken a year. Circle Rep had moved to a new location in the village.

Still, it was a close call to get the play finished for its rescheduled time slot. I rewrote all the scenes in the first act with notations between them, "bridge to come"—that was August's introduction, his memory of the scene. "Bridge to come" became the Circle Rep slang for "later." Marshall rehearsed the first act for a month. The cast went on field trips, they read everything available about the Mound Builders, about archeology, about photography, women novelists, gynecology. Marshall told me he couldn't vamp this much longer. I turned in the final pages about ten days before we opened. It didn't matter, the actors knew their characters so well all they had to do was memorize the lines. They could have improvised the second act.

The crucial moment, the turning point in the composition of the play, had been a wonderful day, six months earlier, that I spent with the archeologist Howard Winter of NYU. The whole story fell into place.

Finally. After a year and a half.

I knew why these people were there, I knew how they would succeed and how they would fail. I knew why Chad was there. I knew why Delia was there. The design of the play had for some time been that the "family" would save Delia—who was quite ill when she arrived—and with their support she would grow stronger during that summer. Strong enough to comfort the others when they fell.

Dr. Winter gave me what I was looking for that day. I asked him, "What is the — dream, Doctor Winter?" His eyes shone and he leaned back in his chair. "In all our work," he said, "we have never found the grave of a God-King. If we have, then it was not materially remarkable. These people had trade routes into the country where there was gold, it's logical that they would have it, but, in all this time, we've never found gold."

ORIGINAL PRODUCTION

The Mound Builders received its first production at Circle Repertory Company (Marshall W. Mason, Artistic Director) in New York City, on February 2, 1975. It was directed by Marshall W. Mason; the set design was by John Lee Beatty; the costume design was by Jennifer von Mayrhauser; the sound design was by Charles London and George Hansen; the slides were by Charles London and Robert Thirkield and the production stage manager was Peter Schneider. The cast was as follows:

PROFESSOR AUGUST HOWE	Robert Thirkield
CYNTHIA HOWE	Stephanie Gordon
KIRSTEN	Lauren S. Jacobs
D.K. ERIKSEN	Tanya Berezin
DR. DAN LOGGINS	Jonathan Hogan
DR. JEAN LOGGINS	Trish Hawkins
CHAD JASKER	John Strasberg

ACKNOWLEDGMENT

The author expresses his thanks to the Rockefeller Foundation for support during the writing of this play, and to Dennis Logan Schneider and Marlyn Baum for their assistance in the research, and especially to Dr. Howard Winters of the Department of Anthropology, New York University, who kindly helped with the archaeological data, spoke with the cast and production crew of *The Mound Builders,* and generously gave us a hint at an archaeologist's dream.

CHARACTERS

PROFESSOR AUGUST HOWE An archeologist, forty.
CYNTHIA HOWE His wife, thirty-five.
KIRSTEN His daughter, eleven.
D.K. (DELIA) ERIKSEN His sister, thirty-eight.
DR. DAN LOGGINS His assistant, an archaeologist, twenty-nine.
DR. JEAN LOGGINS Dan's wife, a gynecologist, twenty-five.
CHAD JASKER The landowner's son, twenty-five.

THE SCENE

August's study in Urbana is indicated only by a desk or table that can be easily incorporated into the house at Blue Shoals. When August is alone, the lights confine us to his immediate desk area. From this light he wanders, while recording, off into the dark, and back again, sitting, standing, messing with things on his desk.

As we move into the previous summer, the house around him is revealed: An old farmhouse with a large living-dining room transformed into a living-dining-working area by the archaeologists. A stairway leads off to the bedrooms, a door opens to August's office, doors lead to an unseen front porch and a back porch that might be incorporated into the set and used as a playing area for a number of the scenes. An arch allows us to see part of the kitchen, in which there is a refrigerator.

The back wall of the set serves as a screen onto which are back-projected slides from the previous summer that serve August as the backbone of his recorded notes. He need not literally control the projector.

The house is seen from August's memory of the wrecked expedition and may be represented as he sees it — not in photographs but in his mind's eye: a house that lifted up like an ark as the lake flooded the valley and floated down some great flood-struck current, wrecking in another place.

Scenes in the house are accompanied by a dense orchestration of the outside sounds, opening the house onto its surroundings. The night is filled with noises of the country and the day with the sounds of bulldozers and workmen preparing the lake bed, which will flood the valley.

THE TIME

February in Urbana and the previous summer in Blue Shoals, Illinois — located in the extreme south of that state, in the five-state area of Kentucky, Missouri, Indiana, Arkansas, and Illinois — at the confluence of the Wabash, Cumberland, Ohio, and Mississippi Rivers.

The Mound Builders

ACT ONE

AUGUST. *(Sits at a desk, speaking into the microphone of a small tape recorder.)* One, two, three, four, five… *(Getting up, walking a few paces away.)* The quick gray fox jumped over…whatever it was the quick gray fox jumped over. *(He returns to the desk, clicks off the tape, rewinds it, and clicks it on. We hear his voice repeating "…three, four, five… the quick gray fox jumped —"* He clicks the machine off then back to record.)* Dianne…ah…good morning. Or, knowing your habits, I should probably say, good afternoon. *(Pause. He walks away a few paces.)* After months of procrastination, with which I'm sure you're sympathetic, I intend to go through what is left of the wreckage of last summer's expedition. *(He returns to the desk.)* You may type this up, or go out to lunch. I'll understand either. *(He touches something on the desk. The back screen is filled with a scenic photograph of a lake at morning.)* This is the lake, against which we were racing time. *(Slide: the house.)* This is the house in which we were staying. After we spent three summers of excavation *(Slide: dam construction.)* on the mounds — within earshot of the construction of the Blue Shoals Dam — *(Slide: bulldozer.)* Engineers preparing the lake bed — *(Slide: the dig.)* uncovered evidence of an extensive village site not six hundred yards from the front door *(Several slides lead us past the lake-bed construction to the house, as we hear a car stopping outside, doors slamming, and the lights of the stage begin to reveal the house in Blue Shoals.)* of the house in which we stayed. Excavation of the Jasker Village site was a salvage operation undertaken literally as the lake basin filled behind us.

CYNTHIA. *(Coming down the stairs, followed by Kirsten.)* God, I thought they'd never get here. They must have come through Blue Shoals. *(She goes to the door.)*

CHAD. *(Off.)* Window's been opened for a week, I was telling the professor we had a hell of a spring. Thought it wasn't gonna be any good for you folks, but it's dried up the last week.

AUGUST. Thank God you're here. *(As Dan, Chad, and Jean enter, carrying luggage, etc.)* Everything possible has conspired to work against us.

DAN. Girls getting to you?

AUGUST. I'm going to have to go to the Paducah airport. How far is Paducah?

CYNTHIA. If there is such a place.

CHAD. About an hour.

CYNTHIA. Auggie's sister is being dumped on us.

AUGUST. It's nothing to talk about; just one more thing.

CYNTHIA. Let me help with the rest of the jazz.

JEAN. There's not much more, Dan said to travel light. Dumped on you?

CYNTHIA. *(As they go out to the car.)* On us. Auggie's sister. *(Kirsten follows them.)*

AUGUST. The place looks like a resort. You've never seen so many tourists in your life.

CHAD. *(Going out to the car.)* I told him.

AUGUST. It gets worse every year. The girls? No, the girls are fine. They pitched their tents, made a cooking pit. Every goddamned one of them is an eagle scout.

DAN. *(He disappears for a moment, taking folders into August's office.)* Or whatever.

AUGUST. They're happy as bugs. Ask about you and Jean every ten minutes.

DAN. Don't say anything about Jean being pregnant, she doesn't want them pestering her.

AUGUST. I doubt I'll see them till September. My sister is dying again; she was scraped up off the street in Cleveland; apparently the hospitals there haven't the facilities or the will. How the hell they found us here — the man came to install the telephone, ten minutes later it was ringing.

DAN. She's dying?

AUGUST. Of course not, and she claims poverty so — Well, it's not worth talking about.

DAN. I've never met the lady.

AUGUST. I'm afraid there's no way I can protect you from it now.

CHAD. *(Re-entering with equipment, etc.)* I had the windows opened forever. It's been a sopping spring; thought it wasn't gonna be any good for you guys, but it's cleared up some the last week.

DAN. Thank God.

AUGUST. Conditions are excellent. *(Jean, Cynthia, and Kirsten re-enter with suitcases and knapsacks.)* We've got the bulldozer lined up for day after tomorrow; you might even be ready for it.

DAN. Oh, hell, let me help.

JEAN. That's it.

AUGUST. Jean, I'm really sorry about this.

JEAN. What's wrong with her?

AUGUST. *(Speaking in Chad's presence as one might speak before a waiter.)* ...I wouldn't know.

CYNTHIA. Acute "I wouldn't know," chronic "I suspect."

AUGUST. The hospital is flying her down tomorrow, unconscious and incognito.

CYNTHIA. And collect. *(To Jean.)* You and Dan are upstairs.

KIRSTEN. You're going to hate it. It's worse than last year.

CYNTHIA. Help carry that up and please don't be impossible.

KIRSTEN. *(Going.)* If I was you, I'd have sent me to camp. *(Cynthia follows her up.)*

CHAD. You visiting again, Doctor, or you planning to stay awhile?

JEAN. No, I'm booked for the duration.

CHAD. We'll have to get her out with us.

JEAN. Don't tell me Blue Shoals swings.

DAN. Out fishing, out to the lake. *(He takes what he can carry of the baggage upstairs.)*

JEAN. No way. What happens when the lake comes in? Will you move the house?

CHAD. Electric company charge you eight hundred bucks for every line you cut...probably cost six, seven thousand to move it up the hill.

JEAN. You couldn't build it for that.

CHAD. Nobody'd want to either. Beams probably rotten, you couldn't get a block under it.

JEAN. *(As she goes upstairs, followed by Cynthia.)* Is it haunted?

CYNTHIA. Not that we've noticed.

CHAD. *(Going upstairs.)* What do you want? You want it haunted or you want it unhaunted? I'll go either way.

AUGUST. *(Slide: townspeople.)* Townspeople who awaited with bated breath our discovery of King Tut's tomb. *(Slide: students.)* Alleged students. We were assisted last summer by eight girls and one presumed male from Dr. Loggins's class in field archaeology. *(Slide: Cynthia.)* Ex-relation by marriage. *(Slide: campsite.)* This is the campsite of the students, pitched well out of earshot of the house. *(Slide: Cynthia.)* Ex-relation. *(Slide: Kirsten.)*

Alleged daughter. *(Slide: picnic.)* Picnic. *(Slide: people playing.)* Horseplay. *(Slide: bathers.)* Horseplay at the lake. *(Slide: Cynthia.)* Horse.

DAN. *(As he comes back downstairs, followed by Jean and Cynthia.)* Come down to the site, you've got time.

AUGUST. I've got to talk money with some St. Louis real-estate men this evening. This isn't going to be much of a vacation for you, Jean.

DAN. *(Leaving.)* Sure it will.

JEAN. Sure it will.

CYNTHIA. *(Opening refrigerator.)* Sure it will. How about a drink? *(She slams the door, effecting a blackout, except for a flashlight beam that investigates the deserted room.)*

DAN'S VOICE. Is someone there? Hello? *(Flashlight out.)* Hello? *(Sound of a stumble. Mumbled.)* Oh, damn it. *(The flashlight comes on. Dan in pajamas gets up, goes to the lamp, turns it on.)*

CYNTHIA. *(Entering from the door, opening a carton of cigarettes.)* Good Lord, I thought you'd be asleep hours ago.

DAN. I was, heard the weirdest ...

CYNTHIA. Probably the kids on the dig.

DAN. Thought we were being burglarized.

CYNTHIA. Not much worry about that.

DAN. Are you just getting in? It must be two in the morning.

CYNTHIA. Cigarettes. You working tomorrow?

DAN. Oh, yeah, I'll be up and —

CYNTHIA. *(Cutting him off. Reaching for the lamp switch.)* Better get to bed then. *(Blackout.)*

KIRSTEN'S VOICE. Mother. Mother. Mommy?

AUGUST'S VOICE. They won't hurt you. You were dreaming.

KIRSTEN'S VOICE. They were talking.

AUGUST'S VOICE. They're only shadows.

KIRSTEN'S VOICE. They were talking.

AUGUST'S VOICE. Shhhh.

KIRSTEN'S VOICE. They were talking. *(Sundown the next evening. Chad opens the front door as Cynthia and Kirsten come downstairs.)*

CHAD. Got a delivery for you. *(August enters, carrying Delia.)*

AUGUST. Please don't squirm. I'm not that strong and you're not as dissipated as you'd like to believe.

DELIA. There is no point in dragging me inside. I'm not staying —

AUGUST. If you want to fight, wait till I set you down!

CYNTHIA. Just here on the —

DELIA. I'll go to a state hospital.

AUGUST. *(Panting.)* No state has that kind of money. *(August carries Delia to a lounge.)*

DELIA. I'm not going to die in this godforsaken Grant Wood mausoleum.

AUGUST. *(Beat.)* Good.

DELIA. How the hell did they find you?

AUGUST. I was wondering.

DELIA. You're making quite a name for yourself. That must be gratifying after all these —

AUGUST. — I've always been satisfied to leave the limelight to those—

DELIA. — That's the God's truth.

AUGUST. — to those who required it.

DELIA. *(Beat.)* Yes, well, just as well.

AUGUST. Why were you in Cleveland?

DELIA. I don't know. It was important to go to — I met someone from Cleveland, or I don't know. I was in Casablanca. Detroit with palm trees! Vile people! Vile air! Vile climate! I went to Annaba, I went to Benghazi, I met someone from Portugal, I started to go back to Lisbon, I changed my mind and went to — *(Interrupted by a violent coughing spell.)*

AUGUST. *(Stands unmoved, watching Delia. Finally, as she relaxes.)* Where?

DELIA. *(After relaxing. Calmly.)* Cleveland. *(Pause.)* How long did they keep me? They kept me a month, didn't they? Why?

DAN. *(Off calling.)* Jean?

DELIA. I don't mean that; I'm not that bad.

JEAN. *(From upstairs.)* I'm up, I'll be down.

AUGUST. *(Taking medicine and papers from Chad.)* I've got instructions, yet. You were glad enough to get away.

DELIA. They were trying to kill me in that goddamned hospital. *(Jean comes down.)*

AUGUST. They were not trying to kill —

DELIA. Whether they were killing me through malice and intention or killing me through ignorance of medicine is immaterial. It amounts to the same torture.

DAN. *(Entering, dirty and mildly refractory.)* What a day. Hi. Be glad you didn't come down.

JEAN. Cynthia said.

AUGUST. *(Handing the paper to Jean.)* Jean, can you make any sense of that?

CHAD. You're going to have a lot of fun with her.

KIRSTEN. For your information, she isn't well.

CYNTHIA. We can do very well without that.

AUGUST. Thank you very much, Mr. Jasker.

CHAD. Yeah, I'll see you around. *(Chad exits.)*

AUGUST. Jean, I don't think you and Dan have had the pleasure of meeting my sister. Dan and Jean Loggins, D.K. Eriksen.

DAN. I talked to you on the phone once.

AUGUST. Dan's my assistant. Jean's an intern gynecologist. If you're interested in discussing medicine, I'm sure she'll listen to you.

DELIA. "D.K." Call me Delia, that's the name Dad gave me.

JEAN. I've read your books, of course.

DELIA. That was another life, Doctor.

JEAN. If you're going to call me doctor, I'll have to call you Miss Eriksen.

DELIA. You know me. I don't *meet people.*

AUGUST. You're not to be moved.

DELIA. You know quite well this is just the sort of cozily scientific, cenobitic community that'll drive me bananas.

DAN. Oh, fine. Scientific. You should see it down there. It's a mob scene.

DELIA. No, thank you.

CYNTHIA. *(Getting a glass of wine.)* Anyone else?

DAN. I'm trying to direct some jerk with a bulldozer ...

CYNTHIA. That was worth seeing.

JEAN. I saw the cars from the house.

DAN. All day long it's been a cavalcade pouring into the field. Every family from the Mississippi to the Wabash. They got their kids, they got their picnic lunches, it looks like a fucking fairground. Where you been, people? I mean, we been here twenty-four hours already. You missed Professor Howe pulling up a patch of ragweed.

CYNTHIA. I enjoy the people showing up.

DAN. Oh, sure. "What's that thing?" Well, ma'am, that *thing* is a surveyor's alidade. It sits on a tripod and you look through here and see a family from Carbondale eating fried chicken.

CYNTHIA. They go away when they find out August isn't going to let them volunteer.

DAN. A girl says, "Why did they build those mounds?" What mounds? Oh, the one over there. That they're using for a parking lot. Well, honey, we excavated that mound last summer and we found they had built that mound over ninety-three Paducah High School cheerleaders. *(Begins to roll a joint.)*

JEAN. He loves it, of course; he performs for them like a dancing bear. The girls line up for his classes. They eat him up. I don't know if they learn anything.

AUGUST. Any number of things, I'd think.

CYNTHIA. After August explains what we hope to find, the crowd gets so bored they leave him talking to himself.

JEAN. *(Re: the medication.)* This is morning and evening — this is four times a day.

DAN. "Why did they build the mounds?!" They built the mounds for the same reason I'd build the mounds. Because I wanted to make myself conspicuous; to sacrifice to the gods; to protect me from floods, or animals; because my grandfather built mounds; because I was sick of digging holes; because I didn't have the technology to build pyramids and a person isn't happy unless he's building something.

CYNTHIA. There are people who'd be perfectly happy tearing something down.

DAN. A person isn't happy unless he's building something. Scratch a fry cook, you'll find an architect. Listen to Chad Jasker tell you about the restaurant he's going to build. I mean, he knows the kind of light fixtures he's going to have. Every society reaches the point where they build mounds. As the society becomes more sophisticated, the rationalization for building them becomes more sophisticated. For an accomplishment, honey, to bring me closer to Elysium; to leave something behind me for my grandchildren to marvel at. To say I'd built something!

AUGUST. *I.e.,* if we find out, we'll let you know.

DELIA. Jesus, dear God, but it's bleak here. Bleak, bleak, bleak, bleak.... Bleak farmland on a bleak pond by a bleak — I can't stay here, I —

AUGUST. Normally I might try to excuse her egocentric excen —

DELIA. *(Riding over.)* But my exploits are so notorious it's useless to closet my presence here and we are forced to admit that I am convalescing from a riding accident...I fell from my horse.

AUGUST. It's rather more serious than it might sound, as it was a flying horse. *(He is pouring medicine for Delia.)*

DELIA. Jean, what is he giving me? I can't breathe. They gave him something to give me, it's preventing me from —

AUGUST. The only drugs in your system are residual from your binges in Benghazi and — wherever.

DELIA. I can't get air.

JEAN. You're breathing perfectly normally; if you weren't getting air, you'd be turning purple, or —

DELIA. — What the hell does a gynecologist know about cirrhosis of the liver?

JEAN. Absolutely nothing; except that it doesn't occur in the respiratory system.

DELIA. All right, I'm a hypochondriac, Jean. Ignore all requests for medical advice.

JEAN. Delia, after one week in the clinic I could spot a hypochondriac at forty feet.

DAN. *(Who has been rolling a joint; passing it to Cynthia, who takes it, and Jean, who passes it back.)* She's not on call this summer, Delia, she's taking off eighteen months to have a baby.

JEAN. After that I might have a better idea of what I've been talking about.

DELIA. It doesn't take eighteen months to have a baby. It takes eighteen months to have a rhinoceros.

DAN. *(Regarding the joint. To Jean.)* Take it.

JEAN. No, I said.

DAN. It's not tobacco, it won't kill you.

JEAN. Not now, thank you.

DAN. Only girl I've ever met who's a bigger drughead than I am, she gets pregnant and goes cold turkey on me.

JEAN. Don't mention the offspring to the girls, we don't want it generally —

DELIA. I will not be cross-examined by a mob of swaddling adolescents.

CYNTHIA. Never fear; they aren't allowed near the place.

JEAN. I thought they might.

CYNTHIA. — That's verboten. No students, no dogs.

DAN. I mean, I can understand giving up alcohol and meat. Well, meat, but an innocent joint.

JEAN. *(From "giving up.")* Oh, come on, really — I don't know why it should bother you; I'm the one who's straight.

CYNTHIA. You can't give up meat. You need all the protein you can get.

JEAN. *(Overlapping.)* No, I'm eating perfectly normally; I'm just trying to avoid toxins. And you don't require nearly the amount of protein you're led to believe. We just thought we'd give it every opportunity to make its own problems.

CYNTHIA. Don't think it won't.

DAN. I can imagine the little bugger deprived of —

JEAN. O.K., so it will. That's a person's prerogative; we'll try to help, and undoubtedly screw up completely. Good God, it's lousy grass anyway.

DAN. O.K., O.K., go to bed.

JEAN. *(Leaving.)* I am, thank you.

DELIA. *(Overlapping.)* Get me out of this thing. I'm going to be sick.

DAN. Where's she staying?

KIRSTEN. Up in my room with me.

DELIA. Oh, dear God —

DAN. I'll take you. *(Picking Delia up and carrying her off)* If you bite me or throw up, I'll drop you right on the floor. *(Kirsten follows them off. Beat.)*

CYNTHIA. Is she all right?

AUGUST. She's fine.

CYNTHIA. I realize she's down and out; she's undoubtedly broke.

AUGUST. I don't think so.

CYNTHIA. And although she's not bothered to contact us more than three times in ten years, you could feel that we've neglected her —

AUGUST. Not as much as she's neglected herself.

CYNTHIA. Or been neglected by her reading public.

AUGUST. I doubt she ever had much of a reading public.

CYNTHIA. August, it is a challenge enough to maintain civilization on these summer-long bivouacs without nursing —

AUGUST. Ignore her; Dad did. Laugh at her.

CYNTHIA. She isn't funny. Could you at least get someone out here to look after her so —

AUGUST. We can't begin to afford it.

CYNTHIA. One of the girls could help —

AUGUST. Their parents are paying a thousand dollars a head for a credit in field archaeology, not for a nursing —

CYNTHIA. They're paying to get them out of the house.

AUGUST. Jean is a practicing intern at —

CYNTHIA. — You can't expect Jean to take up residence as the —

AUGUST. Ignore her, damn it, you have enough to do. Ignore her. She doesn't like you anyway.

DAN. *(In from upstairs, out the door.)* I'm going to take a walk. The girls said someone was snooping around the dig last night. We haven't even started, we've got prowlers; I don't know what they think we're going to find. What do they think we're going to find?

CYNTHIA. *(Going upstairs.)* She likes me fine, August. She always has. It's you she can't stand.

AUGUST. *(Alone.)* Well, fine, fine, fine, good, good. *(As the slides change furiously.)* Dianne, this wreckage appears to be in a state of organization you will undoubtedly recognize as typical of my ex-wife. Please throw away those works of her genius which do not pertain to the excavation. Mrs. Howe, with stunning evidence to the contrary, persists in believing she is Diane Arbus. My sister, for instance, is of marginal archaeological interest. *(Slide: site.)* This is the rather unprepossessing site as we found it. The trial pit — stratigraphy exposed seven separate layers of occupation on the site. *(Site.)* A bulldozer was employed to remove a dense growth of weeds and about four inches of root-bearing topsoil. The remaining four to six inches of humus above the plow sole was cleared by hand and screened. *(Slide: projectile points.)* This soil proved to be the repository of Late Woodland artifacts of surpassing mediocrity which were joyfully displayed to me chip by chip. *(Six quick slides of the lake.)* This is the lake. *(As Jean comes down, dawn arrives and Chad enters.)* This is the lake. This is the lake. This is the lake. This is the lake. This is the — *(Chad framed against the lake.)*

CHAD. *(Immediately, as August stands in stunned remembrance.)* Last summer I didn't really figure you to marry Dan. You seemed to be pretty sure of what you wanted.

JEAN. Dan and I wanted more or less the same thing, I think.

CHAD. I tell you what, I got the car out front; there's something I want to show you.

JEAN. I don't think so.

CHAD. — You don't even know what it is.

JEAN. — I know, but nevertheless —

CHAD. — You only live once.

JEAN. I'm not sure that's been proved.

CHAD. The courthouse. What can happen? Who's gonna miss you?

JEAN. I've seen it.

CHAD. Inside?

JEAN. No, I haven't been inside.

CHAD. — See, now, you don't know. I want to show you.

JEAN. What?

CHAD. Will you come?

JEAN. No. I can't, Chad; what?

CHAD. You'll promise to see it?

JEAN. When I go into town again.

CHAD. There's a model of damn near the whole county laid out — it's huge — guess what it's called. The whole model —

JEAN. I can't guess, I really don't think —

CHAD. *(Overlapping.)* — O.K., O.K., I'm not playing with you — you promised. It's called Jasker's Development. The Jasker Development. They got…the hills, they got all the buildings, the mounds are on it — the ones that are left — they even got little trees set up — and this big, beautiful blue lake — like — not round, but maple-shaped, hand-shaped. We been talking six years to get Washington to give it to us.

JEAN. The mounds that are left?

CHAD. Four of them will be left, the other five the Interstate will take out. It's all part and parcel with the development. The lake and the new Interstate. See, we got 57 from Chicago already, which they're widening, and the new Interstate cuts across us the other way with all these interchanges and all. It all goes — aw, hell, it'll just take fifteen minutes to see the damn model and understand what's happening —

JEAN. — No, I'm sure. You can feel it. We're an anachronism. Squint your eyes and you can already see girls water-skiing over the tops of the hawthorn trees. Restaurants with dance bands. It's all changing. The lake has become the fact, hasn't it?

CHAD. Pretty much.

JEAN. And you'll own a lot of the shoreline, won't you?

CHAD. Good piece. I could show you if we —

JEAN. — Come on, really —

CHAD. — Well, it's not how much we own, it's where it is. See — Dad was smart enough not to sell. Only thing he ever did — Guys were coming down from Memphis — See, we're sitting on the lake and the interchange.

JEAN. So you're right in the middle of it.

CHAD. We *are* the middle of it — we didn't even know. You wouldn't recognize this town if you'd seen it five years ago. Like, it didn't start being a tourist attraction till a few years ago; but all of a sudden Lily-Tulip is buying up twenty acres to build a new home office, a national headquarters with landscaping, and another one — a box company — cardboard boxes, and everybody's trying to buy our place. These guys from Memphis are talking to brokers and the brokers are driving out to chew it over with us, you know. And their offer goes up and it goes up, Dad just sits tight on it — and finally these guys come down to talk to us themselves, and they say, all right, you're not going to sell — you got the place we want to build on — what would you say about giving us a *lease*.

JEAN. Oh…that could mean a lot more.

CHAD. Every month, month on month for as long as they're in operation. They been working over a year. Memphis is the main office of the

Holiday Inn people. They've got their market studies, their books full of figures, they've got their artists'-concepts drawings already. They got their 800-unit motel, they got their swimming pools, and the facilities to the lake, they got a layout would amaze... *(Floating.)* ...Dream of something. Dream of something you want...anything. A restaurant with twenty-four-hour service — dream of anything you want. They showed us rug samples that thick — with padding under it. See, we're sitting on the lake and the interchange.

JEAN. All first-class stuff.

CHAD. A barber sh — ah, beauty parlor. A uh — the clubs, the little — with clubs ...

JEAN. Sauna?

CHAD. No, you hit the damn ball, the little setup for a —

JEAN. Tennis court?

CHAD. Tennis court, too, but those — oh, shit. Golf! Little golf —

JEAN. Miniature golf.

CHAD. No, that's kids, that's toys — Chip and putt! Chip and putt. For practicing.

JEAN. Never heard of it.

CHAD. It's like where you learn, you practice — *you* never heard of it! *I* never had a golf club in my *hand*. There's a golf course at Marion, eighty miles off, probably the closest place you could go — I probably couldn't hit — *(Enjoying himself, nearly laughing.)* — I'd dig up the green; they'd kick me off the — but I'm going to! Hell! Go out chipping and putting; get me a pair of the shorts and the socks and the cap and those gloves they wear — Chip and putt with the pros, man. Lee Trevino's.

JEAN. You'll be terrific.

CHAD. You know what we get? Three percent. On every dollar spent.

JEAN. That's amazing; that's a lot.

CHAD. Of everything except food. One percent on food and drink...that's the deal they're offering us.

JEAN. You will be rich. That's what I find so profound about politics; the grace notes of that kind of power. The signing of an energy bill in Washington transforms rural areas into resorts — field hands into bus-boys.

CHAD. Yeah.

JEAN. They shall beat their plowshares into Pontiacs.

CHAD. *(Almost holding his breath.)* ...I...got six acres all my own. For a house. On an island. I got an island — it will be. Out a little bit on the lake. Looks right across to it. Be able to sit on the lawn and watch people drive up off there to the motel — say that's another ten bucks. That guy over there's havin' himself a beer, that's two cents! —

JEAN. You'll get a kick out of it. *(A long pause; as she starts to move.)*

CHAD. Hey... *(Jean stops.)* I'll give it to you...Anything you want, it's yours. I'll sign it over. You're the only thing I ever saw I really wanted.

JEAN. *(Long pause.)* No.

CHAD. I want you to —

JEAN. — Chad — get lost. *(Cynthia enters with Kirsten.)*

CHAD. Thought I'd come over and see if you people got rained on last night.

CYNTHIA. Did we? You didn't say anything about it.

JEAN. No.

CYNTHIA. Of course no one's out at the dig till it dries up this afternoon; we're all holed up here. *(Jean leaves, Kirsten follows her.)*

CHAD. I'm gonna need some bread. About thirty dollars.

CYNTHIA. *(Beat.)* So you can have another night with the locals on rye-and-ginger?

CHAD. Come on, I got some buddies waiting for me in town. *(Cynthia reaches for her purse as they exit.)*

AUGUST. *(Alone — no slide.)* Note to myself. Separate personal from professional. Discard personal. Separate separate from separate; separate personal from imaginary, illusion from family, ancient from contemporary, etc., if possible. Organize if possible and separate if possible from if impossible. Catalogue what shards remain from the dig; celebrate separation; also, organize (a) brain, (b) photographic material, (c) letter of resignation, (d) health, (e) budget, (f) family, (f-1) family — ties, (g) life. Not necessarily in that order. Dianne, if you're still with me, copy that out and don't worry about it. *(Slide of a pot. Delia is on the lounge; Jean is repeatedly doing a sit-up exercise during the following scene. Kirsten sits watching Delia.)* This is a shell-tempered pot that we found four years ago in one of the mounds. What the hell it's doing in here only God and the photographer could tell you.

CYNTHIA. *(Entering past August.)* My eyes are driving me crazy. I don't think the muscles have the strength to focus on anything more this morning.

JEAN. Spots?

CYNTHIA. *(Falling back into a chair.)* Worse: one spot. I've been batting at a nonexistent fly all day. Everyone at the site waved at me.

JEAN. I might wander down and see how they're doing later.

CYNTHIA. They'll be up. Don't go today, it's too slow. They're digging out post molds. It takes forever and they're not uncovering anything but dark spots. *(To Delia.)* I hope you weren't cold last night; it can get pretty nippy in June, we —

DELIA. I froze.

CYNTHIA. What?

DELIA. I froze.

CYNTHIA. *(Getting up again.)* I'll get the blankets from our room. We all practically sleep outside from March to November.

DELIA. *(Overlapping from Cynthia's "all.")* I'm fine now. I'm fine now.

CYNTHIA. Do you have clothes or anything that we should send for? Other than what's in the trunk?

DELIA. What trunk?

CYNTHIA. The trunk you shipped from Oran.

DELIA. Did I? Good.

CYNTHIA. The hospital discovered your identity by redeeming the claim check on your trunk.

DELIA. That's — resourceful of them.

CYNTHIA. Do you have anything that —

DELIA. Don't worry about it.

CYNTHIA. We're so schizophrenic since we've been coming down here. Just as I begin adjusting to a life stripped down to what I can carry on my back we —

JEAN. — pull up camp —

CYNTHIA. — migrate back to eleven rooms of memorabilia.

JEAN. I don't think Delia's a collector.

DELIA. I collect with one hand and mislay with the other. The world's unclaimed-baggage departments are crammed with my paraphernalia.

CYNTHIA. I know it's going to sound fatuously supportive, but you're looking better. How are you feeling?

DELIA. Better.

JEAN. Don't rub your eyes.

CYNTHIA. Oh, I know ...

DELIA. Don't stare at the Gorgon, Kirsten; you'll turn to stone.

CYNTHIA. You have a fan.

KIRSTEN. Where's Oran?

DELIA. Tunisia — Algeria.

JEAN. That sounds very glamorous to us landlubbers.

DELIA. It isn't. Oran was Camus's model for the *locus in quo* of *The Plague*.
We were host to every fly on the Mediterranean.

KIRSTEN. Were you there with your husband?

CYNTHIA. Kirsten, she isn't married anymore, you know that.

DELIA. *(Simultaneously.)* Good God, I haven't been married since before you
were born. I don't even remember being married. I can't believe —
(Trailing into laugh.)

KIRSTEN. You remember being —

DELIA. — I was very young, darling; I was terrified of rejection; what I
remember is an anxiety to please so severe I could hardly fight down the
panic long enough to get drunk. I was bonded, I wasn't — *(Coughs.)*

KIRSTEN. You don't remember what he looked like?

CYNTHIA. Honey, don't bother her.

DELIA. No, it's fine — He was a strong, hirsute, sweating, horny cocksman.
He sold drilling equipment. I was so captivated that that didn't strike me
as funny until years after I got out from under him.

KIRSTEN. I thought he was an artist.

DELIA. God, no, God, no — God no! He had not eyes in his head! We traveled through the East. He traveled, I trailed.

JEAN. You were working, though.

DELIA. Self-defense.

KIRSTEN. New England or the Far East?

DELIA. Egypt, Lebanon, Syria, Cyprus, Metaxa, Ouzo, Grappa, Cinzano …

AUGUST. *(Off.)* …as long as it's considered subservient to anthropology.
We'll never have sufficient clout till we have a separate autonomous
department.

DAN. *(As he and August enter.)* Man, it's hotter than a pistol out there.
(August goes to his office, Dan to the refrigerator.)

CYNTHIA. Tell me about it.

KIRSTEN. And you split.

CYNTHIA. Don't bother her Kirsten —

DELIA. And I split. But once set in motion, the moving object tends to
remain in motion.

CYNTHIA. Well, maybe the stationary object now will tend to remain stationary.

DELIA. Couldn't do that. Couldn't do that. I have a very real terror of gathering moss. *(Dan opens a beer.)*

CYNTHIA. I don't know how you stay thin —

JEAN. I'll catch up with him.

DAN. *(To Delia.)* I think I might welcome a little moss after your experiences.

DELIA. After how many years? Eight, nine —

JEAN. Don't, I'm counting —

DELIA. — After living in the liquid world, wouldn't I welcome being washed up onto some sandy lakeshore-front property in the sun to dry out. Out in the thin air where the hand is quicker than the eye and noises are distinct and occur at their source rather than inside your head. Well, I'm — vaguely conscious of allowing myself to float up toward the surface — at least to look around.

CYNTHIA. Good.

DELIA. Whereupon I'm certain I'll want to drown myself.

DAN. Again.

JEAN. *(Giving up the exercises.)* Oh. Uncle. A hundred ten.

KIRSTEN. Up toward the surface to look around.

DELIA. Hello. Good morning What's for breakfast? I hope you weren't cold last night.

JEAN. Is that O.K.?

DAN. *(Looking through typed pages.)* All that only typed up to four pages?

JEAN. How are the post molds coming?

DAN. "Post molds?" You've been reading books.

JEAN. Talking to Cynthia.

DAN. *(To Cynthia.)* We're ready on the third section while the girls are taking a lunch break if you want to get at it.

CYNTHIA. They can wait.

JEAN. What were the posts for?

CYNTHIA. Walls. You've never seen so many holes in your life.

DAN. These are for the walls of a roundhouse. They set posts around in a circle about every two feet then filled in the walls with mud and dabble. Walls about yea thick — fire pit in the middle — no chimney, only one door — must have been smoky as hell. Men only — sat around telling hunting stories.

CYNTHIA. Then there must be about forty houses.

DAN. We won't get to them all, just a general configuration.

JEAN. This isn't really a typical village, is it?

DAN. Oh, yeah, pretty much.

CYNTHIA. Boringly so.

JEAN. In your notes you say that the typical village configuration is a large plaza with a mound at each end —

DAN. The downtown area. A mound for the high muck-a-muck God-King, and a mound for the temple.

JEAN. — and a street running around the plaza with houses all around the four sides of the plaza, all very geometrically laid out.

DAN. Very good. Roundhouse we're working on is down here in the corner.

JEAN. Swell. Only where are the mounds in the middle of the plaza?

KIRSTEN. Jasker plowed them under.

DAN. They were plowed under. That's why we didn't know there was a village here.

JEAN. And they weren't burial mounds so who would know —

DAN. No, burial mounds aren't associated with a village. They're a lot earlier. Burial mounds were built by hunters and gatherers; they didn't have a permanent village. There weren't any villages to speak of until the Mississippian Culture moved into the area and began to develop agriculture.

CYNTHIA. Then they had to hang around the house and tend the fields — sacrifice to the gods of harvest and what not.

DAN. There's been at least three different cultures who built mounds in the area — the Adena, back around 600 B.C.

JEAN. B.C.? 600 B.C.?

CYNTHIA. Don't ask; you don't want to know.

DAN. 600 B.C. Then the Hopewell Culture. They both built burial mounds. Then along about A.D. 700 a whole new people moved into the area, and instead of building burial mounds, they built a mound and on top of the mound built a temple. Two mounds. One for their temple and one for their God-King.

JEAN. One at each end of the plaza.

DAN. And we call these people the Temple Mound People. Or for short, the Early Mississippian Culture.

JEAN. And those are our guys.

CYNTHIA. All very filled with pomp and circumstance.

JEAN. Cahokia, up in St. Louis, was one of the Mississippian cities, wasn't it?

DAN. Yeah. Probably forty, fifty thousand. Bigger than Paris or London at the time.

JEAN. I know, I was reading your book on it.

DAN. I knew it; let me tell you, don't read books.

JEAN. Do you get the feeling that they were just the least bit weird?

CYNTHIA. Oh, definitely.

JEAN. There's a grave with six men all laid out ceremonially, with their right hands chopped off.

CYNTHIA. You find that all the time.

JEAN. Well, I mean, really. Do they have an explanation for that?

CYNTHIA. Maybe they were caught abusing themselves. *(Beat.)* Where's your book on circulation? I haven't seen you crack a medical book since you've been here.

JEAN. What's more immediate is a stack of articles I've intended to read for three months.

CYNTHIA. Well, don't hire out as a typist. August spends half his time drumming up money to hire secretaries to type Dan's notes.

JEAN. You don't know how ignorant I am about the —

CYNTHIA. Well, stay that way. I'm not joking. Don't start. *(To Dan.)* Have one of the girls do it. *(To Jean.)* It's a full-time job and you already have one.

JEAN. Two.

DAN. *(Unfazed by anything.)* I'd do it myself but I can't type and I can't spell.

JEAN. What will you do after the Interstate levels the mounds you're supposed to dig next summer?

AUGUST. *(Off calling.)* — Dan? Where'd you put it?

DAN. *(Laying down pages.)* Where'd I put what?

CYNTHIA. Really, don't bother with it.

DAN. *(Giving Jean a pat in passing.)* That's terrific. Come down later.

JEAN. Oh, God. I don't mind correcting your spelling, but please don't pat me on the head.

DAN. *(Laughing, going into the office.)* Where'd I put what? *(He shuts the door behind him.)*

DELIA. *(Aware that August has deliberately interrupted the conversation.)* That was very "Johnny on the spot" wasn't it.

CYNTHIA. *(To Jean.)* Have you learned anything about pregnancy that's going to revolutionize childbirth?

JEAN. Oh…no. The source of that smug glow pregnant women have. You really do feel the miracle of it all. Every woman is the only woman who's ever been pregnant. That — and one moment of blinding damnation that was probably singular to me. After two immediate miscarriages and all kinds of anxiety about it —

CYNTHIA. I didn't realize you'd —

JEAN. Well, as grandmother would say, "Our women have a history of it" — That's why I'm reluctant to accept premature congratulations. Still, when I finally managed to stay pregnant for two months and told Dan that maybe we were O.K. — I felt for one second that in telling him I had breached a covenant between me and the baby. As though I had — forever fallen from grace. Did you feel that?

CYNTHIA. Fallen from grace, I wouldn't remember; the miracle, yes.

AUGUST. *(Re-entering with Dan.)* But that has nothing to do with us.

DAN. Just tell them we've thought of calling the dig the First National Bank of Carbondale Village.

AUGUST. That would do it. Kirsten's coming along and trying to look deprived.

KIRSTEN. I think we do better when I look hopeful.

DAN. *(To Jean.)* Come down and dig out a post mold with us. *(Delia laughs.)*

JEAN. It doesn't sound very romantic. It's more — what — rural than the spectacular cultures, isn't it?

AUGUST. It was quite spectacular — take her up to the Koster Site.

JEAN. I mean like the Aztec Empire.

DAN. The Aztec culture was not really an empire.

JEAN. Well, or the Incan culture.

AUGUST. The Incans had an empire. We'd be working somewhere else if our work here wasn't important.

DAN. If Cortés had landed here in 1250, you wouldn't be talking about the Aztecs at all; you'd be talking about the glory that was Jasker's Field. They had longer trade routes — they just didn't leave anyone around to translate their poetry.

JEAN. They had poetry?

AUGUST. I would imagine. Poetry, drama — the Aztecs did.

JEAN. Do we know any of it? The Aztec —

AUGUST. Yes, otherwise we —

JEAN. What did it sound like?

AUGUST. *(To Cynthia.)* I'll give you a ring about five. *(He exits.)*

DAN. Free verse, rhyming verse; think Emily Dickinson:

Here are our precious flowers and songs
May our friends delight in them,
May the sadness fade out of our hearts.
This earth is only lent to us.
We shall have to leave our fine work.
We shall have to leave our beautiful flowers.
That is why I am sad as I sing for the sun.

DELIA. Who was that?

DAN. We don't know his name, Delia. We only know his work. *(He exits.)*

CYNTHIA. *(Picking up her equipment as Jean begins exercising.)* Do you really think you'll go on with a medical career after you have the baby?

JEAN. *(Stops dead. Beat.)* It didn't stop you. You managed. Don't rub your —

CYNTHIA. I have several thousand photographs of Kirsten. Maybe you'll go into pediatrics. *(Pause.)* If you come down, bring a hat; the sun's murder. *(Starts out.)*

JEAN. Were you into a photographic career before —

CYNTHIA. *(Overlapping.)* Not at all, not at all. I'm sorry I brought it up. *(Jean goes to the door as Cynthia leaves.)*

JEAN. *(After Cynthia has gone, looking after her.)* Oh, brother.

DELIA. Did they fight? *(Jean looks around to her.)* The Temple Mound people?

JEAN. *(Not really thinking about it.)* Apparently. When they came — I think everyone would like to agree that they were runaways from the Toltecs, but haven't found substantial correlation; the books are all very careful about sweeping pronouncements, but it's all looking like a mud version of the Toltecs — so when they came up they fought off whoever was here. And built the first fortifications and all that. Probably kept the first slaves.

DELIA. You feed it all into a computer — all the facts and fancies the doctors have printed or typed or brushed and the computer would print out NOTHING APPLIES. It doesn't scan. The truth is in dreams and nightmares, but you haven't succeeded in getting that down. Rank was the ultimate genius, sure, but he couldn't tell you how to keep from cutting your wrist while you're shaving your legs.

JEAN. So you stopped shaving your legs.

DELIA. Cause and — *(Coughs.)*

JEAN. *(Beat.)* Effect. I wouldn't think you'd have much faith in computers.

DELIA. Well — "faith"…

JEAN. Exactly.

DELIA. It's all going to be facts, Doctor. Art is part of a primitive culture, really. The future is photography. We won't have time for anything more subtle than lies.

JEAN. You have a way of conveying the impression you know all the answers.

DELIA. The answer to which is, Yes, but I don't know any of the questions.

JEAN. Neat.

DELIA. Isn't that neat? It's a lie, but it's neat. I know the questions by rote. I just don't stand up well under them.

JEAN. No, neither do I. I won the spelling bee when I was a kid. Did beautifully, then had a complete collapse.

DELIA. I'd think so.

JEAN. Learned a lot of words.

DELIA. That's usually enough for a good impression. Spelling bee? God.

JEAN. *The* spelling bee. When I was what? Twelve. National Champion.

DELIA. Dear God.

JEAN. No one in the neighborhood went to the dictionary, they all came to me. I was tutored by my grandmother so I was the only kid who used the old-fashioned English grammar school method of syllable spelling. Charmed the pants off them. It started out as a kind of phenomenon or trick — then when my teachers realized they had a certifiable freak on their hands, they made me study for it.

DELIA. We're all freaks — all us bright sisters.

JEAN. It wasn't so bad until the competitions started. I mean, it wasn't like the little girl practicing her violin with her nose against the window pane, watching all the other little girls at play. But I managed to work it into a nervous breakdown. *(Pause.)* I couldn't stop. Every word that was said to me, I spelled in my head *(In an easy, flowing, but mechanical rhythm.)* Mary, go to bed. Mary go to bed. Mar. M-A-R. Mar, "E." Y. "E." Mary. M-A-R-Y. Mary. Go. G-O. Go. Mary go. To. T-O. To. Mary go to. Bed. B-E-D. Bed. Mary go to bed. Mary go to bed: M-A-R-Y-G-O-T-O-B-E-D. Mary, go to bed.

DELIA. Mary?

JEAN. Mary Jean. *(She wanders to the door to gaze out.)* That, and I lost the meaning. Mary, go to bed was syllables, not sense. *(Beat.)* Then there were days when the world and its objects separated, disintegrated into their cellular structure, molecular — worse — into their atomic structure. And nothing held its form. The air was the same as the trees and a table was no more substantial than the lady sitting at it…Those were… not good days.

DELIA. I don't imagine. But you got it together.

JEAN. Oh, yes. Juvenile resilience.

DELIA. And that led one directly into gynecology.

JEAN. That led one directly into an institution, and contact with some very sick kids. Some of them more physically ill than neurotic — who were not being particularly well cared for; and that led to an interest in medicine. And reading your books and others at an impressionable age led to gynecology. *(Beat.)* Also, living with my grandmother and her cronies, who were preoccupied with illness, kept it pretty much in my curiosity. They were always talking about friends with female troubles, problems with their organs. Of course, the only organ I knew was at church. I developed a theory of musical instruments as families. The cello was the mother, the bass was the father, and all the violins were the children. And the reason the big father organ at Grace Methodist Church made such a mournful sound was that female organs were always having something wrong with them.

DELIA. Round John Virgin.

JEAN. Exactly.

DELIA. Have you seen Dad's book on the eye? *Vision*, actually?

JEAN. I didn't know he had one. He was a doctor?

DELIA. Physiologist. Hated practicing physicians. Eye, ear, nose, throat.

JEAN. Somewhat different field.

DELIA. I'd guess. The downstairs of the house was his, his consultation room, his office, his examination rooms: big square masculine Victorian rooms with oversized charts of the musculature of the neck and diagrams of the eye with the retina and rods and cones and iris and lens and those lines projected out into space indicating sight. And it appeared to me — still does — that rather than the eye being a muscle that collects light, those beams indicated that the eye projects vision onto the outside. *(Pause.)*

JEAN. The place has changed since last year. I came down a couple of times last summer — weekends — watching their progress. But something odd is happening now — or not happening. There's something...I don't think it's the pregnancy, I think it's *here.* Or maybe my eyes are just projecting vision onto the outside.

DELIA. No, I don't think that's quite it.

JEAN. I have an intense desire to turn to the end of the chapter and see how it all comes out. You don't happen to have a deck of tarot on you, do you?

DELIA. No, I just look that way.

JEAN. It's only an anxiety.

DELIA. Generally speaking, Jean, ignore the Ides of March, but beware soothsayers. *(Jean laughs.)* The old woman in *Dombey and Son* comes upon Edith in a lonely wood and says: "Give me a shilling and I'll tell your fortune." And Edith, of course, cuts her dead and goes on — Edith cuts everyone dead. And the old woman screams: "Give me a shilling or I'll yell your fortune after you."

JEAN. Oh, God. I'd pay. God, would I pay.

DELIA. That's what I thought.

JEAN. Jesus. Would I ever. What was the fortune? *(Pause.)* What was the —

DELIA. Give me a shilling or I'll tell you.

JEAN. Don't! Don't do that. What was the fortune?

DELIA. Uh, someone intervened.

JEAN. The hero.

DELIA. The villain actually.

JEAN. Do you do that? Turn to the end of a book to find out —

DELIA. No, I don't — I don't read anymore.

JEAN. You do, of course. What's wrong is this inaction. I'm used to doing things. The university funds a clinic, you can't imagine. Coming off that is like coming off speed.

DELIA. And that's your answer. Why do you want to be a doctor when we get such a kick from diagnosing our own case? What seems to be the problem, Mrs. Blue — "Well, Doctor, I'm afraid I'm going to require twenty-five 300-milligram capsules of Declomycin."

JEAN. Oh, it's true. A gargle and forty Ornade spansules.

DELIA. Jean's only coming down off work and Delia is frantically beating the bushes for something to believe in. Something with passion to warm up the blood and make her forget where it hurts. Great blinders is believing in and she's a great believer in blinders.

JEAN. Where does it hurt, Delia?

DELIA. Doctor, it's a pain in the ass.

JEAN. Where does it hurt, Delia?

DELIA. I thought we agreed not to ask. *(Blackout — slide utterly black with a hint of fire somewhere.)*

AUGUST. I think this would be the tribal weenie roast.

CHAD'S VOICE. *(Drunk, pounding the door.)* Goddamn! Cynthia?

CYNTHIA'S VOICE. *(Harsh whisper.)* What are you doing? The house is full of people, none of whom have ever been known to sleep!

CHAD'S VOICE. *(Drunk, urgent.)* I gotta go. I had to come over. I had to come.

CYNTHIA'S VOICE. Shhhhhh! Good God, are you drunk?

CHAD'S VOICE. I drunk thirty dollars' worth of rye-and-ginger since six o'clock.

CYNTHIA'S VOICE. Oh, God. Come outside.

CHAD'S VOICE. When you need it, we go. We gotta go when I need it, damn it.

CYNTHIA'S VOICE. Come outside; come on outside.

CHAD'S VOICE. *(Louder, insistent.)* I'm hot, baby — get down; take it, god-damn it; it'll just be ten seconds; nobody's gonna come in in ten seconds.

CYNTHIA'S VOICE. Shhhh. Come on.

CHAD'S VOICE. Come on.

CYNTHIA'S VOICE. Shh. Come on, come outside. *(The screen-door spring sounds as they are heard to go outside. A flashlight is shone from the top of the stairs.)*

DAN. Is someone there? Hello? *(Flashlight out.)* Hello? *(Stumbles.)* Oh, god-damn it. *(Flashlight on, he's on his knees, the light finds the lamp, he turns it on. Delia is on the lounge, a hand averting the light from her eyes.)* Oh. Oh! Shit. Oh, baby. Oh, wow! I'm sorry. Oh, Jesus…I thought we were being burglarized… Oh, you scared the piss out of me. *(He sits down.)*

DELIA. *(Still with her hand averting the light. Flatly.)* Any time.

DAN. Couldn't you have coughed or something? Were you asleep?

DELIA. No.

DAN. Woooooooow! You expect to see someone. Then you do see someone. Wow! You couldn't sleep?

DELIA. I don't know.

DAN. I'm a light sleeper.

DELIA. *(Only a glance at him.)* Why don't you straighten up like a man? Your posture is a disgrace to the species.

DAN. That's probably from working in —

DELIA. — Oh, for godsake, put your shoulders down, you look like a capon. I'm not talking about your physical health. I'm talking about this Howdy-Dowdy, hale-fellow, nice-guy, innocent-babe-in-the-woods facade you splash over every — I'm a writer, I'm not a chiropractor.

DAN. You still think of yourself as a writer? *(Delia looks at him directly for the first time.)* I mean, I'm glad; are you working? Are you writing? You know, I knew August for two years before I knew you were his sister? We read you at school…Contemporary American Lit. Professor…can't remember. Read half your second book aloud. Second one was *Spindrift?* *(Pause.)* He was wild about it. Read everything aloud because he knew (a) we wouldn't read anything he assigned, and he had this thing that any really good book should be read aloud (b). *(He begins rolling a joint.)*

DELIA. Sounds like a lousy disciplinarian.

DAN. Frustrated actor. Read terrifically.

DELIA. Snap course.

DAN. No shit; that's all I took my last year.

DELIA. Where was this?

DAN. Columbia. Said you were the last defender of a woman's right to make a fool of herself.

DELIA. Oh, surely not the last. Tell him I was drunk.

DAN. When you wrote it? Does that make it bad?

DELIA. No. It makes it easier. No, it doesn't. Nothing makes it easier — *(Mumbles, a light cough.)*

DAN. What?

DELIA. *(Forced out.)* I said nothing makes it easier once it starts becoming difficult! Half of it. Half of it should read very nicely. Half of it was dictated into a tape recorder. Because I couldn't find the typewriter — keys.

DAN. I liked it.

DELIA. The half you heard.

DAN. I read it. I liked it a lot. I realize you couldn't care less one way or the other whether I —

DELIA. *(Overlapping almost from "realize.")* I had a little secretary come in from some agency and type it for me. Temporary help. She looked... "temporary." Very neat, sweet, meek. She typed eight hours a day for five days, never misspelling a word, stacked the manuscript on the desk, put on her neat, sweet, meek gloves while I wrote out a check; took her check sweetly, put on her coat meekly, and left by the front door neatly. And I took the manuscript, put it in a box, wrapped it in vinegar and brown paper, addressed it to my publisher, who had been expecting it daily for over five months, threw it on the closet floor, and got drunk for three days. Wouldn't answer the phone.

DAN. Because it was finished?

DELIA. Because I thought she hadn't liked it.

DAN. *(Pause.)* And after three days?

DELIA. The police, with my publisher, broke the door in. I told him it was going to be a failure. Later on he told me the book was a success but I was a failure.

DAN. I liked it very much. *(Beat. He gets up, looking out again.)* Was that you? That clamor down here?

DELIA. You've been coming here four summers? You and Auggie and Cynthia? I'd think you'd have noticed that you're in the country out here. The natives get restless at night. The dogs raid the hen houses. They get hungry.

DAN. *(Offering the joint.)* Want a toke?

DELIA. How did you ever survive four years in New York?

DAN. Five, I got my M.S. *(Delia laughs.)* It was really intimidating, but I kinda loved it. I had this great roommate who worried about me. Thought he was Seymour Glass. The guy in all the —

DELIA. I'm familiar —

DAN. Studied medieval history, but he was a nice guy —

DELIA. — Well, though, medieval history isn't something to cross off lightly, he could have told you how the Flemish used a virgin to distract the horny unicorn.

DAN. We used to put him on.

DELIA. Yes, I'm sure —

DAN. — Well, then, also, I really believed the only way to feel completely safe on the sidewalks of New York was to be completely, knockdown drunk. I mean visibly, stinking, reeling, dangerously drunk.

DELIA. How many times have you been dangerously —

DAN. On the sidewalks of New York? Once. But it's the only time I felt safe. I was badly drunk. In a bad drunk way.

DELIA. I'm familiar. Sick drunk.

DAN. Sick doesn't even begin. I saw signs, sidewalks, people veering out of my way. Taxis *avoiding* me. I fell off the curb — had no idea what it was — got up, staggered across the street wondering where all the *buildings* had gone — realized just as I got to the other side that probably I was crossing a street — looked around to confirm it, and fell over the other curb. *(Pause.)* In the rain. I remember walking up to a street light. I thought it was a street light, it wasn't a street light, I thought it was a street light, and wrapping my arms around it like it was my mother. Cold hard wet beautiful mother. Stood there forever. Long enough to lose all orientation. Finally opened my eyes and right at my nose this sign says: "You must answer to get help." *(Pause.)* White letters on a red field. "You must answer to get help." Blackout. Next thing I know, my roommate's shaking me awake asking me what time I got in. I said, "You must answer to get help." *(Pause.)* You ever see that sign? *(Pause.)* "You must answer ..."

DELIA. I missed that one.

DAN. One on every block. I saw it about a month later. Old friend. Little letters: "Break glass; lift receiver; answer operator." Big print: "You *must* answer to get help." No more metaphysical than anything else in this world. *(Pause.)* Fire-alarm box. One on every block. *(Pause, looks at her. Delia stares blankly off into space.)* Friend of man and dog. *(Long pause. He gets up, reaches for the lamp.)* Light on or off? *(Pause.)* Delia? D.K.?... light on or off? *(A pause. He turns off light. Blackout.)*

AUGUST. *(Slide: Mr. Jasker.)* This is old man Jasker himself. The wise old bird who owns the place. After being made famous with the arrival of the college, he was looking forward to being made rich by the arrival of the lake and Interstate 64. We see him twice each year, on our arrival and departure. This is a June hello — there was no September good-bye this summer. *(Slide: the moon.)* This is the moon. *(Delia is seated in the shadows. Chad and Dan are noisily divesting themselves of rods, reels, creels, etc. Enjoying the noise; oblivious of the silence of the house. Dan goes to the refrigerator.)*

DAN. Nothing!

CHAD. Nothing?

DAN. Nothing to drink. Do you want to eat?

CHAD. God, no —

DAN. Food?

CHAD. Never again in my life. *(He has found a bottle of Scotch.)*

DAN. Well, then there's nothing.

CHAD. You call that nothing?

DAN. Are you crazy; you want to kill yourself?

CHAD. No — you go. "Beer on whiskey — mightly." Mightly?

DAN. Mightly?

CHAD. What is it? You say it.

DAN. You're saying it. I don't know what —

CHAD. I'm telling you, it's an old wives' tale — there's a thing — a saying that tells you how to judge.

DAN. A what? What's the thing?

CHAD. A thing. You're the educated member of the family — you're supposed —

DAN. But not in FOLKLORE! Not in —

CHAD. I'm not talking —

DAN. — Absolute blind spot in folklore!

CHAD. I'm talking words — it's a epigram or epitaph or aphorism or anagram.

DAN. Axiom.

CHAD. It's not an axiom.

DAN. Well, what is it? Is it —

CHAD. It's not a goddamned axiom. It's an easy word — it's a word! It's a saying — a truth!

DAN. That's the word. It's a truth.

CHAD. It's a truth, but that's not the word — ANYWAY!

DAN. Anyway. How does it go? Tell us! Are we safe? Will we survive?

CHAD. It goes… *(Pauses, trying to frame it.)*

DAN. *(Under.)* How does…

CHAD. *(Under.)* Just cool it a minute, will you? It goes: *(Headline.)* "BEER.
   ON WHISKEY."
DAN. Sounds bad.
CHAD. "MIGHTY RISKY…WHISKEY. ON BEER. NEVER FEAR."
DAN. *(Pause.)* It's an aphorism.
CHAD. So. *(Pours a glass each.)* Whiskey on beer — *(Toast.)*
DAN. Cheers.
CHAD. WHISKEY ON BEER …
DAN. That's what I said: "Never fear."
CHAD. Cheers. *(They drink.)*
DAN. This will probably kills us.
CHAD. Hey! Have you ever seen anything as beautiful as that moon?
DAN. Never.
CHAD. As big?
DAN. Never. When's the harvest moon?
CHAD. October.
DAN. Only the harvest moon.
CHAD. November.
DAN. Only the harvest moon.
CHAD. October.
DAN. Only the harvest moon.
CHAD. September.
DAN. As golden?
CHAD. Never.
DAN. What is it? June 21, 23 — that's the summer solstice — moon.
CHAD. *(Simple.)* It's a full moon.
DAN. It's a full moon.
CHAD. And you're full of shit.
DAN. I'm fulla beer.
CHAD. I gotta piss. *(He goes out the door.)*
DAN. *(Alone.)* What'd we do?
CHAD. *(Off.)* Twelve.
DAN. Twelve's ass. I caught five and you caught what?
CHAD. *(Off.)* You caught five, I caught seven.
DAN. They be all right out in that tub?
CHAD. *(Off.)* You want to clean 'em?
DAN. Hell, I couldn't clean me.
CHAD. *(Off.)* You better manage it; Jean'll kick your ass out on the floor.

DAN. Hell she will. *(He stands, miming rod: casting, catch.)* Strike! Shitfire! Strike! Get the net!

CHAD. *(Off.)* What?

DAN. Get the net, goddamn it, I got another one!

CHAD. *(Off.)* Get your own damn net; I got a seven-pounder out here.

DAN. *(Dropping it.)* He who brags about size of meat — I forget what it was, but Confucius said something very appropriate to that. What'll it weigh? The big one. Five pounds?

CHAD. *(Off.)* Six.

DAN. Was that one motherfuckin' fish? Was that a *fight?* To the *death?*

CHAD. *(Entering.)* That was a fight to the death.

DAN. Was that the biggest bass you ever saw in your life?

CHAD. No.

DAN. Shit.

CHAD. No.

DAN. You've seen a bigger bass?

CHAD. I've seen a bigger bass.

DAN. Drink your beer.

CHAD. I gotta get my ass home

DAN. Would you drink your damn beer?

CHAD. You better get your duds off; get up to that warm bed, you're gonna be diggin' tomorrow.

DAN. Terrific — You know why? 'Cause what's happening is, it's all gone wrong. And that's always very terrific.

CHAD. Get up and have your girl give you a rubdown, huh?

DAN. Everything's looking like a typical village, right? And all of a sudden it's not typical any more. They got something *under* the roundhouse.

CHAD. Isn't that right?

DAN. We don't know what yet. What?

CHAD. You gotta get up to your girl.

DAN. She's beautiful, isn't she?

CHAD. She is that.

DAN. And bright — you wouldn't believe it.

CHAD. No, I'm counting on it. Let's take you up, put you to bed.

DAN. And sweet; you wouldn't believe it.

CHAD. No, I'm a believer.

DAN. You better believe it.

CHAD. Let's get you up to bed, come on.

DAN. I'm all wet.

CHAD. Come on.

DAN. I'm all wet, come on.

CHAD. Well, you said it.

DAN. Drink your — Scotch.

CHAD. Wore your life preserver, didn't you? That's nice out there, just you and me, huh?

DAN. Beautiful.

CHAD. Wouldn't be right with no one else, huh?

DAN. No way.

CHAD. You gettin' warm?

DAN. I'm fine.

CHAD. *(Very close to Dan.)* You gonna be O.K.?

DAN. I am.

CHAD. *(Pulling Dan closer.)* You sure? You sure?

DAN. Yeah, well, I didn't drown, I can survive without mouth-to-mouth resuscitation.

CHAD. Huh?

DAN. I'm fine.

CHAD. You know why you didn't drown — because you got a cork head!

JEAN. *(Entering.)* You've got to be kidding; it's one-thirty in the morning.

DAN. *(Whispering.)* Oh, damn! No! It's the night of nights! People should be up.

JEAN. Do you drink when you're out fishing? No wonder people go fishing. *(To Delia.)* Are you all right? I mean, are they bothering you?

DELIA. Not at all.

DAN. Jesus Christ! I might have sat on you! We're all here. *(To Jean, moving toward her.)* This is the night —

JEAN. Shhh! The night of nights; I hear you. Come on, really. I'm all over calamine lotion…I'm itching all —

DAN. Gently, gently, gently — *(Softly, singing, waltzing her gently a few steps.)* "We're gonna fill an ocean of calamine lotion …"

JEAN. Come on, you'll wake me up; you'll wake me — *(Breaks off.)* Oh, well, hell, it's too late; I'm awake. Damn. Damn. Damn. Are you sure we won't bother you? Were you sleeping out here?

DELIA. No, you won't bother me. No, I wasn't sleeping.

JEAN. *(Opening refrigerator.)* You hungry? I'm starved.

DAN. Is anybody hungry? No one is hungry.

DELIA. Whattaya say, Jasker? You hungry?

JEAN. What are you drinking? Is that straight Scotch?

DAN. Well, yeah, it's… We're sipping.

CHAD. I'm gonna leave you all to your dig.

DAN. Stay. Stay.

CHAD. Later. *(Leaving.)*

DAN. Stay awhile. *(Chad is gone.)* Eat! We'll all eat! What's the matter with him? *(Jean is making a sandwich.)*

DELIA. What's he got on you?

DAN. Got on me? Nothing. What are you talking about, he's not got anything on me — I owe him my life — he's not got anything on me.

DELIA. Nobody owes their life to —

DAN. Well — some things you don't know, do you? He pulled me out of the drink last summer. We were rowing out; I was pulling back on the oar, it came out of the lock, hit me right in the face — I passed out and slid over the side in twenty feet of water.

JEAN. You're really too much.

DAN. Pulled me out by the hair of my head.

JEAN. What did you catch?

DAN. Oh! Incredible!

JEAN. Come on.

DAN. *(Whispers.)* Four very friable, skillet-size bass. And one mammoth ...

DELIA. Motherfucking.

DAN. Motherfucking. President of the Lake. Come and look!

JEAN. No, I haven't got any —

JEAN. — It's wet! I'm barefoot. I hate fish. I mean, I'll eat it, I'm glad you caught it, but I don't like live fish.	DAN. Come out and look. Come — Would you come out here and look.

DAN. What do you do when they got no sense of adventure?

JEAN. How big?

DAN. Very big. Formidable. Six pounds. If she hadn't been here, I'd of said twelve. But a fighter! A very...vicious opponent. Only six pounds, but solid muscle. Look at the moon at least — come look at the moon, you can see the moon from here; you don't have to even — where'd it go? *(He has taken her arm.)*

JEAN. You're soaking wet. Did you fall in?

DAN. I jumped in. I wanted to test my life jacket.

JEAN. Did it work?

DAN. Uh...inconclusive. Anyway! I thought we were getting a late start. I mean, what do I know, right? But it was hot. And bass are hedonists.

When it's hot on top they puddle about down at the bottom, doing whatever they do when it's hot on top. You got to know the psychology of the mothers. To be a fisherman you have to be a kind of amateur —

JEAN. Ichthyologist.

DAN. Ichthyopsychologist. But what do I know. So, no sign. We row miles. Miles. *(Slowing down, tiring. Jean has sat down.)* You wouldn't believe the size of — there's one spot that's surrounded — both sides — with pines. Miles and miles, both sides. Anyway — *(Getting comfortable, against her, or on her lap. Jean continues to munch her sandwich.)* The sun goes down. No big deal.

JEAN. No big deal.

DAN. A little rose, a little amber. Nothing to notice. Basic everyday sundown. Then a bunch of disinterested strikes.

JEAN. Uninterested.

DAN. Uninterested strikes, all in a row. One two three four five six. So. There are fish in there; we just don't interest them much.

JEAN. Is this the fish or is this the moon?

DAN. Shhhh. This is the moon. This is the fish and the moon. This is both…We're busy with the strikes; we don't even notice it's getting dark. Another couple of strikes, nibbles — bait stealings — nothing serious. And all of a sudden it's night. Pitch. Ink. We're two hours away, easily. Might as well turn around. So we start back — and…up…drifts… this…orange. Deep orange…unstable…major moon. *(Beat.)* The lake is like…

JEAN. Glass.

DAN. … Very calm. We're rowing back — it's just beautiful. It's important. We stopped rowing and watched it. And then I threw my line in — *(Simply.)* — just because we were stopping. And — "Galoompba." Immediately. *(Lying in her lap. Swaying with it.)* They swam up to that light like they were mesmerized by the light, dizzy on it …

JEAN. And that's when you caught them.

DAN. All — however many of them. Five and seven.

JEAN. Twelve.

DAN. All twelve of them.

JEAN. And by this time you were stoned.

DAN. Uhhh.

JEAN Importantly stoned.

DAN. Uhhh.

JEAN. You bring back any grass?

DAN. Of course not.

JEAN. And what did you drink? *(Pause. Shakes him lightly.)* And what did you drink?

DAN. We drank...sunshine...and moonshine...and the air...and trees... and singing...singing! And fish...and camaraderie, and... *(Mentally counts.)* Five six-packs.

JEAN. You don't swim that well.

DAN. Chad swims like a duck.

JEAN. Ducks have rarely been known to save anyone from drowning more than once.

DAN. This is true. I'm going to go to bed. *(Gets up.)* Give me a kiss. *(Kisses her lightly.)* I'm going to go to bed. *(Exits.)*

JEAN. *(Pause.)* I don't think I've ever been more awake. *(Pause.)* There's an old Chinese proverb: If you save someone from drowning, you're responsible for them for the rest of their life. I think Dan feels it's the other way around.

DELIA. I wasn't overly enthusiastic about the Orient.

JEAN. I'd like to see India. Japan.

DELIA. No, no...I couldn't take the Indian deities with their fucking Mona Lisa smiles saying: "Well, that's for us to know and you to find out." I made the only rationalization possible. I decided they didn't know at all. Come drift with me on a raft in the sea of tranquillity. I'd go nuts. All of which would have served me very well if I could have forgotten it was a rationalization.

JEAN. Don't you make yourself tired with all that?

DELIA. *(Profound sigh; pause.)* Yes.

JEAN. I mean, they're only pieces of sculpture. They're art objects. They're not Shiva and Shakti themselves. Shakti didn't come down and sit for her portrait. She didn't pose for the artist.

DELIA. *(Beat.)* I believe she did. I think that she did. You're not easily quailed by the inscrutable.

JEAN. Inscrutable. In. I-N, in. Scrut. S-R-U-T, scrut. Inscrut. Ah. A, ah. Inscruta — ble. B-L-E, ble. Inscrutable. Inscrutable: I-N-S-C-R-U-T-A-B-L-E, inscrutable. *(Cynthia, in a robe, comes down, mildly surprised to see them. She hesitates only a second, then, without thinking further about it, crosses the room to the back door and lets herself out. They watch but do not comment.)*

DELIA. *(After a moment.)* Men. God, they're sad — depressing poor bastards, breaking their balls for their families. We're their reflection, I suppose, but

I don't know as they love us for it. *(August enters, goes to the refrigerator, looks in.)* Who would have the time? I wonder, do we drive them to it?

JEAN. Women? *(August takes a bottle of milk from the refrigerator, sets it on a table, goes for a glass, leaving the refrigerator door open.)*

DELIA. No. Wives. I have an odd vision that women are wonderful. It's the wives. Sad old wives. *(August pours milk into the glass, and sits at the table staring off.)* I wouldn't be a man. Not and carry the dumbfounding load they've saddled themselves with. Actually, now that I think of it, being a woman is worse. We're the remains. We're what's left. We're the lees in the bottom of the bottle. You know how the world ends? You know what the "with a whimper" is? A sad old world of widows: wizened old women, lined up on beaches along all the Southern coastlines looking out over the water and trying to keep warm. *(Beat.)* Good Lord. That sounds so horribly right I'll bet it's prophetic. The species crawls up out of the warm ocean for a few million years and crawls back to it again to die. Why don't you make me a drink.

JEAN. No. *(August notices the light from the refrigerator, returns the bottle, closes the refrigerator door. Blackout. A flashlight beam moves slowly across the stage, investigating the chairs, the refrigerator, the floor. The light goes out. We hear the screen door creak and close. A pause.)*

END OF ACT ONE

ACT TWO

Everyone except Kirsten is onstage, Dan presiding.

DAN. Well, it's wrong is what it is. It's all wrong. Show her the Polaroid.

CYNTHIA. *(Handing Jean a print.)* You won't be able to tell much.

AUGUST. Burials have a way of turning up just as the light goes.

JEAN. I can't tell a thing from this.

DAN. *(Looking over her shoulder.)* See, he's laid out straight, head to the right.

JEAN. He isn't missing a hand, by any chance?

DAN. No, he's got the usual number of hands and three feet. Which is kinda funny when you see it.

CYNTHIA. Very awkward for dancing.

JEAN. Are you going to play with me, or are you going to tell me what you've found?

CYNTHIA. The third foot is incursive from some neighbor.

DAN. We don't know what we've found until we go over and see who his buddy is, and how many of them there are.

AUGUST. Tomorrow.

DAN. You're damn right.

CYNTHIA. Come out tomorrow, you might actually see August with a trowel in his hand.

DAN. Something's up; it's all wrong. Remember the roundhouse I showed you? With the fire in the middle? Well, these guys are buried under the roundhouse.

AUGUST. Looks almost as if the house was built over them.

JEAN. And that's not cricket.

DAN. Uh — no. That's not cricket.

JEAN. Does he have artifacts around him?

DAN. Very low caste. Not so much as a little stone pipe.

JEAN. You think they had a caste system?

CYNTHIA. All the latest advancements

DAN. As a matter of fact, around 1500 a tribe called the Natchez ended up down in Mississippi, where the French settlers studied them for about fifty years, decided they were dangerous, and rubbed them out —

JEAN. — Oh, God —

DAN. — Exactly. And it looks like the Natchez might have been the last of the Mound Builders. Hey, Deek — want to write a book? Last of the Mound Builders — I'd be glad to advise for a small consideration.

DELIA. Delia or D.K. Not "Deek."

DAN. So. If our guys were anything like the Natchez, they had a really off-the-wall, really bizarre, caste system.

AUGUST. Four distinct castes: The Suns —

DAN. — who were the very big muck-a-mucks, led by the Great Sun, who was a God-King.

AUGUST. Then the Nobles, then the Honored Men, and then the Stinkards.

DAN. Really. Stinkards. Or that's the French translation. And of course most everybody was a Stinkard.

CYNTHIA. So things haven't changed all that much.

AUGUST. — and the Suns, the Nobles, and the Honored Men could only marry into the Stinkard class, with the second generation assuming the class of the mother. So only someone with a Sun mother and a Stinkard father could become the new God-King.

DAN. And everybody married Stinkards. Including the other Stinkards.

CYNTHIA. I didn't realize that.

AUGUST. I thought probably you did.

DAN. So they were an "upward-mobile," matriarchal society with a God-King muck-a-muck. All dressed in swan feathers. Carried on a litter everywhere he went. Like Delia; huh, D.K.?

DELIA. Dan, it has been years since I've dressed in swan feathers.

JEAN. How long did they live? Not the Natchez, our guys.

DAN. Short.

JEAN. How long? How short?

AUGUST. If they reached the age of fifteen, their life expectancy was maybe thirty. *(A light thunder is heard, and gradually a wind rises.)*

DAN. Do not ask how old I'll be my next birthday.

CYNTHIA. You haven't reached the age of fifteen.

JEAN. And won't. The head of the department calls him "Pollyandy" to his face.

AUGUST. The head of the department is an extremely nihilistic individual.

DAN. This is true.

JEAN. What did they eat?

DAN. *(Who has gone back to studying drawings of the grave site.)* Huh? Oh — corn, squash, beans —

CHAD. That's succotash.

DAN. You kill, right? When you can't flunk 'em? They ate everything. Shellfish, deer …

CHAD. For all you know, they were cannibals.

DAN. Of course you know I'd love to discover they were cannibals. Only I doubt if we'd ever be funded again. They had fairly elaborate ritualistic human sacrifices, but they weren't barbarians.

CYNTHIA. Actually, there's evidence that they did practice cannibalism.

DAN. None. Here? None. You're talking about Wisconsin. The people of southern Illinois are certainly not responsible for the perverted table manners of the people of Wisconsin. I personally wouldn't be surprised at anything that was discovered in Wisconsin. I think there's something in the water that twists their minds.

CHAD. Beer.

DAN. Very likely. Exactly.

AUGUST. Is that rain?

DAN. Is it raining? Damn. I better go down and see that they got everything covered. *(Getting a slicker.)* Let up already. *(Going out.)* My God, it's pouring.

JEAN. Put the hood up.

DAN. *(Off.)* What?

JEAN. Your hood, dummy. Put the hood up. *(Several slides of rain and the lake.)*

AUGUST. *(Isolated by the light to his desk area.)* Up, up, up, up. Every morning Dr. Loggins pushed a stake into the edge of the lake, trying, I think, to kill it. And every evening the lake had covered it. Nine tributaries empty into the basin, draining almost all of two counties. By the time the lake over-ran the site, it didn't at all matter. *(Chad knocks at the door. After a moment, Jean comes down.)*

CHAD. I've been wanting to talk to you.

JEAN. *(After an audible sigh.)* I think maybe if you didn't come here…I mean, I know it's your house, and Dan likes you, you're a terrific relief from his gaggle of volunteers, but — you're putting yourself through something that seems so unnecessary.

CHAD. I thought we should talk. Just with nobody —

JEAN. We're talking, I don't mind; I'm perfectly willing to talk, but you can't expect it to be the sort of talk —

CHAD. *(Overlapping from "expect," letting himself in.)* What? Are you trying to make a fool of me? We're not talking; I got my boat over here. We'll go over to the place, the six acres I told you about — it's gonna be an island when the lake fills, I want to show you. There's a cave. It's going to be under water in another couple of days …

JEAN. *(A long pause.)* No.

CHAD. I thought you said we'd talk.

JEAN. Say whatever it is you want to say. It won't improve with the change in scene.

CHAD. It's just down at the landing —

JEAN. You have some kind of romantic fantasy going on that frankly frightens —

CHAD. I gave it a paint job; you ought to look at it.

JEAN. Chad, for godsake, I don't even swim, I don't like water, I don't like boats, it's pouring rain, and I'm not at all attracted to you.

CHAD. You don't know anything about me, you don't know —

JEAN. That is absolutely true, but I can live with it. You said you wanted to talk; you don't want to talk, you want to bludgeon. I'm married to a guy you claim is your friend — I'm going — I'm very much committed to him — I'm really sorry, but you make me feel foolish.

CHAD. O.K., O.K., O.K., you don't want to be with just me. Maybe what you want is for the three of us to get together. Go out fishing ...

JEAN. (Going.) You're too much of a sport for me, Chad, you're too sporty for me.

CHAD. I thought you said we'd talk.

JEAN. Please put it out of your head, I don't like it. You make me uncomfortable.

CHAD. You said we'd talk. (August enters with Kirsten.) Bitch of a day, huh?

AUGUST. (Shaking water from his hat.) None too bright. (Chad exits.) I don't know, Jean — I think it's not a good idea to socialize too much with our little surrogate landlord.

JEAN. Socialize? — Dan seems to like him.

AUGUST. Well, Dan, for all his ebullience, is quite tactful really.

JEAN. And I'm not — or women aren't.

DAN. (Entering soaked.) Brother! Drowned.

JEAN. You really are. (Hands Dan a towel.) You get the girls into the motel?

DAN. Yeah, their tents were almost washing out from under them; they're game, but they're stupid. The lake is insane; it's ten feet higher than it's supposed to be — if it's raining tomorrow, we're going to have to work anyway.

JEAN. You get dried off?

DAN. Yeah, I'm fine.

KIRSTEN. (At the table.) What's in the sifter?

DAN. Seeds.

KIRSTEN. Maize? (Pause.) Maize?

DAN. Grass. *Cannabis sativa.*

KIRSTEN. Oh. (*Delia, dressed in a clean robe, walks unsteadily but unaided down the stairs.*)

DAN. Well. It walks, it talks. It takes nourishment from a spoon. (*August moves into the office.*)

DELIA. Spiritually it still crawls on its belly like a reptile. — And it no longer takes nourishment from a spoon.

JEAN. You didn't.

DAN. You know the Contemporary Lit. professor I told you about? Used to read your stuff out loud?

DELIA. (*Sits.*) Don't push.

DAN. Thought of his name. Dr. Landau. Had a great voice. Said — what do you think about this? — said —

DELIA. I don't want to know what he said.

DAN. No, you'll get a kick out of it.

JEAN. This is about which one, this is *Spindrift*?

DAN. Yeah, said you were checking off the possibilities of the species. You know, if it hadn't been for the —

DELIA. That's such a load of crap, what a load of — you know what I wrote? How I teased myself through it? I set a simple problem and tried to solve it. Write a Chinese puzzle box. Write a Russian doll. A box within a box within a box within a box. Every time something was solved, within the solution was another problem, and within the solving of the second riddle another question arose. And when that riddle was unwound there was still a knot. And you know why I failed? For me? Because either a Chinese puzzle box must go on *ad infinitum* or there must finally be a last box. And when that box is opened, something must finally be in it. Something simple like maybe an answer. Or a fact, since we all seem to be compulsive compilers. Look at you, digging your evidence, piecing together shards, fragments, sherds. Clues, footnotes, artifacts, pollen grains, bones, chips.

DAN. (*Overlapping from "pollen grains."*) Not of themselves — in association. Where are they, why are they there?

DELIA. Boxes in boxes.

DAN. (*Simultaneously overlapping second "boxes."*) Boxes in boxes. And when you got all the knots unwound in your book, and all the problems untied, and got down to the final little box —

DELIA. The Russian doll.

DAN. — and it was opened, what was inside?

DELIA. (*Pause.*) Another book.

DAN. *(Pause.)* I didn't know there was another ...

DELIA. Well, that shows what you know. I thought it should be for Dad. A simple...simple.... Then, of course, Dad died, and I — *(Pause.)*

JEAN. What?

DELIA. "In Memoriam" never interested me much.

DAN. *(Softly.)* There wasn't another ...

DELIA. For you to see? For Dr. Landau to read aloud? I heard it — I saw it down there somewhere...that graceful, trim, and dangerous leviathan that got away — it moved in the cold depths of some uncharted secret currents where the sun has never warmed the shadows. Graceful and taunting. Moving through a spectrum of dark colors alien to the unaided eye. I could have captured it and displayed to the light some undiscovered color. But it was deaf to my charms and tokens and incantations. I called the son of a bitch, but it wouldn't rise. So I went down to find it.

DAN. *(Pause.)* And it got away ...

DELIA. *(Laughs.)* Well, I didn't get away. It caught me!

DAN. Tell me about —

DELIA. Tell me about the three-footed skeleton you've found.

DAN. We can't work, Delia; how can we work in this? *(Goes to office door.)*

AUGUST. If it's this bad tomorrow, we'll put up tarps.

JEAN. I've thought about that house you grew up in. Big old masculine rooms with medical charts.

DELIA. Oak floors and old oak furniture. And light. The whole place filled with sunlight. Especially in the winter.

AUGUST. She left when she was seventeen; I'm surprised she'd tell anyone about it.

DELIA. I'm the one who liked it, so I'm the one who remembers it.

AUGUST. I never said I didn't like it.

DELIA. He liked it so much he sold it the first week he could. Without mentioning to me that it was up for sale —

AUGUST. You were being sick in Mexico, as I recall, and couldn't come to the funeral.

JEAN. Boy, you two make me glad I'm an only child and grew up with grandparents.

AUGUST. It's all quite past. That's all past. Water under the bridge. Water under the bridge.

DAN. Water, water, water, water, water — *(Slide: bone awl.)*

AUGUST. This bone awl you might as well enter as made by one Mr. Cochise Mississippi, around A.D. 1100.

DAN. *(Overlapping.)* Mississippian; around A.D. 1100, give or take fifty years; it's made from a turkey metacarpal bone.

JEAN. You get into some far-afield studies, don't you?

DAN. Umm.

AUGUST. Most everything we're finding here is remarkably well preserved. *(Cynthia enters.)*

DELIA. *(Handing the bone awl to Jean.)* Well, that's a real keen bone awl, Cochise, but what have you done recently?

CYNTHIA. More recently they vanished without a trace. Along with the whole Mississippian Culture.

DELIA. Along with nearly everyone; vanished without a trace.

DAN. *(Still leaning against the screen, watching the rain.)* Vanished without a trace, vanished without a trace, vanished without a trace? God, I wish it would stop raining. Vanished without a trace. Nine mounds and a hothouse do not constitute without a trace. We've seen the outline of the foundations of houses used for gentlemen's clubs, complete with fireplace, never mind the ventilation. Vanished without a trace. It happens that this awl is one of the finest-crafted utilitarian tools discovered in North America — Cochise did not disappear without a trace. I think we have palpable evidence of his craft, of a subtle skill and imagination, of his care and conscientiousness. I think with his example his family stood proud and neat. I think his wife fashioned for him quilled buckskin aprons and kilts of surpassing brilliance that dazzled the tribe. Past? Vanished? Without a trace? Cochise? His passing, women, was mourned by tribes up and down the length of this river. I think his friends told histories around the fire of his craftiness in trapping game. Women cried and brave warriors walked out into the woods to be alone and fathom his loss. I think odes were composed and spoken and learned and repeated down the generations; songs were sung. I think so sure and strong a warrior stood as an example that young braves and children held up to themselves; I think Cochise was extraordinary beyond precedent. He danced with grace, he bathed twice a day, he spoke with simplicity and truth, and nursed the sick back to strength; he tamed wild animals and laughed when the children were frightened at night. I think he spread his arms out in an open field in the sun and yellow-green parakeets that he had tamed to sit on his hands came when he called them. I think wolves nuzzled his thighs and allowed him to walk in the wild as their comrade a thousand years before anyone named Francis walked in

Assisi! Goddamn this rain! *(He grabs his slicker, kicks the screen door open, and charges out into the rain.)*

JEAN. Put the hood up! *(Pause.)* I have a feeling he really believes that. If it weren't for August, nothing they write would ever get published.

CYNTHIA. If it weren't for Dan, the work wouldn't get done in the first place.

DELIA. Parakeets?

CYNTHIA. Don't get him started. Parakeets were as common in Illinois as the sparrow is now.

JEAN. They weren't tropical?

DELIA. Some things we don't know, huh?

AUGUST. We have no clear idea what the bone awl was actually used for, but it was undoubtedly used for something. This is a particularly good one. *(He goes into the office.)*

CYNTHIA. Chad Jasker said he'd drive me into town; I think he's changed my plans.

JEAN. He was —

DELIA. I just left him standing on every corner; all the Mediterranean youths are hustlers.

CYNTHIA. Hustlers? I don't know why you call him a hustler. The Mediterraneans are probably poor, and he's poor.

DELIA. Not by their standards he isn't. Poor hustlers, rich hustlers —

CYNTHIA. You talk about how rich they're going to be —

JEAN. They are though —

CYNTHIA. Oh, they are not.

JEAN. No, really. When the lake comes in, God, they own about a mile of the shoreline.

CYNTHIA. Poor people don't become rich. It takes capital to develop a lakeshore — they're rich with fantasy. They'll sell for what they think is money and be ripped off. They're not going to be rich.

JEAN. To hear him tell it, it's settled. You've heard about the Holiday Inn and all that…the place is going to be a spa…they're sitting right in the middle of it.

CYNTHIA. I'm sure they'll borrow from the usurers and have the whole property extorted out from under them.

DELIA. I was only thinking, there are those who hustle and those who get hustled.

CYNTHIA. There are winners and losers, givers and takers; there's the quick and the dead; Chad tries to be among the quick. Sometimes it shows. What are you? Or do you know?

DELIA. I'm a nomad.

CYNTHIA. And you're happy with that?

DELIA. Happy has nothing to do with it, Cynthia.

CYNTHIA. Well, it sure as hell wouldn't seem to.

DELIA. *(Pause. Friendly.)* If it applied, I could ask you the same thing: Are you happy with that? But it doesn't apply.

CYNTHIA. *(Backing down.)* Forgive me for bringing it up. There are things I need that you perhaps don't.

DELIA. We all need them. It's a question of what you're willing to pay.

CYNTHIA. Well. You're willing to pay a good deal more than I am.

JEAN. No. She isn't.

DELIA. I'm used to shopping in bargain basements, peasant bazaars. You're paying the gold of the realm for bazaar merchandise.

CYNTHIA. All that glitters …

JEAN. I don't believe that.

CYNTHIA. *(Letting it pass.)* I thought you had given up on men. Wasn't there some woman sculptor or someone?

DELIA. Good God, no. Never. I know — I should have. A long time ago; I just never got around to it. Isn't it pathetic, it's too late to change.

JEAN. I don't think I could get into it. *(They laugh.)* Is that funny? I guess it is. Wasn't there a story about you and some woman? About tearing up some bar?

DELIA. Which bar?

JEAN. In Spain or somewhere. Oh, no! You were fighting. You were arrested.

DELIA. Not in Spain; I'd still be there.

JEAN. Did you know you made all the newspapers?

DELIA. Of course I knew. Why do you think I did it?

CYNTHIA. They used to call us for comments; we hadn't heard from her in four years.

DELIA. Now no one has. That was Cannes, Nice…along that winding, cliff-hanging — in a Mazerati. That was P.R. That wasn't me. A couple of times I allowed myself to cause a brawl or pass out in the middle of the ring because I knew it was good for the biographer. If there's such a thing as sin any more, that must be high on the list. Which of the command-ments would that come under? It's not really so bad to lie; sometimes it's kinder. Go ahead and steal, really, most of the bastards deserve to lose it. But I've "sinned." I've humiliated myself because people expected it of me.

CYNTHIA. *(Closing the refrigerator in disgust.)* Christ, this house is crammed with drugs. Doesn't anybody drink any more? *(Blackout.)*

AUGUST. Dianne, would you just note marginally that I have decided I am definitely sick of aesthetics. Aesthetics and all the representatives of the humanities ransacking anthropological collections for pots they find pleasingly shaped and carrying them off to museums, where they lecture without content on form — and without the least ethnological information or understanding. Aesthetics is becoming an enemy to thought. *(Pause. Slide: college graduation.)* What the hell is — Christ, this is my graduation — notice the innocent and hopeful countenance. Prepared to conquer lost worlds with a doctorate in one hand and a trowel in the other. *(Slide: Dan — a pause.)* A man's life work is taken up, undertaken, I have no doubt, to blind him to the passing moon. I have no doubt that in an area of his almost unconscious he knows this and therefore is not blinded but only driven. The dig at Jasker's Field was unfinished. A salvage operation from which we salvaged nothing. Slides of picnics, slides of houses, slides of water, slides of ducks, slides of boats, slides of pain, slides of need, slides of spear points. A great amount of work has been done on the early cultures of North America and we have found only the periphery of the culture. Three hundred mounds, numberless graves have been opened, usually seconds before the builders plowed them under. And of the Mississippian Culture — never before had the grave of a God-King been discovered. The most important find in forty years of work. We do not allow ourselves to dream of finding what we might find and dream with every sweep of a trowel. And what is salvaged? Nothing. Nothing. *(To the slides.)* Nothing. Nothing. Nothing. Nothing. Nothing. Nothing. *(Jean and Delia are reading. There are approaching sounds of girls yelling, everyone yelling, Dan's voice heard approaching. They stand as he enters. The slides continue flicking repeatedly across the screen.)*

DAN. Jean, Jean, Jean, Jean — come out — come down — the muck-a-muck. The high and holy muck-a-muck —

JEAN. — What? Who is it? In the grave? —

DAN. Not one — I'll be very calm, I'm not trembling, shit, I'm fine — We started clearing away toward the third foot — you remember the — grave, the —

JEAN. — Sure, sure…. The Stinkard —

DAN. — Third foot? He isn't a Stinkard, he's a retainer, dozens of them — all over the place — and in the center the ground is dark — a big black square where there has been a log tomb. It's all rotted away, but the ground is dark. August said, Oh, my God. Oh, my God. It's the tomb of a God-King. Nobody's ever found — *(Breathes deeply.)* You have never seen anything like it. Never. We didn't know if they had gold — but a gold thing on his face — and copper — Beautiful copper breastplates — everywhere — pearls like — obsidian axes, beads, thousands of tons of — come on. Delia, if you don't come out and see this, I'll never read another word you — I swear to you, two more days and the lake would have flooded it. We're going to have to break our asses.

JEAN. A muck-a-muck? A God-King?

DAN. Oh, God, what a god he must have been! Pottery. *Glazed* pots — fifty, sixty of them. It's going to be dark in no time; hurry up, it's soaking wet — we're up to our knees — Oh, my God, how famous we're going to be! You gotta write the book, Delia, you really gotta write it.

DELIA. I'll come down and see. If I can't make it, I expect to be carried on the muck-a-muck's litter.

DAN. I'll carry you on my back.

JEAN. Pearls?

DAN. A room full — and maybe *gold*. This mask thing. We thought they might have gold. They had trade routes into country where there's gold. Copper armbands, bracelets. I am perfectly calm. I am a mature and balanced scientist. I wish you could see August up to his ass in mud. He said, "This is a very high muck-a-muck." *(Delia and Jean hurry off.)* What am I supposed to get? I was supposed to get something. *(August, Chad, Cynthia, Jean, Delia, and Kirsten, all carrying boxes, overrun him, pass back and forth, busy with things, working, tired and high, but preoccupied. Kirsten goes upstairs.)*

CYNTHIA. Pitch black, it's absolutely maddening. You know you're not going to keep it under your hat.

AUGUST. For a while; for a day.

CYNTHIA. *(To Chad.)* You're pledged, you know that — not a word. Because if it gets out, it's all over; we'll have to set up guards.

CHAD. You could get lights, you could work at night —

AUGUST. That would be subtle.

DAN. We'd draw a larger crowd than the World Series.

AUGUST. You called Croff?

CYNTHIA. Yes, again. You want to know what he said again? *(They go back to working — she tells the women.)* He pissed. He was absolutely wetting his pants. He kept saying, Where's August? I said, he's down at the goddamned dig, where would you be? He started looking up charter-plane companies. I said, Croff, don't sweat it, we won't be doing anything until it gets light; drive down in the morning. He's already calculating the size of the grant the college will be getting from this. He has his picture on the cover of *Newsweek*. He honest-to-God asked me when *Scientific American* went to press.

DAN. Jasker's the one who's going to be famous, you know that, don't you? *(As the work organizes itself Dan is painting green copper beads with clear nail polish; August is cleaning something as delicately as an artist; Cynthia is writing the location and date numbers on projectile points, pottery shards, and small envelopes of pearls; Jean is entering the numbers on a chart.)*

CYNTHIA. It's going to be the most important archaeological dig in America.

DAN. Well, north of the Rio.

CHAD. You know, no bull, I admire you people. You're really trying to make something of yourself. You could have been on vacation like everybody else. I'd just make a bet — you're not doing it for what you get. I've watched you down there and I wouldn't have the patience for it.

CYNTHIA. They wouldn't have the patience to bust down a transmission or any of the tinkerings that —

CHAD. — No, you do that 'cause you got to do it; 'cause you'd be embarrassed not to. But, see — you guys are finding little pieces of charcoal last week and stuff if I saw on the ground I wouldn't bother to bend down for, but now that you found something — what's something in that grave that's valuable? I mean, that you could sell?

CYNTHIA. Almost everything.

DAN. — No more hitches with funding, you realize that. We'll be turning people down.

AUGUST. Well, now, no point in being high-handed.

CHAD. If someone came along and offered you — where's the thing? The gold thing? The bead?

DAN. Jean?

JEAN. On the table.

CHAD. See? Sitting on the table. If someone offered to buy this —

AUGUST. Very carefully, Mr. Jasker. That's the first gold ever —

CHAD. I know, I watched you with it. How much would you ask for that, how much is that worth?

AUGUST. *(Carefully.)* The gold in it — is worth maybe two or three dollars. It's beaten very thin and spread around a wooden bead. The wood has long since disintegrated. *(Taking it.)* You can hear it rattle inside. You felt how light it was.

CHAD. See, two dollars. You'd only ask what it was really worth — you wouldn't try to make anything for — Like what you really want to know is — aw, no — well —

AUGUST. I suppose if we knew that —

CHAD. *(Over.)* No, forget I said it, I can't say it; I'm not saying it right; I don't know what I'm trying to say. What are these?

AUGUST. *(Taking them from him.)* Why do you come here?

CHAD. *(Beat.)* Beg pardon, Doc? Whatta you mean?

AUGUST. You could be any number of places.

CYNTHIA. We undoubtedly have our attractions, August.

AUGUST. You were down at the dig last week watching the excavation of a fire pit. Charcoal and split rocks. Anyone could see there was no intrinsic material value in that find.

CHAD. Yeah, I know, but it's —

AUGUST. You asked when it had been built, how old it was — which were the precise questions we were asking ourselves.

CHAD. No, I'm not putting it right.

AUGUST. People are drawn to speculate. Even my sister, who has no curiosity about anything —

DAN. I'm going to get her to write us up, though. Fictionalized, of course.

AUGUST. I think archaeology can survive without that.

CHAD. Now you got your boss impressed; he's going to be down —

DAN. Something like this, we need people to verify that we aren't faking it — it's —

AUGUST. *(Minimizing.)* He's the sort that likes to check up on his employees. He's come down a number of times. Generally unannounced.

CHAD. I gotta have another beer. See, that's why I come here; I can always count on Dan to turn me on.

CYNTHIA. Oh, I think you can be turned on by any number of things.

AUGUST. *(He lifts from the table the fragile gold mask he has been cleaning.)* Look at this, coming out beautifully.

CYNTHIA. *(Getting her camera and a flash unit.)* I want to get this.

DAN. It's a death mask — we guess. It might have had feathers around it here. We have to guess. We've never seen anything like it before. *(He holds it up to his face, and almost inadvertently it stays in place.)* Is that incredible? Tell me I look like a God-King.

JEAN. Don't put that —

DAN. I didn't do a thing.

CYNTHIA. Smile. Or can you? *(Flash.)*

DAN. Let me see. I'm blind. Help me with it. *(August carefully lifts it from Dan's face.)* That's the same design we've seen on gorgets, and assumed it was meant to represent pigmentation.

CHAD. That thing's solid gold, isn't it?

AUGUST. *(A lie.)* That's copper — they valued it above gold.

DAN. It's fragile as hell. He didn't wear it, you know — they made it for him after he died. If you can imagine it completely surrounded with feathers.

JEAN. I really didn't like it on you at all.

DAN. Are you crazy; every dead God-King is wearing one this year. It may take a while to catch on.

CHAD. These are beads; they're copper too?

DAN. Those will fall right apart, Chad, they're corroded right through. They're made the same as the gold — they beat out a solid nugget of copper — they had no metallurgical knowledge, to speak of.

CYNTHIA. What have you got all over your hands?

CHAD. Oh, that's uh — paint; got more on me than I did on the car.

CYNTHIA. You painted your car?

DELIA. It's a different car.

CHAD. Got a new one; painted it black. I had 'em put on the papers that it was black, it was some kind of green, all rusted off; I had to paint it before I got stopped.

CYNTHIA. You sold the blue one?

CHAD. Wrapped it up.

CYNTHIA. The Olds?

CHAD. Couple a days ago, over on 14.

DAN. He wraps it around a tree, gets out, leaves it there, and hitches a lift home.

CHAD. Sheriff comes by, says they towed it to the dump, tried to give me a summons for abandoning it. I told him I was dazed; I didn't know what I was doing …

DAN. How'd you know it was a different car?

DELIA. I'm familiar with all possible transportation in and out of here.

JEAN. What's that stuff you're putting on that?

DAN. Just nail polish, help hold it together.

JEAN. Smells vile.

DAN. You look tired; don't get sick again.

CHAD. You been sick?

JEAN. No. Woozy; tired, not sick.

DAN. I think she's developing evening sickness. You've heard of morning sickness; she's getting evening sickness.

JEAN. *(To Cynthia.)* Did you have that?

CYNTHIA. Boring as hell, isn't it?

CHAD. What from?

DAN. Who knows the metabolism of a pregnant woman? She'll feel better tomorrow; she can diagnose what was wrong with her and write a paper on it.

JEAN. Might do it too.

CHAD. Since when was you — *(A long pause. His face registers the implication of the statement. They do not notice and continue working.)*

AUGUST. *(To Dan.)* What are you hiding there? *(Dan gives him a box, which August begins to sort through.)*

CHAD. *(Finally. Pinched.)* When's it due?

DAN. December, January.

CHAD. Hell, probably ought to celebrate.

DAN. Thought I told you.

CHAD. Not me.

DAN. As big as the hole is in the gold bead, what would you think — these are all small — if several ropes of copper beads came down like this and then the strings went through the gold one.

AUGUST. Where's the Polaroid of his chest; how was the copper situated?

CYNTHIA. *(Overlapping Dan from "gold bead.")* What did you say you were going to show me on your car?

CHAD. Me?

CYNTHIA. I don't know; you said you had something in the trunk.

CHAD. Trunk's locked. I don't have the key for it.

CYNTHIA. Maybe it was the hood, I don't know.

CHAD. I think you're thinking of someone else.

CYNTHIA. *(Going out the door.)* Well, anyway, I want to see this famous paint job.

CHAD. I ain't got time. I gotta get going. *(Savage whisper.)* Leave me alone.

CYNTHIA. *(Goes to the refrigerator, gets out a beer.)* Anyone else? Auggie?

AUGUST. I'm fine.

CHAD. *(Finally. Hardly audible, but hard.)* Whatta you gonna call it? *(As Jean, who has heard, starts to leave.)* HEY! *(Everyone freezes.)* Said, what name you gonna name it?

DAN. What?

CHAD. *(Almost in tears.)* The baby.

DAN. We're taking all suggestions, putting them in a hat.

CHAD. What then, you'll pull it out like a rabbit? It's no more important to you than that?

DAN. Well, we figure when we have a palpable, honest-to-god kid, with a gender, we'll think of something. *(Kirsten comes down, hangs back at the stairs.)*

CHAD. Boy, you guys are supercool, supercool. Down here in the sticks, you got your little harem of ugly girl students around you watching every little brush stroke and pick and pry like you was painting the world's last masterpiece. You got your pretty wives and your kids and your drug-addict sister. You really got everything going for you. Cynthia says you're going to be getting write-ups in *Time* magazine.

CYNTHIA. I said Croff envisions his mug on the cover.

CHAD. You got the place all tied up so anything you find belongs to you. You're really knocking it.

AUGUST. That was the agreement your father signed.

CHAD. *(Not hearing.)* I really got to admire your supercool.

DAN. We got it knocked.

CHAD. You really got it knocked. You're digging up all these old battle weapons — *(Lifting from the box a foot-long spear point.)* Just look at the craftsmanship on that — what'd you say that was? You called that a spear point. Who'd think those old boys would have the tools to make something like that.

AUGUST. That's very dangerous.

CYNTHIA. You said you had to be somewhere by —

CHAD. Hell, you don't even need — you can break someone's neck just by putting the right twist in the right place. *(He has, as quick as a snake, reached around Cynthia's neck with his arm.)* You know that?

CYNTHIA. I'm sure you could. You're a lot stronger than I. *(He releases her.)*

CHAD. It's a damn shame you're going to have to find yourself some other field of operation.

DAN. We'll be a while on this one yet.

CHAD. I'm talking about next year.

DAN. Next year we can get back to those mounds you think are so important.

CHAD. I guess you can if you can find where the road-construction crew scatters them. Only I don't think the Holiday Inn people are going to much appreciate a scruffy gang of ugly virgins digging up the front yard of their motel.

CYNTHIA. I don't know why you think they're virgins.

DAN. People eating at your restaurant?

CHAD. You think it's cute? You think it's not going to happen? There are some cost accountants and some professional architects from down at Memphis you should talk to.

DAN. The tourists are going to be flooding the place heavier than the lake, huh?

CHAD. You may know a hell of a lot about your grave robbing but you're really full of shit when it comes to commerce. I know you've had your nose stuck in the ground; it's not easy to see what's going on around you from that position, but this is the last trip you fellows are making down here —

DAN. — You don't seem to realize the importance of what's happened here today. Coordinating this site with the information we're going to be getting from the mounds — The information we have already will take years —

CHAD. (Overlapping from "we have.") You're just going to have to go on what you've got, buddy.

DAN. — It's a man's life work here —

CHAD. 'Cause as it hap-	DAN. I mean, it doesn't
pens, I don't want you here.	matter whether you under-
And there ain't going to be	stand or not, but I'd think
any mounds. The mounds	you'd want to be part of
are going to be fucking flat.	that. Goddamn! If you want
The mounds are going to	tourists coming in here,
be under about forty tons	we're going to have to be
of highway interchange.	digging around them.
They're going to be under	
a tennis court.	

DAN. I don't want to hear about your tennis courts.

CHAD. You people are dreaming! You might not like it, but there ain't no mounds next year. There's an interchange coming through you maybe don't know about.

DAN. I know all about it; the site is archaeologically too important to be superseded by —

CHAD. (Overlapping from "to be superseded.") They may be hot shit to you; Dad and me don't happen to want our property —

DAN. You don't realize how important a man like August Howe is. Jesus Christ, you talk like —

CHAD. — My land, baby! MY LAND! MY LAND! It don't belong to your Indian god. It don't belong to you. It's my land and there is an Interstate coming through. Now, if you want to sit in its way, every one of you, good, you're invited.

KIRSTEN. The Interstate isn't coming through your land.

AUGUST. That isn't necessary now.

CHAD. Hell, it isn't. You think they're going to build a motel where there isn't a highway?

DAN. *(Overlapping from "where there.")* Then they won't build it. What the hell difference does it make? You're talking about a goddamn Holiday Inn.

CHAD. They been here! I've seen the plans!

DAN. Goddamn it, there's a law since 1954 — in this state — against public-funded construction defacing Indian monuments.

CHAD. *(Beat.)* Well, guys, I hate to disappoint you, but you're thinking about it a little late.

DAN. We thought about it two years ago. *(Pause.)* When did you last hear from your motel architects?

CHAD. What do you mean, two years ago?

DAN. Professor Howe prepared a —

AUGUST. — Not tonight. In the morning —

DAN. *(Right over.)* — August prepared a report to the legislature on the importance of this site —

CHAD. — Well, I'm sorry he went to all the trouble —

DAN. The highway isn't going to be anywhere near Blue Shoals. It's been rerouted to the other side of the goddamn lake! We got notice before we came down this summer. *(A long pause.)*

CYNTHIA. When was this, August?

CHAD. Shit. "When" — Let on like —

DAN. Two years; after our first summer; after we heard about the highway.

CYNTHIA. It must have been a lot of trouble keeping me in the dark.

DELIA. We're a bad risk, Cynthia.

AUGUST. It was a matter of a brief report, a few pictures, and a phone call.

JEAN. You can't do that.

DAN. Old man Jasker wouldn't allow the land to become a national monument. How else could we protect them?

CYNTHIA. Them? Protect them or protect you?

CHAD. Boy, you're pretending to be my friend; you're listening to me talking about soul food and grilled bass out of the lake; what are you saying behind my back? Leading me on. Where do you get off thinking you're better than the people around here and can take over and take away everything we hope for — where — laughing about my goddamned island — what do you care. Millions! You're trying to steal from me!

JEAN. You don't know what it means to him.

DAN. I know what it means to me; you should know what it means to me.

CYNTHIA. Using my photographs of the dig to surreptitiously —

DAN. Chad, I'm trying to make you see that you'd be better off — understand the value of what you have here, God, the place —

CHAD. *(A howling scream.)* NOOOOOOOOO! *(Silence. A pained plea.)* How can you treat people…? *(Pause.)*

JEAN. Chad. I went down to the courthouse; I saw the model you told me to see, I …

CHAD. *(Fiercely to August.)* — you won't get it. I know what you want, Professor, but you might just have to stay up at State next summer with your whore and fuck her yourself. *(He exits.)*

CYNTHIA. Chad? *(Going out.)* Jasker, goddamn it, stay here. Talk to me! I didn't know.

DAN. What model at the courthouse?

JEAN. Of the motel and the resort; it isn't important.

DELIA. I may take you up, Dan, on writing that book.

AUGUST. I'm glad you're walking, I don't think it's necessary for you to stay.

DELIA. Not at all. Cynthia said Jasker'd be ripped off — I guess —

AUGUST. If I thought it were possible for you to write, I'd admonish against it.

DELIA. You always have. I never needed either your approval or "admonishments"; Dad respected what I was doing, that was enough for me.

AUGUST. What you never realized was that Dad and I were close. You didn't want us to be, so you supposed it to be the way you wanted.

DELIA. *(Overlapping on "you supposed.")* — I was never interested in your opinion of anything I was —

AUGUST. — Thinking you were some kind of wunderkind and assuming —

DELIA. — He respected what I was doing and that was —

AUGUST. — Dad never read a word you wrote. He quoted your reviews back to you verbatim and laughed behind your back because you never noticed. He thought you were a fool.

CYNTHIA. *(Re-enters, goes upstairs.)* Come upstairs, Kirsten; come to bed.

AUGUST. Dan, it's late, I hadn't thought we'd sleep much tonight, but maybe that's the best thing to do. We'll be getting up at five. *(Leaving.)*

DELIA. Dad's opinion was always too important to me. Thank you.

AUGUST. You're welcome. *(He is gone, so is Delia; the others begin to leave as the night sounds increase, along with a weirdly close screech owl, and the lights fade as tractor sounds are heard. As the stage becomes dark, we can hear someone moving about.)*

DAN'S VOICE. Hello? Jesus Christ. Is somebody down there? *(Pause. Flashlight.)* Delia? Hello? *(The beam catches Chad full in the face. He is wearing the God-King's mask, and has the knapsack in his arms. He stands perfectly still.)*

CHAD. The light's in my face.

DAN. *(The beam from the flashlight moves to Chad's loaded arms. Dan stays on the stairs.)* Chad?

CHAD. Cynthia said you was a light sleeper. *(Pause.)*

DAN. Yeah.

CHAD. I got something I want to show you. *(Pause.)*

DAN. You…shouldn't handle… *(Pause.)*

CHAD. It's only copper. They treasured it higher than gold.

DAN. What have you got in — what are you doing?

CHAD. There's something outside I want to show you.

DAN. What?

CHAD. Come outside. *(He moves to the door.)*

DAN. Don't go out with that …

CHAD. There's something I want to show you.

DAN. Chad? *(The light plays across the empty table.)* Chad? *(Back to the door through which Chad has disappeared outside.)*

CHAD. *(Off.)* I want to show you something. *(Dan moves down the stairs and out. As a slow dawn begins, a girl's voice is heard calling, "Dr. Loggins?" repeatedly, then another girl calling the same. August, barely awake, stumbles down, buckling his belt, yells out the window, "Yes, goddamn it," and goes off. Kirsten follows him almost immediately, but stops at the bottom of the stairs as Delia, fully dressed, enters.)*

KIRSTEN. *(Sullen.)* Good morning.

DELIA. Good morning. *(Kirsten goes out as Delia takes a bottle of tonic from the refrigerator.)*

JEAN. *(Entering.)* My God, real clothes.

DELIA. The better to leave your enclave. *(The light continues to intensify.)*

JEAN. Oh. Well, I guess you know what you need. Did Pollyandy sleep down here last night or did he even get home?

DELIA. I don't know.

JEAN. I woke up; then I managed to get pissed off enough to go back to sleep. He said something about celebrating the God-King's discovery with a mescaline trip, but I think he was blithering.

DELIA. Where would anyone get mescaline in Blue Shoals, Illinois?

JEAN. You've been away longer than you know. *(Going out.)* It's gorgeous out. *(There are a few noises, girls' voices, August's.)*

CYNTHIA. *(Off.)* What? *(Muffled answer.)* I'll be down — Said, I'll be down. *(She appears.)* The son of a bitch. I'll kill him.

DELIA. You'll kill whom?

AUGUST. *(Off.)* It's mad — He's a madman, it's crazy —

JEAN. *(Off.)* August, where is —

AUGUST. *(Entering.)* Not now, damn it; not now.

CYNTHIA. Chad Jasker.

AUGUST. Everything's gone. He's carried everything off — the bulldozer's been run over the site — the bulldozer is out in the lake in six feet of water, apparently where it got stuck — *(Cynthia goes out.)*

DELIA. Is Dan out there?

AUGUST. What's to do? There's nothing to do. Let him sleep it off.

KIRSTEN. *(Entering.)* The girls are calling you.

DELIA. *(As Jean enters.)* Jean, you'd better go in and call the county sheriff.

JEAN. Tell him he's wrecked the site.

DELIA. Tell him Dan is missing. *(Jean stands transfixed for a second. Turns and goes into the office.)*

AUGUST. Oh, God, no.

CYNTHIA. *(Entering.)* I tried to tell August he didn't know what he was dealing with.

AUGUST. Cynthia — I want you to sit down. *(Takes her hands.)*

CYNTHIA. What? *(Breaks away.)* Oh, please.

AUGUST. Please.

CYNTHIA. What? What is it? Don't hold on to me, you know I don't like to be grabbed at. What on earth... *(Freeze. Looks around.)* He's left. He's run off ...

AUGUST. No, no, no, no ...

CYNTHIA. Where?

AUGUST. There's the possibility —

CYNTHIA. Oh, damn your possibilities —

AUGUST. Dan hasn't — Dan isn't here. Did you talk to Jasker last night?

DELIA. Did he tell you anything?

CYNTHIA. I couldn't find him.

DELIA. What is Jasker capable of? I never looked at him twice until last night.

CYNTHIA. He'd do anything.

DELIA. You know what I'm talking about; I want to know if the madman is capable —

CYNTHIA. — Yes, yes! He's capable of anything —

DELIA. He hurt you; you know.

CYNTHIA. — Yes, repeatedly. Yes. *(Delia exits. Pause.)* You didn't tell me about the highway because you knew I'd tell him. I would have.

AUGUST. What matters is finding Dan.

CYNTHIA. We have nothing to show for our dig, August. We have nine pictures I took last night.

AUGUST. I know.

CYNTHIA. The little bastard thought he wiped us out completely, but we fooled him.

AUGUST. That isn't important to me.

CYNTHIA. What a stupid thing to lie about. *(As August starts to move away.)* Well, I can do one thing for him. *(Takes up the camera, ejects the film, and begins unrolling it.)*

AUGUST. Stop it! CYNTHIA!

CYNTHIA. *(Throwing the unrolled film on the floor as he reaches her.)* There! I can do that much for him. There's your dig.

JEAN. *(Entering.)* There are two police cars turning into the field if you want to go out. I'm trying to think where they might have... *(The light immediately confines August to his desk area.)*

AUGUST. At eleven that morning an oar from Chad Jasker's boat was found floating near the center of the lake. At nine that night townspeople turned their car headlights out across the water to assist the divers who had come down from Marion. *(Car headlights swing across the room. Delia turns on a lamp.)*

JEAN. Where the hell are all the people coming from? Why don't they stay away?

CYNTHIA. People from town, volunteers; there's almost no police force.

KIRSTEN. They've got men with diving equipment.

JEAN. I can't help; I can't go outside; I'm swamped with commiserations. Keep those damn girls out of here; keep them all out.

CYNTHIA. August does that. They know better than to come here.

DELIA. Who's the old man?

CYNTHIA. Old man Jasker.

DELIA. What are all the goddamned people doing here; the cars keep turning into the area, there must be fifty cars.

CYNTHIA. They see the lights, they think we've discovered something.

DELIA. Can't they keep them away?

CYNTHIA. There's no law.

DELIA. All the laws are the wrong goddamned laws.

CYNTHIA. Someone heard we had discovered a monster in the lake. The sightseers will go away; the men will work all night.

KIRSTEN. They've got a lot of machinery for a small town.

JEAN. *(Running to the screen door.)* THEY ARE NOT TO DRAG THE LAKE. THEY USE GRAPPLING HOOKS TO DRAG THE LAKE, THEY ARE NOT TO DRAG THE LAKE! They said they'd send for divers!

DELIA. Shut up!

JEAN. I'm going to be fine.

DELIA. You can't help. Shut up.

JEAN. Why did he go out? Why didn't someone hear him? Why did the girls stay at the motel? WHY DID HE HAVE TO HEAR NOISES IN THE NIGHT? WHY DID HE TRUST PEOPLE, WHY DID HE BELIEVE IN THINGS? *(Delia slaps her across the face. Holds her a moment. Jean sits. Delia sits beside her.)* Morbid, morbid, stupid people. Vanished without a trace. I'm going to be fine. Cochise. Co-C-O-co. Vanished without a trace. I want the bone awl. I want the —

CYNTHIA. *(Going to her.)* Jean, please. Please. We don't have it. It's gone.

AUGUST. Dianne, Dianne.... We left the house for the last time August 8. I went back in January, only hoping to see the lake take it away. In my mind's eye the river's currents swept the house before it as a great brown flood bears off everything in its path. That was in my mind's eye. The lake had risen to half-cover the house. Much of the second level was above the water. The house looked more scuttled than inundated. The lake rises as a great long hand-shaped pond, slowly... *(Stops, turns the machine off. The women hardly move. Cynthia stares off, Jean sits, her head in Delia's lap.)*

CYNTHIA. August won't work without Dan.

JEAN. Does it matter?

CYNTHIA. No.

DELIA. Yes. Of course it does.

CYNTHIA. He doesn't know he won't work.

DELIA. Yes, he does.

JEAN. *(Not moving.)* I'm too heavy on you.

DELIA. You weigh nothing.

JEAN. Are they gone?

DELIA. The divers will be back at nine.

CYNTHIA. They won't find them.

DELIA. Shhhh.

CYNTHIA. They won't find them.

DELIA. Shhhh.

CYNTHIA. They won't.

DELIA. Shhhh.

CYNTHIA. They won't find them. *(August presses the tape recorder. It plays.)*

AUGUST'S VOICE. *(On tape.)* ...to see the lake take it away. In my mind's eye the river's currents swept the house before it as a great brown flood bears off everything in its path. That was in my mind's eye. The lake had risen to half-cover the house. Much of the second level was above the water. The house looked more scuttled than inundated. The lake rises as a great long hand-shaped pond, slowly... *(He turns the machine off a second, then turns it on.)*

AUGUST. Dianne... *(Turns machine off. After a moment he turns it on.)* Dianne... *(The women fade. August tries to frame a statement. The machine continues to record the stillness. August stands with the mike in his hand, very still. The tape continues to turn. A long pause. The lights fade on him.)*

END OF PLAY

ANGELS FALL

For Lou Fink

The shepherd's brow, fronting forked lightning, owns
The horror and the havoc and the glory
Of it. Angels fall, they are towers, from heaven—a story
Of just, majestical, and giant groans.
But man—we, scaffold of score brittle bones;
Who breathe, from groundlong babyhood to hoary
Age gasp; whose breath is our memento mori—
What bass is our viol for tragic tones?

Gerard Manley Hopkins

Nancy Snyder and Fritz Weaver
in the Circle Repertory Company production of Angels Fall.
Photograph ©1982 by Gerry Goldstein.

INTRODUCTION

Angels Fall was part of a huge commission (plays, operas, ballets, symphonies, the works) by The New World Festival, Inc., whose intention was to attract tourists to Miami in the punishing heat and humidity of a Florida summer. I suspect it didn't work, the festival, scheduled to be yearly, wasn't repeated. They contracted me with the offer of a generous commission two years before the festival date. I said I would accept if Marshall could direct Circle Rep actors. They thought that was great. Then I forgot about it. Completely. Until about a year before the festival.

I had been working on *A Tale Told*, which a few years later would be rewritten as *Talley & Son*. Almost the moment *A Tale Told* opened I remembered I had a commitment to Miami. I hate commitments. They make me very anxious; I don't like people expecting things of me, I'm always certain I'll fail them. I don't work well in an anxious state. I panicked. I drove all my friends mad, running about yelling, I have to write a play and I have no idea at all. They all said, "Don't panic, you've got a year for Godsake, you wrote *Lemon Sky* in two weeks." I continued to run about frantic for eight months or so. Then I had only four months.

I'd just taken a new apartment in the West Village. To acquaint myself with the neighborhood, I walked down West Street to Sneakers, a bar about six blocks south. The place was nearly empty. I sat at the bar and looked at the wall in front of me. Someone had stuck a postcard over the cash register. It pictured a barren and completely uninteresting landscape, a barely discernible hill, scrub brush, a blank sky. I was thinking, "Why would someone even take a picture of that, let alone produce a postcard of it?" I decided one of the bartenders had sent it back from vacation. Maybe it was some desolate area of New Mexico or Arizona, maybe he had been born there, God help him. I had been to New Mexico on a painting jaunt when I was in college. We painted the pueblos, the adobe churches, but that was colorful, this was just a — what kind of church would be in such a barren place? Then one of those weird visions occurred, those whammies that happen only a few times in a life; or at least in mine (it had happened with *Lemon Sky*, and would happen again with *Burn This*). I saw the interior of a dirt-poor church, a professor and his wife (he taught at maybe Yale or Brown) rushing inside to escape the blinding light and heat; the professor was agitated. He was much older than his wife. They had been turned back on the highway, a bridge was out or something. Other people would soon arrive in the same predicament. This vision was all in one — what's the opposite of blinding — I guess eye-opening — flash. I thought what in the hell was that? Then I realized it was a situation for a play. As a matter of fact, it was a situation play — what is called a Locked-Door play. Everybody gets trapped in a place and can't leave and the experience of being cooped-up changes them — or not. The locked door play is a genre play. I don't write genre plays, they're always dismissed as genre plays. I dismissed it — even though I had heard what would become the first two pages of dialog.

A month later, after I had had not a sign of another idea, I started considering it. It may be a worn-out form, but damn it, better genre than nothing. The challenge would be to make it as good a play as I could muster, and to hell with what kind of play is was. *Lemon Sky* and *The Glass Menagerie* are memory plays, that's a genre, isn't it? So is *Long Days Journey into Night,* if you stretch the rules a little. You see the sort of rationalization that's necessary to get started on something.

I had to work quickly. (It was April by now, we were scheduled to *open* in June.) I grabbed at the first things at hand: the somewhat older "mentor" of a young tennis pro — I had written a character very similar, in the same relationship, in a teleplay. Her boytoy (a word I may have coined, I hope not, and if so forgive me), Zappy, is new but this is how I imagined him when I wrote the TV script. Niles is a character I had been thinking about for some time, trying to generate a play that takes place in the teacher's lounge of a progressive college. Vita is new. And the priest is a reaction to all the drunken, swearing, disbelieving priests in so many plays and movies I'd seen recently. I thought: how novel, how interesting, how absolutely retrograde to write an intelligent priest who actually believes in God and the betterment of the species. The Brave-with-Arrow Doctor is a composite portrait of some of the Maddening Native Americans I Have Met — including my uncle Tony who was full-blooded I forget what.

The writing and production were so rushed it's a wonder we got the play on at all. The first dress rehearsal, with lights and costumes, was the first performance, and, taking their cue from opera, the producers invited the critics to that show! Every run-through had been ragged and halting. The performance that night was a miracle. The actors, the direction, were dazzling. One wanted to have carnal knowledge of Dennis Parichy's lights. John Lee's set was gorgeous. This production was by a considerable measure the most beautiful Marshall and I and our design team had so far accomplished. The only things wrong with that night were an inappropriately garish blouse and earrings for Marion — and the script.

We were scheduled to do the play at Lucille Lortel's White Barn Theater in August before we opened Circle Rep's season in October. My first out-of-town tryout. It's the workout you've always heard it is. I rewrote most of the play that summer and fall, working full-time for the first time and for the first time with a full-time assistant. I got it, if not as good as it could be, as good as I could get it at that time and in that time. We opened to pretty good reviews and, after the run at Circle Rep, moved to the Longacre Theater on Broadway. I'm sure we were the last Broadway show to open for less than $90,000. The set had already been built by union hands, only the trucking and load-in had to be paid for. The actors, I've always assumed, were making next to minimum with the promise of a later raise. And we opened with almost *no* advertising budget! I've written that (and in italics) before, but it always amazes me when I think of it. I'm sorry, but if you don't get blistering raves in most of the New York papers and national magazines, if the gal who decides whether or not to run a feature in the *Times* decides not this time, you damn well better have a healthy reserve for advertising. I watched the show die on the vine. I went to almost every performance, in support of the actors. I *bought* ten tickets for friends one night, expecting the house to swell, it was smaller. The audience dwindled nightly. It was the most disheartening experience I've had in the commercial theater (and I've had my share) to see fewer than two hundred people in a house that seats eleven hundred. Bernie Jacobs of the Schubert Organization told me people must not be talking about the show because nobody was coming. I told him word of mouth may not be the most effective form of advertising but it certainly was the cheapest. He actually smiled. You'd have to have known Bernie for that to astonish you.

After the play closed in February I limped back to my house in Sag Harbor, completely whipped. I promised myself not to think of an idea for a new play for a year. (See the introduction to the translation of *Three Sisters*.) I didn't think of an idea for a new play for two years. By that time I was frantic again.

ORIGINAL PRODUCTION

Angels Fall was commissioned and first presented by The New World Festival, Inc., in Miami, Florida, on June 19, 1982. The director was Marshall W. Mason, Setting by John Lee Beatty, Costumes by Jennifer Von Mayrhauser, Lighting by Dennis Parichy, Sound by Chuck London Media, Stewart Werner, Production Stage Manager by Fred Reinglas. The cast, in order of appearance, was as follows:

NILES HARRIS	Fritz Weaver
VITA HARRIS	Nancy Snyder
DON TABAHA	Danton Stone
MARION CLAY	Tanya Berezin
SALVATORE (ZAPPY) ZAPPALA	Brian Tarantina
FATHER WILLIAM DOHERTY	Richard Seff

Barnard Hughes (for whom the role was written) replaced Mr. Seff as Father Doherty when the play opened at the Circle Repertory Company in New York City on October 16, 1982. Original music for this production was by Norman L. Berman.

This production was moved intact to the Longacre Theatre on January 18, 1983. It was produced by Elliot Martin, Circle Repertory, Lucille Lortel, The Shubert Organization, and The Kennedy Center.

CHARACTERS

NILES HARRIS Fifty-six, an art historian and professor. He is tall, elegant, and disheveled.

VITA HARRIS Thirty, his wife, thin and strikingly attractive.

SALVATORE (ZAPPY) ZAPPALA Twenty-one, almost skinny, quite energetic, a professional tennis player.

MARION CLAY Early forties, a gallery owner, handsome, well turned out.

DON TABAHA Mid-twenties, half-Indian, intense.

FATHER WILLIAM DOHERTY Sixty-five, the parish priest.

PLACE

A small and very plain adobe mission in northwestern New Mexico. We see the entrance, where a bell hangs just outside the front door, and the entire interior of the church. Wooden benches without backs, a simple altar painted with faded blue and yellow, the only decoration is a washed wainscoting and a primitive painting of the Madonna, painted on a round barrel top. The front door leads to a sandy parking lot where (offstage) there is a telephone. Across the room from the front door is another door leading to an equally sandy garden that might, space permitting, include a few wooden crosses over bare graves. On one side of the altar is a door to the living quarters.

It is five in the afternoon, Saturday, early June.

Angels Fall

ACT ONE

The interior of the church is dark and cool. White-hot sunlight streaks in from the narrow, deep-set windows. Outside, the light is intense. Don Tabaha sits alone, staring at the wall. We hear people approaching the front door from the parking lot. After a moment Don rises and goes into the residence.

NILES. *(Offstage.)* We'll look at the map and see if we can find some semblance of a decent highway.

VITA. *(Offstage.)* It's enough just to get out of this glare.

NILES. *(Offstage.)* It must be two hours to the nearest motel.

VITA. *(Appears at the doors. They open. Sunlight illuminates the interior of the church.)* Hey, it's open. We're in luck.

NILES. *(Standing in the open doorway.)* Thank God.

VITA. *(Her voice lowered.)* It's wonderfully cool; that sun is blazing. *(For the first time they look around them.)* You sit, and I'll go see if that telephone works.

NILES. I don't want to sit. I want to get back on the road. *(He sits.)*

VITA. I'll be a sec. *(She goes off. Niles moves to the window, looks out after her. He takes a prescription bottle from his pocket, has difficulty opening it, peers into the bottle, dumps the only pill onto his hand.)*

NILES. Sanctuary. *(He looks into the empty bottle, carefully breaks the pill in half, and returns half to the bottle.)* Well, half a sanctuary. *(He looks around the church. There is water in the font; he decides against that and moves to the garden doors. As they open, the interior grows lighter. Niles sees what he is looking for and goes out the door. The church is empty for a moment.)*

VITA. *(Entering.)* Niles? Are you all right?

NILES. (Offstage.) Just a minute.

VITA. (Notices the pill bottle, picks it up, smiling at the half pill. Calling.) Where have you got to? (Puts the bottle in her purse.)

NILES. (Offstage.) I found a water faucet I'm sure hasn't been opened in twenty years. I'll die of typhoid, but I'll die refreshed. (He re-enters, wiping his face with a damp handkerchief.) I must have half of New Mexico on my face.

VITA. You were beginning to look a little like a cinnamon doughnut, yes.

NILES. Sixty miles on a dirt road with nothing to look at except sagebrush, only to be turned back by the highway patrol and have to look at the same sagebrush all over again from the other side. You told Dr. Singer we'll be a day late?

VITA. He's in a meeting. His secretary has gone to the bank.

NILES. At twelve hundred dollars a day, you'd think Singer's institute would own the bank by now.

VITA. I left the number of the pay phone out there.

NILES. Darling, I'm not going to stand in a church in the middle of the wilderness waiting for some secretary to return our call.

VITA. If we don't hear in ten minutes, I'll try again. (Niles notices the pill bottle is gone.) I've got it.

NILES. Good. I may need it. (Looks at his watch.) We'll give her five minutes. (He spreads a handkerchief on the deep sill of the window, and sits.) Even when we get there, Phoenix is going to be no fun for you. Living down the road from the asylum — in some sleazy motel.

VITA. Holiday Inn. No surprises.

NILES. Probably be crowded with husbands and wives of the other patients, all brightly pretending nothing is wrong. Keeping active and interested and fit. Forming a slow-pitch softball team. I see T-shirts emblazoned with WIVES OF THE LOONIES. (He gets up again.)

VITA. I'll duck that, I think. I might even get some work done.

NILES. I'm sure after one session of whatever it is they do to me, I'll be infinitely grateful for your presence close at hand. (Looking around.) Good Lord, this church is unrelentingly severe. No self-respecting Catholic should tolerate this degree of austerity.

VITA. I imagine the locals would rip off anything not nailed down. There's a sign over the pay phone that says: "This phone is for medical emergencies only. If you need money, break the Coke machine."

NILES. Oh, dear.

VITA. I checked. Sure enough, the Coke machine is broken.

NILES. *(Looking out.)* Can we even hear the telephone from this distance? Hello. One of those desert surprises. There's a wonderful broad luteous patch of something. I don't have my glasses. A really marvelous yellow hazing over by the road. Some thriving cactus or other.

VITA. That's a bulldozer.

NILES. Really.

VITA. It looks like they're widening the road.

NILES. Of course they're widening the road. We didn't pass a single car coming or going, what better place to widen the road?

(Don says something in Navaho offstage. He enters from residence. Vita jumps. Don wears a University of New Mexico T-shirt.)

VITA. Oh!

DON. How'd you get in here?

NILES. I beg your pardon?

DON. The church is closed on Saturdays. This isn't a tourist attraction here.

NILES. Yes, we gathered as much.

VITA. We just stopped to use the phone.

DON. That phone is for medical emergencies only.

VITA. Yes, I saw the sign. My husband is checking into a clinic tomorrow. We're going to be delayed. I wanted to let them know nothing serious is wrong.

DON. Then there's no emergency.

VITA. We seem to be encroaching on alien territory.

NILES. Are you the vicar around here?

DON. The more devout of my tribe come in to pray for the maize.

NILES. In the event the summer corn dance doesn't suffice.

VITA. Are you at the University of New Mexico? *(Beat.)* They had another really great basketball team this year.

DON. Come on, the church is closed.

VITA. I noticed a *portale* out back. We can wait back there if we can hear the phone.

DON. Don't go back there. That's private back there. The Tabahas live in back.

MARION. *(Offstage.)* At least get out of the damn heat.

DON. *(Going to the door.)* Marion! What the…?

VITA. *(Overlapping.)* There's someone else. Where did they come from?

DON. *(Turning to them.)* Cameras are against tribal law. Outside of that, like I said, make yourselves at home. *(Exits into parking lot.)*

VITA. Oh, my.

NILES. There are people who, when you meet them, bring to mind all the things you might have done but neglected to do. Such as learn to handle firearms.

(A motorcycle starts up and drives off.)

VITA. Apparently that was his Honda out there. He's kicking up a dust-storm.

MARION. *(Offstage.)* Don!

VITA. It amazes me how cool you become in the face of those types.

NILES. Altogether too much experience. Much too much experience.

MARION. *(Offstage.)* Ridiculous! Is this the pits? If we can't get the airport, I'll try the damn base or the — I don't know — weather. Of all the stupid. *(Enters counting change. Zap hangs back in the doorway.)* I'm blind from that damn sun. Twenty, thirty, forty — give me your change.

ZAP. *(Sees Niles and Vita.)* Hi.

VITA. Hi.

NILES. How do you do.

MARION. Oh, hi. Sorry. Pisser of a situation, isn't it?

VITA. Very inconvenient for anyone with a tight schedule, yes.

ZAP. We're trying to make a plane.

VITA. Oh, no.

MARION. *(Leaving.)* I should be used to it by now. *(To Zap.)* Stay. Stay where it's cool. *(She exits to lot.)*

ZAP. No, I'm okay. Good to meet you. *(Exits.)*

VITA. Good luck.

MARION. *(Offstage.)* I forgot my purse. Go get my purse.

(Zap comes back for Marion's purse; exits.)

VITA. What do you suppose is the nature of that relationship?

NILES. *Le coeur a ses raisons que la raison ne connait point.*

VITA. I'm hip.

NILES. *(Looks out front door.)* There goes the phone for the next however long. Ah, well. I wish you had talked me out of buying these shoes. They're wonderfully comfortable, but they're very stupid-looking.

VITA. I think they're cute.

NILES. Ummm. Cute. I'm afraid I agree with you. I wonder if I dare smoke.

DOHERTY. *(Entering from the garden, talking to himself.)* "And the road was a ribbon of moonlight, over the purple moor." *(Sees Niles and Vita.)* Oh, dear goodness.

NILES. Perhaps not.

DOHERTY. I have no concept of time. I'm sure I've kept you waiting.

(*Calls.*) Maria! (*Back to them.*) Well, she won't come out as long as you're here. Well, then, just to leap right in with both feet, we call these little talks pre-Cana conferences. Water into wine, remember. *Accipite armaturam dei.*

VITA. No, Father, we're not here for religious instruction.

DOHERTY. You're not here for the conference. In spite of everything you've undoubtedly heard of me, I do that rather well. Then you're — Don't help me, it'll come to me.

VITA. No, we're just — No, you see, we — No, we're just stopping —

DOHERTY. No, no, no, no, now. (*Beat.*) You know, I'm not even going to try. This is terrible. I'm an absolute blank. You'll have to fill me in.

NILES. Oh, dear.

VITA. We have no appointment. We're just taking advantage of the open door to wait for a telephone call. We just ducked into the church to get out of the sun.

DOHERTY. Oh, I'm very glad, because right at the moment I have kinda a full plate.

VITA. (*Looking out.*) Well good, she's giving up. I can try again.

NILES. (*Grabbing at her.*) Darling.

VITA. There are so many green valleys and such beautiful mountains. And we expected New Mexico to be a burning desert from end to end.

DOHERTY. That's south of here. You're lost, then; no one finds the place unless they're lost.

VITA. No, we were turned back at the fork, so to speak. There's a bridge out.

DOHERTY. There's no bridge out. Where would there be a bridge out?

NILES. Route 57, about twenty miles north of here.

DOHERTY. No, no, no, no. There couldn't be a bridge out. There's no bridge. I've never heard of the road being impassable in June. We'll be in for the light rains soon, if they come; the gentle rains, the "she-rains" they call them, isn't that lovely? There's no bridge out. It's some problem with the nuclear thing again. The radio was saying something about it. I never listen, but it's good company when you're driving along. I'm not really so rushed, I'm just like this. I'll learn to relax one day. (*Singsong.*) Learn to relax, learn to relax. Now. Maybe I can interest you in the fifty-cent tour.

NILES. Some problem with the nuclear thing again?

DOHERTY. There usually is, and they usually say something coy like the bridge is out. We don't pay much attention anymore. Don didn't come through here, did he? Short, dark, surly…?

VITA. In and out.

DOHERTY. In from where and out to where?

VITA. In from there and out on a Honda in a cloud of dust.

DOHERTY. *(Sitting.)* Oh, no. Oh, dear.

VITA. Is there something wrong?

DOHERTY. *(Gets up, goes out the front door. Pleasantly.)* Yes, of course, anything you like.

NILES. He's not really rushed, he's just like that.

VITA. You are going to be nice.

NILES. I am not. I have every intention of being inordinately difficult. What nuclear thing?

DOHERTY. *(Entering, crossing to the residence door. Happy; to himself.)* Ho-ho-ho, ho-ho-ho. He's down at the intersection having a violent argument with Arthur, our highway patrolman.

NILES. Excuse us, but —

DOHERTY. Ho-ho-ho. Ho-ho-ho. *(Exits.)*

NILES. This country would do it to the best of them. On the other hand, I doubt if they'd send the best of them to this country.

DOHERTY. *(Re-enters with binoculars.)* Now we'll see. Ho-ho-ho. *(Leaning into the window, looking off.)* Oh, what an argument. Arthur's not going to let him pass. Ho-ho-ho.

NILES. Excuse us, but what problem are they having with what nuclear thing again?

DOHERTY. *(Not turning from the window.)* No, no, no alarm. Nothing to be alarmed about. They just have these little...emergencies.

NILES. Do you find that at all reassuring?

VITA. Let's go with the idea that the bridge is out.

DOHERTY. We had a wonderful fright three years ago. Radioactive clouds drifting across the street. You couldn't see the store. We all hid inside, waiting to be evacuated, but I guess they thought we weren't worth the trouble. Nobody came, nobody came. The next morning men went through in Jeeps, mind you, dressed for the moon, with little radioactive bleepers that were clicking their heads off. You've never heard such a racket. Like a nest of rattlesnakes. And they said: "No, no, no problem. Nothing to be alarmed about. Minor levels, minor levels." They had to yell it out over the sound of the clickers, you understand. And off they went. I had a good laugh at myself when I realized that I had been concerned about the possibility of being rendered sterile. *(Turns to the window.)* Oh, now they're both angry. Our patrolman was a classmate of

Don's and he enjoys teasing him. Ho-ho-ho. Well, I had better make myself scarce.

NILES. Excuse me, Father —

DOHERTY. Doherty. Bill Doherty. The Indians can't pronounce it — they call me Father Bill. When none of my superiors is around.

NILES. Niles Harris; my wife, Vita. Not that we're alarmed, but what sort of nuclear thing is having these little emergencies?

DOHERTY. Oh, does it matter? I'm sorry, but you would ask. They're trying to install a dump south of here. We're not going to let them get away with that. And over west are about seven mines and mills, and east of here the Rio Puerco goes awash with some kind of waste every few months, and of course there's the reactor at Los Alamos and the missile base down at White Sands, and all kinds of things are seeping into everyone's water. It's all the Perils of Pauline, but I just get into trouble every time I say anything about it. We aren't supposed to notice. Apparently they own this part of the state. Or everything that isn't owned by Texas.

ZAP. (Offstage.) I can't leave them in the car. They'll warp in the heat, you know that.

DOHERTY. (Looks out.) Good gracious, what's Marion doing down here? Of course, settling the estate. Poor dear woman. Such a waste. So sad. Still, there's hope. Well, we get them all.

ZAP. (Entering with a bag of tennis rackets.) Jeez. Boy. Hi. Boy oh, boy oh, boy.

DOHERTY. This is the only public phone in the village, I'm afraid.

VITA. So we gathered.

DOHERTY. So this is the hot corner. (Exits into quarters.)

VITA. No luck?

ZAP. Oh, boy. Who knows? We can't get through; everybody's callin' everybody. The airport's busy, the highway patrol's busy, the weather station's busy. We've been listening on the car radio.

VITA. (As Marion enters.) What did they say?

ZAP. Something went wrong trying to get a plane loaded over at the Chin Rock mine.

NILES. We were turned back on Route 57. They said the bridge was out.

MARION. I love the way they don't even try to make their stories plausible.

VITA. There's no bridge on 57?

MARION. Not one. The radio said there's no cause for alarm, but as a precaution they've stopped traffic for a hundred miles.

NILES. Oh, lovely.

ZAP. Oh, boy; oh, boy; oh, boy…

MARION. Stay inside. There's no point in wearing yourself out.

ZAP. I know, I know.

MARION. We're due in San Diego. He has a tennis match tomorrow in the opening round of the WCT.

VITA. Oh, no.

ZAP. And this is just great psychological preparation. This is just the perfect psychological preparation.

MARION. I know.

ZAP. Assuming we even get there at all, this is just the best preparation I can think of. Boy, boy, boy, boy, boy. *(He exits.)*

MARION. We'll get there. *(Calling.)* Don't walk around in the sun. Well, don't fall down. Get the thermos and come and take your zinc. Okay? *(Turning back.)* Oh, Lord. Total child.

NILES. *(Rather private.)* Ah, well…what route did you decide on?

VITA. *(Consulting the road map.)* How do you feel about…There's Taos. We could visit their little art colony. That might be fun.

NILES. Under no circumstances.

VITA. They would love you. After your review of that dreadful book…?

NILES. *Contemporary Paintings of the American West.*

VITA. Some of the things you said about — what did you call it?

NILES. Regional Art. Exactly. We'd both be stoned at the gate.

VITA. It's way out of the way, don't worry. I think maybe take something that's actually called Hot Water Road to Route 44. We may have to backtrack.

MARION. Excuse me, but you're not taking Hot Water Road and you're not taking 44. We were headed for 44. They're turning everyone back. All routes east, west, and north.

NILES. You're joking.

MARION. I'm afraid not. Unless you want to go down to Mexico.

NILES. I would love to go down to Mexico. I would especially adore going down to the Yucatán Peninsula. I unfortunately am going to Phoenix, Arizona.

VITA. We can be late; we're in no rush.

(The noise of a helicopter approaches, growing deafeningly loud.)

VITA. What on earth?

NILES. What in hell.

VITA. *(Looking out.)* Helicopter. Very low. *Very* low.

HELICOPTER. *(From speakers above, a stentorian voice.)* The roads are closed. Please stay indoors.

MARION. *(Yelling.)* Well, that's a new one.

HELICOPTER: Please stay indoors. The roads are temporarily closed. *(It passes by.)*

NILES. Dear Lord, the dust.

VITA. *(Overlapping.)* My ears are ringing.

MARION. *(Overlapping.)* Do you believe it? "Temporarily closed." The last time they said that, the traffic was rerouted around the area for four days.

NILES. Still, there doesn't seem cause for these alarums and excursions.

MARION. Some of the houses don't have electricity or radios.

ZAP. *(Enters.)* You hear that?

MARION. I may never hear another thing, but I heard that.

ZAP. What is that supposed to mean?

MARION. Just a precaution, everything's fine.

ZAP. Sure, sure, we're probably dying here, everything's fine.

MARION. There's no point in getting a stroke.

ZAP. I know, I know. The radio's still saying any minute, so we're cool. It wasn't a plane crash, they're saying it was a truck and something about high winds.

DOHERTY. *(Enters, picking up trash.)* Get her to take a little water and slip some broth in when she isn't looking. I don't know. Did you hear that? Aren't they exciting? I threw a rock at one of them, I think they laughed at me. Over the loudspeakers. I'm picking up trash. Where does it come from in a week? On top of everything else, Mrs. Valdez has stopped eating. Says she's going to die. I told her that was certain if she didn't eat. She said she'd lived to be ninety, and that's all she'd planned on.

MARION. What are you doing here? I didn't expect to see you.

DOHERTY. I've changed my schedule. Our little genius is running away. You've settled the estate?

MARION. What with the sale and the transfer of the paintings, I've signed my name in the last two days more than most rock stars.

DOHERTY. Are you all right? You're not, of course, neither am I. I have to ask and you have to say "I'm fine."

MARION. I'm fine.

DOHERTY. As bad as that?

MARION. I'm fine.

DOHERTY. *(Looking out the door.)* He's turned around. The little ingrate. Those choppers must have done the trick. He's coming back. Not a word.

VITA. It looks as if we're detained for a few minutes. Is it all right if we wait here?

DOHERTY. Oh, yes. Maria will be very happy. Happy, happy. She always makes refreshments when she sees a car stop, so we'll have a little treat. She loves people, but she's terrified of them. Wouldn't go near one. But this sort of thing makes her day.

MARION. Lucky for her that it happens all the time.

DOHERTY. Marion can tell you. No alarm, no alarm. *(Exits into residence.)*

VITA. I'll bring in the hamper and we'll have a sandwich. You haven't eaten a bite.

NILES. I haven't been hungry, I don't know why.

VITA. Even if you don't feel hungry, you should eat. You look terrible.

NILES. Thank you, I'm fine!

ZAP. *(Pill in one hand, thermos in the other.)* This ain't cocoa. What is this? I can't take a pill with gin. This is the martinis.

MARION. It's zinc. It's a mineral. Alcohol won't affect that.

ZAP. I'm not talking chemical reaction, I'm talking swallowing. I can't slug back gin like that.

MARION. You don't need that much liquid.

ZAP. You don't. I do. What if that got stuck in there?

MARION. Just work up a mouthful of saliva, then. It's down before you —

ZAP. Oh, fine, I'm dying in the middle of the desert, I'm supposed to work up a load of spit.

MARION. Concentrate. Think of a lemon. A nice…tart…juicy…sour…

ZAP. Come on, what are you trying to do to me. I need a glassful of water. You know that.

VITA. Apparently there's a faucet out there.

NILES. I wouldn't trust it for drinking. Unless you're desperate.

ZAP. Where's the hot chocolate?

MARION. *(Patiently.)* You read that chocolate was ninety percent cholesterol, and cholesterol causes cardiac arrest, and you said you didn't want me to make hot chocolate this trip.

ZAP. *(Overlapping from "cardiac.")* It ain't that important, I won't take it now. It doesn't matter, it's cool. *(To Vita and Niles.)* Excuse us, okay? *(To Marion.)* I was gonna bring a soda, it's my own fault.

MARION. It amazes me how you can make a simple thing like taking a pill into a Rain Dance.

ZAP. *(Serious.)* You okay? Something wrong? I'm a little weird about pills.

MARION. No, I just forget what a baby you are.

ZAP. *(Lighter.)* No, now, no. This has nothing to do with babying myself. This has to do with a basic fear that runs in my family. My mother had this. This is the fear of choking. This is just a simple preventative thing that when you take a few precautions is no problem to anybody. *(To Vita and Niles.)* Excuse us, okay? *(Back to Marion.)* The way I grew up, you take a pill with one full glass of water.

VITA. Did someone in your family choke?

ZAP. *(Point made.)* Never.

VITA. We have some seltzer in the car.

ZAP. No, miss. Don't go to any damn trouble.

VITA. *(Exiting.)* It's no damn trouble at all.

ZAP. Why do you always do this? *(Marion is laughing.)* The simplest thing and you bring attention to me. You're as bad as my sister. When I was fourteen, we go to a dance, I'm standing outside cruising the chicks, my sister spits on a handkerchief and starts washing my face. Sportswriters all over the country every day eat me for breakfast; I don't need it from my old lady, you know?

MARION. *(Still laughing.)* I don't like "old lady," don't say "old lady." It's too close to home. I'll ask Father Doherty if he can get you a glass of water from the kitchen.

ZAP. Fuck it, gimme it, fuck it. I'll drink the gin.

MARION. Not if it's going to be such a problem. She's gone to get a soda, you don't have to.

ZAP. *(Takes the pill, drinks from the thermos, sputters enormously.)* Oh, boy. Oh, boy. Oh, wooo! Oh, great. That is one very dry martini. Woooo!

MARION. You okay?

ZAP. *(Red-faced and coughing.)* Give me your handkerchief. Oh, boy.

VITA. *(Enters.)* Here you go. I'm afraid it's warm.

ZAP. *(Immediately fakes cool. Takes a handkerchief from Marion.)* Oh, thanks, but like I said, everything's cool. No problem.

MARION. Save it. There's a different one every half hour. Packing for a trip is a logistical nightmare.

ZAP. No, that's fine. We're cool. It's down there. It's doing its thing.

VITA. You look the picture of health.

ZAP. I'm healthy, I'm healthy. I'm a physical specimen.

(Don comes in front door, sees them, turns on his heel and leaves.)

ZAP. Hi.

MARION. Don!

ZAP. Boy oh, boy oh, boy. If we even get out of here alive, this is just great preparation, I'm telling you.

MARION. We'll get there. Please don't work yourself up into a flither.

ZAP. I'm in a flither, I'm in a flither. *(Exits into garden.)* It's okay, I like it.

MARION. Total child. My name's Marion Clay.

NILES. Niles Harris; my wife, Vita.

MARION. Pleased to meet you. Under any other circumstances.

VITA. We'll make the best of it. I love him, he reminds me of my brother.

MARION. Salvatore Zappala. Zappy Zappala.

VITA. Is he any good?

MARION. How do you mean?

VITA. Tennis.

MARION. Oh, I think so. A lot of people expect him to go all the way. Unfortunately, he has the worst luck in the world. The last four... *four*... tournaments he's drawn the eventual winner on the first round.

VITA. Oh, no.

MARION. And all four times he's fought them to a tie-breaker in the last set before he lost. Forget the burning bush, give him a break on the first-round draw. That would be a miracle.

DON. *(Charging back in.)* Marion, do you know anything about this?

MARION. What did Arthur say?

DON. Arthur doesn't know his ass.

MARION. Some accident up at Chin Rock mine.

DON. That bastard won't let me go there.

MARION. Don't you have a pass, some sort of ID?

DON. He knows who I am. The son-of-a-bitch can't understand anything except he has orders to stop traffic. I can't get Chin Rock on the phone.

MARION. You can't get anything on the phone.

DON. Was anyone hurt?

MARION. I don't know, love. We were listening on the radio, but they didn't tell us anything. Chin Rock probably owns the radio station. *(To Vita and Niles.)* Did you meet Don?

NILES. Not formally. Niles Harris; my wife, Vita.

MARION. Don Tabaha.

(A phone rings in the distance.)

VITA. Do you have a call in?

MARION. No.

DON. I'll get it. *(Exits.)*

VITA. *(Jumping up.)* That's for us. Well...

NILES. This nonsense has us a little — I don't like delays. Ah, well…It's cool.

MARION. I know…it's cool.

NILES. I meant the temperature, actually.

DON. *(Entering.)* You said you're Mrs. Harris?

VITA. Yes. *(To Niles.)* Are you okay?

NILES. Fine, fine; briefly.

(Vita exits.)

DON. Don't tie up that line. They may try to reach me here. Damn it!

MARION. You have Rhode Island plates.

NILES. Providence. The city.

MARION. You're driving to Phoenix?

NILES. Yes. Our first trip West, so we're taking in all the out-of-the-way sights. Hence these interesting local…diversions. *(He looks out the window to make sure Vita is on the phone, goes to her purse, and digs for his Valium.)* When I told a colleague of mine we were going out West, he said: "To Las Vegas in a hand basket, I presume." I suppose you had to be there. I was always relating some half-witty anecdote to my class, who stared back vacantly in just that manner.

MARION. You teach, then?

NILES. I taught. Or I lectured. Rather too steadily for thirty years. I'm on a sabbatical that had originally been scheduled for the purpose of writing yet another book, but it will now conform to the ancient Israelite sabbatical in which every seventh year the field was left untilled.

MARION. Ummm. And slaves were released and debts were forgiven.

NILES. Let's hope there's no necessity to go as far as that.

MARION. Were you at work on the great American novel?

NILES. No, no. I would have wanted it to sell. My field was the only somewhat less fictional one of art history.

MARION. And art history sells.

NILES. Like beer at a ball game; you have no idea.

MARION. I do. I own the Clay Gallery in Chicago. I'm Marion Branch. Ernest Branch's wife.

NILES. Ernest Branch!

MARION. The Regional Artist.

NILES. Good Lord, I thought he died.

MARION. He did.

NILES. Oh, forgive me. How tactless of me —

MARION. No, no, my fault — I should have said Ernie used to be my husband —

NILES. No, no, thank you; but in any case, how asinine and rude. Forgive me — *(Vita enters carrying a picnic basket.)* Darling, Miss Clay is the wife of the painter Ernest Branch.

VITA. I'm glad to meet you all over again. I liked his work a lot. I have to talk about anything later than the seventeenth century behind Niles's back. I've seen articles about your place. What's it called?

MARION. I'm afraid it's called the Branch Ranch. And there's a sometimes creek that runs through the middle of the property that's called the Branch Branch.

VITA. I didn't realize we were that close to it here.

MARION. Eight miles. There's only sixteen acres, but the buildings are good and the situation is spectacular, of course. One of those private green valleys.

NILES. Everything all right with Phoenix?

VITA. Oh, it's a bother; you don't want to know. His secretary will call us back. She has to get him out of a conference; he'll want to talk to you.

NILES. Absolutely not.

VITA. He'll just want to understand the circumstances of —

NILES. I said no. When have you known me to say no and mean anything other than no. Absolutely not. I've no intention of talking to him.

VITA. Fine. I'll talk to him.

NILES. Admirable.

DOHERTY. *(Backing in, carrying a tray with lemonade and sugar. He is talking to someone inside. Don stands.)* Well, come in and take a bow. Make an appearance. *(Laughs.)* She gets so embarrassed. What did I tell you? *(Sees Don.)* Hello, Don. Don't you look surprised to see me. I hear you had a fight with your uncle. *(To Niles.)* His uncle goes off into the mountains and yells at the sky for two days when they fight. He comes back so hoarse he can hardly speak. *(To Don.)* I see you've packed your knapsack and have your motorbike working again for your getaway. I'm making Saturday evening the Sunday obligation tonight. I rearranged my schedule so I could see you off.

DON. I didn't see your car.

DOHERTY. No, I parked around back. Aren't I cunning? *(To the others.)* Now, Maria has made lemonade. Isn't that musical. *(He is passing the glasses around.)* Cheers. To Maria.

NILES. No, no, no, don't go to any — I don't really care for lemonade. I always think it's doing something to the enamel on my teeth. Well... thank you. That's fine. To —?

MARION. Maria.

DOHERTY. Or maybe we should drink to Don's newfound fortune.

MARION. What fortune?

DON. Skip it.

DOHERTY. Newfound opportunity, then.

DON. If I didn't know better, I'd think you arranged this roadblock.

DOHERTY. The efficacy of prayer? No, nothing this alarming.

MARION. Does Maria have the paper from Gallup? Zap has a match tomorrow. They had the draw this morning.

DOHERTY. *(Trying to remember.)* Zap. Zap, zap, zap, zap.

MARION. Never mind, I'll get it. If I don't scare her to death.

DON. I'll get it.

MARION. It won't be in any of the local papers, but it gives me something to do.

DON. Terrific party, Father. You really know how to throw it.

DOHERTY. You'll be back. We should have a nice talk before you leave. *(Don exits into residence.)* Young Tabaha is going through his lapsed phase just now.

VITA. He lives here?

DOHERTY. Oh, yes. He's the nephew of our little church mouse, Maria. His mother abandoned him to her sister. Said she had no idea who the father was.

NILES. But the father wasn't Indian?

DOHERTY. We wonder lately if he was even human. *(Offers Vita sugar.)* Sugar?

VITA. I have honey, thanks.

DOHERTY. This has been Don's playroom since before he could walk. Right up through high school he's done his homework here, invited his friends here, so he's a little possessive about the place. I always had to let him ring the bell. He's had an alarming change of heart since he's been at the medical school. The big city works its wiles, but I'm sure we can set him straight.

NILES. Medical school?

MARION. He's on a full scholarship, of course.

DOHERTY. Always was brilliant, and that's never easy.

MARION. He's interning now. Goes up to the Indian hospital once a week. That's what he always wanted.

DOHERTY. Wonderful to see that. Went about that high with a stethoscope around his neck. A real one, not a toy. No idea where he got it. Dragging to his ankles. Said he'd been working on the reservation. Where you been, Dr. Don? "I been working on the reservation." Now he is. Wonderful to see that. *(Sings.)* "I've been working on the reservation…"

MARION. He should be at Chin Rock — that dope Arthur wouldn't let him through.

DOHERTY. Before he heard about Chin Rock he was trying to run away, so I'm grateful for Arthur.

VITA. Oh, yes. I was talking to Phoenix, and I'm afraid we're international news. This is the third time something's gone wrong at the Chin Rock mine.

NILES. What, dear God, is the Chin Rock mine?

MARION AND DOHERTY. Uranium.

NILES. Oh, lovely. You've known that all along?

VITA. We learn these little things one at a time.

MARION. If they don't have us on the road in ten minutes, this is going to cost me a thousand bucks to charter a plane.

VITA. At the risk of being an alarmist, I heard them say it might be an hour or more before the highway is reopened. *(To Niles.)* Don't pace.

NILES. Why ever not? It seems the perfect physical expression of the situation. One suddenly understands polar bears.

VITA. Are you all right?

NILES. Oh, my dear, of course I am. There's no need to feel my forehead, I'm fine.

VITA. I'm not used to all this unfocused energy.

NILES. I've never been what one might describe as lethargic.

VITA. No, one would have described you as focused.

NILES. Very well, *do* feel my forehead. *(As she does, he smiles forbearingly.)* We must look a couple of complete asses, Mr. Zappala and I. You baby us too much, as he said.

VITA. You're burning up. Are you coming down with something?

NILES. *(Takes off jacket.)* Lord, I'm perspiring like a — something that perspires. Heavily. Ah, well…

MARION. I should warn you, it doesn't pay to get sick in this country. There isn't a doctor within eighty miles.

DOHERTY. And Don is a genius, but I wouldn't give you a nickel for his bedside manner.

NILES. No, no, quite the contrary. I'm just recuperating from the effects of a — traumatic nervous breakthrough.

MARION. When do you get back to the college?

NILES. No, no, no, I've quite burned my bridges. I won't be going back to the college.

DOHERTY. You're a professor, that explains it.

MARION. Art history.

NILES. I used to be a professor, and I used to be an author. But fortunately I experienced what you might call a crisis of faith, or a disturbance in my willful suspension of disbelief that allowed me to see what I had done for what it was. You see, while framing the schema of my new book, I made the tactical error of rereading my other books.

MARION. Oh, no.

NILES. I'm afraid so. They are, of course, the authoritative statement on the subject. Both in style and in fact.

MARION. I remember.

NILES. Of course you'd be familiar with them.

MARION. A long time ago.

NILES. Let's not discuss how long ago.

MARION. That's a deal.

NILES. Well, Miss Clay, to every didactic, authoritative sentence I had written, I said: "Yes, of course, and exactly the opposite could be as true." Or: "Whereas we have assumed the artistic expression of a culture was the mirror of the people's soul, and that from that mirror we can posit an aesthetic for our own enlightenment — it is also possible that the expression of an artist tells us nothing whatever about the people and from it we can posit — nothing."

MARION. I *think* I followed that.

VITA. There'll be a quiz later.

NILES. Never again, never again. All I said, really, was that I reread the three books that I had written and didn't believe a word of them. Not one. So, naturally, I asked myself what on earth I had been doing for thirty years, and woke up one morning to discover that I suspected that I had been bought.

VITA. Not bought.

NILES. Worse. That I had been subtly conscripted as part of that elite corps who have been given the necessary task of "breaking the bronco from dancing." Or brainwashing the little bastards.

VITA. Not that the little so-and-sos appreciated what you were telling them.

NILES. I have the comfort of knowing that I made my statement.

VITA. Oh, and vividly. He has rather a flair for the dramatic.

MARION. We hardly noticed.

DOHERTY Not at all.

NILES. *(Laughs.)* Oh, dear, if I say so myself, I was magnificent.

VITA. Three weeks before the term final, he burst into his classroom —

NILES. Certainly not. I walked majestically and deliberately to my desk and did not sit down.

VITA. And announced to his class that the course was useless.

NILES. I said it was something akin to buffalo chips.

VITA:— took his three published books from his briefcase and ripped them in half.

NILES. And flung them in the air. I was exalted. *The Imagination of Ancient Greece. (Rips in half.)* There! to *The Imagination of Ancient Greece.* I know nothing about it, and neither does anyone else. Oh, it was wonderful.

VITA. And in his exaltation he had mislaid his glasses, so on his way to class he drove the car straight across the iris bed at the entrance to the college.

NILES. I was fired with the message of truth.

VITA. And coming back he drove the shortest route to the street, which was directly across the badminton court.

NILES. *Nolo contendere.*

VITA. Then he stopped off to have a celebratory drink, and he doesn't drink. It's a miracle you got home. God protects drunkards and little children, both of which would cover him.

DOHERTY. That's blasphemy, of course.

NILES. Unfortunately, several of my students are reactionary little —

VITA. Nerds.

NILES. And their parents are worse, and they are suing the college.

VITA. Our class would have stood up and cheered. Carried you over our heads about the corridors.

NILES. Your class was unruly, unwashed, and very nearly undressed. It's one of my most cherished memories.

MARION. You were a student of his?

VITA. That's where we met.

NILES. A-minus, and she had the nerve to come to my office to discuss the minus.

VITA. That wasn't the reason I came to your office. That was just the excuse.

NILES. Do you mean that after nine years of marriage I discover that you deliberately contrived —

VITA. Anyway. The professors convened with the provost. All except Whittington...

NILES. …head of the botany department…

VITA. …who was still saying: "Look what that brute's done to my iris bed!"

NILES. And I was completely exonerated. Enough, now.

VITA. Unfortunately, the Board of Governors was not quite so obliging.

NILES. Certainly not. They're capable of recognizing sick behavior when they see it. Enough now. We're telling stories out of school.

MARION. Do you care?

NILES. Not a fig.

MARION. Imagine Ernie ripping up his life's work.

NILES. Another fig for my life's work.

MARION. I might pace back and forth, after something like that.

DOHERTY. But you experienced a disturbance in your willful suspension of disbelief.

NILES. Coleridge had it as "willing," I believe.

DOHERTY. Wonderful phrase. I don't think I'd like the experience. That would be a real doozer.

NILES. Isn't that a doozer? Well, better now, on only slightly the downside of the prime of life than on…say…one's deathbed. That would be a doozer. *(Old voice.)* Oh, my God, I've just realized that I'm full of shit.

VITA. *(Offers him lemonade.)* Why don't you sit and join us, Niles.

NILES. Thanks, no, darling. I don't like lemonade. I'm sorry, it's probably fine as lemonade goes, but — why am I trying to be nice? Do you suppose I'm growing considerate in my old age?

VITA. I doubt it.

NILES. Sorry about the profanity. I don't usually.

DOHERTY. No, no. The scatological comment was very amusing. "Oh, my God, I've just realized I'm full of beans" doesn't have the same ring. The "Oh, my God" was unnecessary, but I never scold about that sort of thing.

DON. *(Offstage, shouting in Navaho. Enters, sees Marion.)* Oh, damn it. *(Exits back into the residence.)*

DOHERTY. Something about money. It usually is lately. Did you have violent arguments with your parents over money when you were young?

NILES. No.

VITA. Yes.

MARION. Yes.

DOHERTY. So did I.

DON. *(Enters with newspaper.)* Here's the paper. It's not going to be in it. *(He goes out.)*

MARION. I know, I know.

VITA. *(Looking off after Don.)* A brilliant doctor, hm? Well, if you say so.

MARION. Ernie painted him. It's the only painting I know I'm going to keep. It's one of the best things he did.

DOHERTY. Don pretended to hate Ernie, but he didn't, really.

MARION. I know. That's exactly what Ernie painted. The smugness, the fear, the belligerence, the uncertainty, the superiority, the distrust of the painter, the love. All staring right out at you. It's beautiful.

(Zap enters, wearing earphones.)

DOHERTY: You're Zap. I knew I knew Zap. Hello, Zap.

ZAP. Hi.

DOHERTY: Zap, zap, zap, zap, zap.

ZAP. I'm probably dying here. My skin is probably falling off. I'm getting the report here.

MARION. Zap, you did not dig through the suitcase for the radio. I spent two hours organizing — *(Zap removes earphones to hear.)* — well — good boy! *(Don enters.)*

ZAP. Hi.

DON. What's up?

MARION. *(Looking at the dust on the seat of Don's pants.)* Look at you. *(She brushes dust off him.)*

DON. Come on, Marion. Zap's your boytoy, I'm not your boytoy.

ZAP. *(To Don.)* Hey, Doctor, you go to New York, you go down to the Village, you dress like that, you'll pick up a lot of Jewish girls.

MARION. Have you two ever actually been introduced?

ZAP. Yeah, I know him, he's "Brave with Arrow." She's got you hanging over her fireplace in Lake Forest. Least he's not in the room where we eat, right?

DON. What's up?

ZAP. It ain't good at all. You don't want to know. A guy's already died.

DON. Who?

DOHERTY. Who?

ZAP. Some Indian. They're not releasing the name till they tell the family. Boy, that gives me the crawlies.

NILES. Died?

ZAP. What's yellow cake?

DOHERTY. Where was this?

ZAP. Up at the Chin Rock mine. It's a mess. This truck was supposed to be being loaded and instead it backed up over the containers and they busted, and the wind blew all this yellow cake stuff all over the guys that were loading it. Those helicopters were coming to take the guys who are still alive to the hospital in Los Alamos.

MARION. Up from White Sands. Wouldn't you know they'd get into the act.

VITA. Yellow cake is pure uranium, refined at the mill. That's from my protesting days.

ZAP. How far away is that Chin Rock mine?

DOHERTY. Twenty miles? Thirty miles?

MARION. Twenty miles as the buzzard flies.

ZAP. What really gripes you, though — what they're saying is, anybody not in the immediate area won't get sick for about twelve years.

DOHERTY. Minor levels, minor levels.

NILES. Don't panic the populus.

ZAP. You get the picture, twelve years from now you're walking down the street, you're feeling great, all of a sudden you're a spot on the sidewalk. *(Pause. They look to Doherty, who has his fingers pressed to his forehead, his eyes closed. His lips are moving. He prays silently. After a moment he crosses himself, looks up, smiles. Vita moves to a window, looking out.)*

VITA. I keep envisioning us all being slowly covered with Chin Rock ash. Like the people of Pompeii. A thousand years from now this will be an archaeological site with markers saying: This is a professor, this is his wife, this is a hopeful tennis player, with his rackets.

ZAP. Come on.

DOHERTY. No, no, it sounds very minor. We're not that close. People all over the country are going to be terribly disappointed. They'd rather have a big gaudy cataclysm. They've been preparing themselves for years.

VITA. Look at it. It looks so clean and immutable.

DOHERTY. No, no, quite mutable. Mute, mute, mute. Those solid-looking mountains, if you tried to climb them, would mute right out from under your foot.

VITA: I keep looking for an eagle. Can they really pick up children and fly off with them? Would that be too scary?

NILES. She doesn't mean that literally. Vita writes stories for children.

DOHERTY. You do? Wonderful.

VITA. They're nothing. They only sell because I have a very clever partner who does the illustrations. In spite of all this, I envy anyone who has a place here.

MARION. You either love it or you hate it. I sold it.

VITA. Oh, no.

MARION. I couldn't hack it. The first freezing night I spent here I woke up to Ernie carrying a rattlesnake through the bedroom at the end of a pair of fireplace tongs. They come in to warm themselves on the hearth.

NILES. We learn these little things one at a time.

MARION. He throws them back over the fence. To grow, I suppose. The romanticism completely escapes me. I think he'd read Georgia O'Keeffe did that. I'm sorry. I left without packing a bag. Drove to Chicago before I called him.

NILES. He wasn't a complete hermit, then. He had a phone.

MARION. Oh, by the swimming pool. And a large house and a large studio and a salon with a gaggle of fawning admirers.

NILES. It can't be easy being an artist today.

MARION. Nothing simpler, believe me.

DOHERTY. I'm going to hate to see you go. Isn't that what we're supposed to say? But I will. Marion used to spend a month here in the summer and a month in the winter.

MARION. Shaking my shoes out every morning in case a scorpion had holed up inside during the night.

DOHERTY. Very possible, of course, very possible. But I wouldn't leave here. They'd have to blast me out.

VITA. You don't have a choice, do you? Aren't you assigned?

DOHERTY. Yes, yes, we're sent. We don't just move where we'd like. They sent me all the way from Worcester, Mass. But they'd have to drag me away. Wild horses. (Singsong.) "Wild, wild horses couldn't drag me away." Now, why is that? It isn't healthy for me. Why would I fight for my inch of land to the bitter end? The grave of my dear little daughter who died that first hard winter is definitely not out on the hill behind the old corral. My father and his father before him never laid eyes on the place. Ah, well…Silly Billy. (To Marion.) Do you miss him? I miss him terribly. (Beat.) I miss our Sunday afternoons. Ernie used to come here after his struggles at the studio. Silly Ernie. He had to get away from all those people. I think he only invited them to come so he'd have someone to get away from. He'd steal an hour away, and I'd steal an hour away. We sat out back under Maria's arbor. He'd drink wine and I'd drink tea, and we both got drunk. I miss all that. I don't sit there anymore. He liked his friends at a little distance, didn't he? Not in a position to grab anything. Like some of the limelight. Sunday afternoons.

ZAP. Let up, okay?

MARION. (With energy, thrusts paper aside.) There's nothing in the paper, of course. They've had the draw hours ago. The only thing to do is call San Diego and get it over the phone.

ZAP. You okay?

DOHERTY. Was I being insensitive?

MARION. No, I need something to do.

ZAP. You want me to call?

MARION. I want me to call. Excuse me. *(Exits.)*

DOHERTY. Button my lip.

ZAP. Yeah, well, you get used to talking to yourself, you sorta just talk to yourself if someone's there to listen or not, you know?

DOHERTY. I know, I know. Silly Billy. Button my lip, button my lip.

ZAP. It ain't too easy on her coming back down here. I'll ask her to marry me again. I ask her every coupla days. She always gets a good laugh outta that.

VITA. *(To Don.)* Scorpions aren't that dangerous, are they? I think I've read that.

DON. How would I know?

VITA. There's no reason you should. I thought you might. When do you finish your internship?

NILES. We've been talking about you behind your back, Doctor.

DOHERTY. No, Don has decided he doesn't want to be a doctor anymore. So he won't have to finish his internship now. *(Don looks at him.)* You didn't know I found out, did you? *(He exits through the front door.)*

VITA. Why wouldn't you finish your internship? I thought you were doing so well.

DON. *(Beat.)* There's a species of scorpion in Mexico that's been known to be fatal to infants. It wouldn't seriously harm an adult.

ZAP. Scorpions. Oh, man.

DON. The tarantula's the same, rarely fatal. Unless the bite gets infected with gangrene.

ZAP. Gangrene?

DON. But that could happen from — tennis elbow.

VITA. I thought tarantulas were deadly.

DON. White wives' tale. Sorry.

ZAP. You got those here?

DON. White wives? Not many.

ZAP. Tarantulas!

DON. Tarantulas, oh. Pick up a rock. Little ones; six inches across.

ZAP. Oh, give me a break.

DON. Won't hurt you. The coral snake is really deadly, though. We understand you don't feel the bite.

VITA. *(In mock awe.)* You don't feel the bite?

DON. You just start feeling numb around the area; then a paralysis starts to set in —

ZAP. No, no, no, no. Don't talk symptoms. I can't hear symptoms. This is truly. I can't hear that.

VITA. Snakebite, Zappy. Snakebite.

ZAP. I can't hear symptoms without getting it. I know. This has happened.

DON. With snakebite it usually requires the snake.

ZAP. Not with me it don't require no snake.

NILES. They're putting you on.

ZAP. Yeah, well, he's putting me on, but he isn't making it up.

DON. I tell you, Zappy, it's a jungle out there in the desert.

DOHERTY. *(Enters behind Zap. Zap jumps a foot.)* No alarm, no alarm.
(Marion re-enters.)

ZAP. They got the draw?

MARION. Lines are busy. I'll try in a minute.

VITA. So. Why aren't you going to finish your internship and be a doctor?

MARION. What? That's news to me.

DON. Dr. Lindermann has asked me to join his cancer research team at Berkeley.

MARION. Oh, bullshit. Excuse me.

DOHERTY. *(Mumbled.)* Under the circumstances…

VITA. How did you get into cancer research? Not that I know anything about it.

DON. The last year or so I've been interested in gene structure, protein production, cellular experiments.

VITA. Is that like DNA?

DON. Like that.

DOHERTY. My goodness.

DON. There are some fairly complicated machines and equipment involved that I seem to understand better than some.

MARION. I'm sure, but I thought you turned them down. You talked to Ernie about it.

DOHERTY. Oh, that's last year's news. That was a lab in Pittsburgh. But those poor devils toil day and night for little reward. Dr. Don got very indignant and told them — quite movingly I thought, Don — that he must follow his calling and minister to his own people.

MARION. The Indian on the reservation doesn't respond well to outsiders.

DON. You've deliberately misunderstood everything I've said for the last year.

DOHERTY: Nothing you've said has made sense. But the lure of Dr. Noah Lindermann is not to be sneezed at. One of those charismatic "leaders of his field," always being interviewed on TV.

VITA. We've met him. I think we were less than impressed.

NILES. To say the least.

DOHERTY. Well, he's been at the college for the last three months. But now the Famous Man is returning to his research project and luring away his brightest star with the offer of an astronomical salary in a glamorous position.

DON. *(Very angry.)* If I were interested in being glamorous and making money, I could stay right here and be glamorous as hell and rake it in by the kilo. What do you think, Marion? Maybe I should hang up my shingle as the half-breed podiatrist. All those seven-foot Texans in Santa Fe walking around in their pointy boots. Their toes must be killing them.

MARION. Mine too, but I'm not sure I'd put my feet in your hands.

DOHERTY. Neither would they.

DON. And with this sun they'll need a dermatologist.

DOHERTY. *(To Don.)* Tell us about the respiratory disease among the Navaho mine workers.

DON. And a handsome young endocrinologist could make a killing.

DOHERTY. *(Rather heated.)* Talk to us about the rate of birth defects on the reservation.

DON. And there's a pretty penny here for a proctologist.

DOHERTY. I've never seen a pretty penny.

DON. And the entire desert is weeping for an anesthesiologist. I know I am.

DOHERTY. I know I am.

MARION. Wasn't that fun. Only now you're both hyperventilating.

DON. Not I.

VITA. Why would there be a higher rate of birth defects on the reservation than there would be in the rest of the area?

MARION. They live right in the middle of the uranium mines.

DOHERTY. Most of the men work there.

DON. *(Still quite angry.)* Congenital anomalies, lung cancer, tuberculosis, chromosomal aberrations, sperm morphological distortion — begins to get scary, doesn't it?

VITA. I can see why Father Doherty doesn't want to lose you.

DON. I'm just getting started, honey. Kidney disease, glaucoma, and there's no time for one person in a hundred years to begin to correct a millennium of genetic neglect.

VITA. So you just wave good-bye to it.

DON. In abject humiliation, yes.

VITA. You think that's all just romantic folly now?

DON. No, darlin', I think that is a deep and abiding tragedy.

NILES. I would have welcomed the idea that you were a practicing radiologist.

DON. We're not so skittish about radiation as you are. Having been forced to live with it all our lives.

NILES. Well, you won't be any longer.

DON. Who put a straw up your butt?

NILES. I would have thought there would have been a need on the reservation for a nutritionist.

DON. There is, Doctor.

NILES. Professor. A pediatrician.

DON. There is, Doctor.

NILES. Then I guess I miss the point of your little sally.

DON. You can't imagine.

NILES. I can imagine the horrors of the ninth circle, but if you mean it's ignorant speculation, you're quite right.

DON. *(Very hard.)* There is no time, Doctor. No time for any of it.

NILES. *(Angry.)* I'm never addressed as doctor, and I've recently turned in my badge. "Professor" was preferred to "doctor," but I didn't insist on it. *(Doherty stands.)* I'm sorry. I'm being snide and I don't know why. My wife and I are accustomed to being mildly insulted by students. I'm not myself, as I said. And whoever I am, I seem to have little control of him.

VITA. You're fine.

MARION. Zappy could give you one of his Valiums. Goodness knows, he has them to spare.

VITA. I don't think Dr. Singer believes in tranquilizers.

NILES. Please!

DON. Singer's!

VITA. What?

NILES. Really!

VITA. What?

DON. Well, goddamn. No wonder he's off the wall. He's on his way to the nuthouse.

NILES. Nothing of the kind.

DON. Hold on to your tranquilizers, Zappy; he's so doped up now he's not responsible for anything he's said all afternoon.

NILES. *(Overlapping.)* I'm just constitutionally ill-equipped for changes in plans. Surprises annoy me. And though the lessons in local ophiology and arachnology are diverting, I'm sure you'll understand.

DOHERTY. *(Overlapping.)* Pooh, pooh, pooh, pooh. Winnie the Pooh. Pooh out of the bag. *(To Don.)* Settle down now. Nothing to be embarrassed about. We know all about Doc Singer.

DON. Ernie and his crowd knew every expensive psychiatric hangout in the West.

NILES. Not at all, not at all.

DON. He's going off to be shock-treated or warm-bathed...

NILES. I won't be shock-treated — I won't be warm-bathed —

DOHERTY. We've seen it a hundred times. You'll come back placid as a cow.

NILES. Not at all. *(To Vita.)* You see what silliness you started?

MARION. It costs a fortune, I hope you realize that.

NILES. We know, of course, that it's exorbitant — *(Sighs.)* Oh, well.

VITA. *(Pause.)* The pretense that this was a vacation was beginning to wear a little thin.

NILES. Especially between the two of us, yes. I only agreed to go to such a ridiculous high-class funny farm to humor the Board of Governors of the college. They're picking up the tab, of course. They feel it will appease the parents if they can tell them I've had a complete collapse.

ZAP. Don't take the medicine if you don't need it.

MARION. Cool it, Zap.

NILES. Well, actually, Zappy, two months ago I was fabulously healthy in mind and limb. But since we've had the appointment I've prepared myself for the place by becoming a total basket case. I think my mind has a natural aversion to wasting money.

ZAP. Sure.

DOHERTY. Well, good. You'll be in wonderful hands. Best in the West, best in the West. Don is a little skeptical about that sort of place, but that's to be expected.

DON. Out of my field. Dude-ranch psychiatric hospitals are not the Indian's bag.

NILES. It sounds like the Indian's bag is out of your field now.

DON. Enough, okay?

DOHERTY. It's best never to look back, Don. Don't you agree, Professor?

NILES. I wouldn't know.

DOHERTY. You're running away from school, Don is running away from his practice.

DON. I'm running away from nothing.

NILES. As the young man said, I know nothing about what he's running from.

DON. No, and you're damn well not likely to. Working in your ivy-covered ivory towers back East.

NILES. Oh, hardly. Ivory towers?

DON. The matrons and the patrons who go to Singer's usually fly straight from their penthouses to the padded cells without touching down. They don't usually drive to the loony bin through the wilderness. It's very egalitarian of you to take a tour through the real world. I hope you learn a lot.

NILES. The real world, the real world, dear Lord. I thought I'd heard the last of the real world. And certainly the idea that academics know nothing of the real world. *(To Vita.)* We used to have wonderful talks about the real world, remember? In your class? *(To Don.)* Begging to differ with you, the real world has come slouching into my room hourly for thirty years. The real world is too much with me. I would expect the young today to see things more clearly. They certainly clamor more loudly. But it appears youth wears blinders. Endemically, or, "it comes with the territory."

DON. You don't have to translate endemic. I know the meaning of endemic. It comes with the territory.

NILES. It would. But you appear as blind to the fact of school life around you as I was at your age. I'm not surprised, I am disappointed.

VITA. Darling.

DON. You're full of it, too.

NILES. Oh, completely, but by all that's holy, man, open your eyes.

VITA. Don't get upset.

NILES. I am not upset. I am strident and overbearing.

VITA. And a touch irrational —

NILES. This young person is justifiably sickened by the effete performance of professors of my ilk —

VITA. No one is quite like you, I'm sure.

NILES. Oh, let us hope. No, people are snowflakes; there's none quite like any. I'm sure there is no comparison to the deprivation you have lived with and are running from, but the fact is that the ivory tower is a bloody shambles. How can you be in school and not know that? The fact of the graceless routine of my life in academe is being awakened at three in the morning, called to the village morgue to identify the mutilated and alcohol-sodden corpse of the victim of a car crash. The fact is — let go of me — is having the brightest light of my fraudulent teaching career quench itself by jumping off the bridge into the bay because in your enlightened age of sexual permissiveness, he was afraid he was sexually deviant. *(Mumbles.)* Ivory tower…There have been, in fact, seven suicides in the past ten years; in fact, one third of my class each year, and of yours, I'm sure, if you had bothered to look around you, burn themselves out on drugs and overwork and exposure to the pressures of academic life, and are unable to return, probably to their everlasting benefit, if they knew it. Dear God, how can anyone with eyes *(Vita touches his arm.)* — stop that, please — think that we are out of touch with the real world. If that's the real world, I beg to plead very familiar with the real world, thank you. The calumny, Lord! *(Vita takes hold of his arm.)* Stop touching me, please! What are you trying to do? Make it better? It will not be better, thank you! I won't embarrass you again. You won't have to endure that again. I wish in God's name the door to this building wasn't so heavy, so I could slam it. *(He strides out the front door.)*

VITA. Niles, don't go out there! I'd better — well, I'd better not, is what I'd better. He'll walk around. He's been getting very — lately — irrational. *(To Don.)* Still, it was unnecessary for you to goad him like that. He's unwell physically as well as — I'm sorry.

(Distant helicopters heard overhead.)

DOHERTY. They must be taking the injured mine workers to the hospital in Los Alamos. My goodness, what a racket. Our poor little church mouse, Maria, must be under the bed. I must say, when she called me this morning, it was a wonderfully comic picture. I don't want to make fun, but she's afraid of being electrocuted by the telephone instrument and won't even go near it. Yells and jumps when it rings. Imagine her even getting through to me. The Archangel Gabriel must have intervened for her. She said: "You must come immediately, Father, our doctor is running away." And you almost did. *(Pause.)* You used to come to me and say: "It's all so impossible. I don't know if I'll ever do anything right." And I said you would. And here Dr. Lindermann has presented you with such a golden opportunity to make something of yourself.

DON. What do you know about it?

DOHERTY. Oh, pooh. What do I know? I never know anything.

DON. I can't talk to you.

DOHERTY. You try. *(Don exits to parking lot. To Marion.)* Is he going to his bike?

MARION. No, he's charging straight down the road.

DOHERTY. Good. Zappy, take these. *(Throws a set of keys to Zap.)*

ZAP. What are they?

DOHERTY. Just hide them and don't tell me where.

(Zap exits into garden.)

MARION. You ought to be ashamed of yourself.

DOHERTY. Well, I'm not. Not a bit. *(He turns to Vita.)*

VITA. I thought he'd be all right if I came with him. He's just been getting worse. Well, he'll be fine.

DOHERTY. Oh, yes. Quite possible. Always possible.

VITA. I'm kind of at the end of my tether here.

DOHERTY. Why don't we talk?

VITA. *(Pause.)* No, thank you.

DOHERTY. You sure?

VITA. Thank you.

MARION. I'm going to call San Diego again. *(Exits.)*

DOHERTY. Yes, yes, yes. Back to work, back to work. Everybody back to the salt mines. *(Sings.)* "I've been working on the reservation...All the livelong day..." *(He exits into the residence.)*

(Vita, alone in the church, folds Niles's jacket, holding it on her arm. She turns to the front door, to the garden. A second helicopter goes over, higher, the sound farther away. She looks up and then slowly turns, following the plane's path, ending to look at the altar. She stands facing the altar, her back to us. The first time the altar has been our focus.)

END OF ACT ONE

ACT TWO

Half an hour later. Zap is lying on the floor, listening to his headset. Father Doherty is at the altar, kneeling. After a moment Vita comes in from the garden. The priest rises. He might speak a little less brightly in this act.

VITA. Don't let me disturb you.

DOHERTY. No, no, impossible. You can't disturb me. I'm full up. I was just asking for the usual. Nothing special. Step up to the altar and say, Give me the usual!

VITA. What would that be?

DOHERTY. Oh...courage, perseverance, strength.

VITA. Make it a double.

DOHERTY. Oh, I'm sure. After the sun goes down, it gets beautifully cool here. Nights are lovely.

VITA. We spent last night outside Clovis, I know. I hadn't seen stars before. It's the first time I'd had the feeling that the earth was a planet moving through a galaxy of stars. Niles came back to the car and picked up his hat, so he isn't completely irrational.

DOHERTY. So I saw.

ZAP. *(Flat on his back.)* That's it. Interstate 40 is definitely moving now. Everything's under control down there. Up here they're still saying eight o'clock, so we're cool. *(Rising.)* Who am I talking to? Where is everybody?

VITA: Marion is calling about your schedule again. She was talking to someone, so she seems to have got through.

ZAP. I don't want to know. I know already. I can't talk about it; I want to hear this.

VITA. What are they saying now?

ZAP. *(Earphones off.)* What?

VITA. What's the radio saying, now?

ZAP. No, this is the Moody Blues. *(Earphones back on, he stretches back out on the floor.)*

DOHERTY. Moody Blues. I hear all those in the car. They're good company, very cheering.

VITA. You drive a lot?

DOHERTY. Oh, yes. All my missions are thirty or forty miles apart. Saturday night at one mission, back to my own at Dry Lake for seven o'clock Sunday Mass, eleven o'clock here, four P.M. at a grammar school assembly hall. I carry a portable altar. And back to Dry Lake for Mass at eight o'clock Sunday night. Little Santa Clara has the Sunday obligation on Wednesday.

VITA. How many are there in your congregation?

DOHERTY. Very good, I think. Most of them are fifteen…twenty.

VITA. (Looking out.) Mr. Tabaha is sitting on his motorcycle all slumped over, his head down, looking into the dust. He looks like an updating of the painting "End of the Trail."

DOHERTY. Yes. This little show of power has interrupted everyone's plans. "Tabaha," "by the river"; that's Navaho for "by the river." I wonder which one? The young miner who died at the Chin Rock mine was twenty-three. His wife is eight months pregnant with their first child. Four others are ill. I listened on Zappy's headset. Very interesting apparatus. Occupational hazard they're calling it. A uranium mine is no different from a coal mine; coal dust, they're saying. Each is a slow, painful death, they say. But then what isn't? Courage, strength, and perseverance. Moody Blues. Blue, blue, blues.

VITA. What time is Mass?

DOHERTY. Eight.

VITA. If we're still here, I'd like to see the service.

DOHERTY. No, no, nothing to see. I'm afraid there isn't anything to watch. Not even picturesque, I don't imagine. Twelve, fifteen stoic Navahos shuffle in, kneel, I mumble sincerely, they mumble sincerely, and they shuffle out. Nothing to see. Nothing on their faces, probably nothing on mine. In and out. Shuffle — shuffle.

VITA. It must mean something to them, though. And to you.

DOHERTY. Oh, it's what we live for, but there's nothing to see. You're welcome to stay, but you'll be on the road. They'll get all this cleared up, they'll have a good cover-up story by tomorrow. Bad publicity for the mines if they don't, and the mines are already complaining that the price of uranium has dropped thirty percent in the last ten years. Must be the only price that has. No, you'll be on the road. On the trail by then. Living your life.

MARION. (Entering.) What are they saying?

ZAP. Hi —

VITA. They're playing the Moody Blues, so it can't be all bad. Interstate 40 is moving. We'll be okay soon. You get through?

MARION. I was calling for a plane. They're ready when we are.

DOHERTY. I-40. Used to be Route 66. I think they do those things deliberately. Don't want us to get too attached to anything.

VITA. Probably just as well.

DOHERTY. Oh, yes. *(Beat.)* I don't have the energy for tonight, not what's going to be necessary. Not what I'd like to have, but whoever has what he'd like to have. *(Exits to residence.)*

MARION. I broke every damn nail I own. Oh, boy. I sound like Zap. The last three days I've been showing a crew of blithely incompetent Indian carpenters how to crate paintings.

VITA. No fun, I'd imagine.

MARION. I shouldn't try; they drive me — oh, well. They would have done fine left on their own if I hadn't kept butting in. They were slow, I was nervous, and you've never seen canvases that size. He had the good sense to leave the pots to a museum in Albuquerque. And don't think they weren't Johnny-on-the-spot. Labeling and wrapping and generally being underfoot — Oh, well, I suppose I should be grateful...

VITA. Are you taking the furniture? I was remembering the pictures I saw in *Architectural Digest.*

MARION. The rugs and Savonarola chairs and the Mexican refectory tables? No, thank God, everything was sold with the buildings. It looks very good here, but for Lake Forest it's much too "Goodbye, Old Paint, I'm Leaving Cheyenne." It's more the trauma of seeing the place in such a shambles than anything.

VITA. I hate moving, breaking up households.

MARION. It's the worst, isn't it?

VITA. All us kids came back to help Mom sort through the years of mementos when Dad died.

MARION. Oh, thank God, I was spared that. Ernie wasn't a hoarder.

VITA. Dad kept everything. His dad's cavalry sword from the First World War. Old ribbons from high school track meets, his own Second World War stuff — snapshots of D-day. We even found an old Western saddle stashed away. He had some secret cowboy fantasy maybe. I made a few calls. Local preservation societies. It wasn't like he was famous. Small-town lawyer, state assemblyman, respected family man. Good money, well-meaning, who cares?

MARION. What did you do with it all?

VITA. Mom took a few things, we all took something, and we burned the rest. Soon as it was gone I felt I'd broken a law. All that crap belonged to the race, not to me. Every scrap should be stored somewhere. You never know what one little piece of paper, photograph, will be the key that unlocks the secret of the universe.

MARION. *(Smiles.)* I expected it to be morbid: going through the studio, looking back over all the paintings, getting them ready for a retrospective. It didn't happen. I hadn't seen most of them in years. It turned out to be very exciting. I sat in the middle of the studio with all the paintings around me. It was like a big blowout with a lot of old friends. I wanted Ernie to be there so I could congratulate him. Even Zap felt it. It's going to be an important show.

VITA. Where are they going?

MARION. Open in Chicago —

VITA. At your gallery.

MARION. At the Art Institute of Chicago. He always wanted that. The bastards had to wait for him to kick off before they gave it to him.

VITA. I imagine he knew it would happen eventually.

MARION. On good days. Then go from Chicago to Denver, then Los Angeles, Dallas, probably not New York. Maybe a few other places. They're all designated for different museums after that. That'll be the hard part, seeing the collection broken up. But it's what he wanted. *(She is trying not to cry.)*

VITA. I'll have to see it.

MARION. Try to catch it. *(Moving to the window.)* The radio said soon, you said? I think the professor has cooled down a bit. Looks like he might be wandering this way.

VITA. Good. Did Zappy know him?

MARION. Ernie? Yeah. They got along. Ernie was working rather furiously the last few years. He felt better if I had a project. They got along. It's been good for me, it was good for Ernie. Maybe it hasn't been completely fair to Zappy. He gets a little confused. Father Doherty thinks we should "sanctify our relationship" now. I think not. I'll be there 'til he needs something else. So we do learn from our — Zappy, are you hearing this?

ZAP. Sure.

MARION. I forgot you were there, creep.

ZAP. Yeah, I got that problem. You ready to hit the road?

MARION. Soon as it's open.

ZAP. You are getting so weepy, you know? The last week you can't talk about me, you can't talk about Ernie, she can't talk about tumbleweed without the faucet. Yesterday she was crying over the damn sunset.

MARION. Shut up.

ZAP. I can't wait to get you out of here. Get you bossing everybody around again.

MARION. It can't be too soon. *(As Niles enters.)* Well.

ZAP. Hi!

NILES. *(Tapping his hat.)* Don't I look jaunty?

VITA. Almost.

NILES. Forgive me for that astonishing exhibition. I have no idea what causes those —

VITA: *(Overlapping.)* No, I'm sorry if I blurted out something you would rather have left as just between ourselves —

NILES. *(Overlapping.)* Of course not, what care I? There's no explanation except petulant infantilism —

VITA. We could move the car into the shade now.

NILES. No, darling. I needn't be ostracized to the car. I've walked myself to a frazzle and feel I'm almost fit for social intercourse. *(As Don enters.)* Dr. Tabaha, I want to apologize for my spectacularly tasteless attack. Nothing personal, believe me. *(Pause.)* And you say…

DON. No, I just can't deal with Father Doherty. He likes to stir everyone up with his "Don't you think, Don?" and "Wouldn't you agree, Professor?" Anyway, it's interesting to see someone freak out for a change.

ZAP. You like that, I'll take you to my house sometime.

NILES. Freak out. I think that characterizes it perfectly. Walking around out there, I've never felt so twitchy in my life. Aside from knowing that I'm exposing myself to terminal radiation poisoning, I keep thinking enormous ants are going to come up over the hill. Giant spiders. Great amorphous blobs slithering across the sands.

ZAP. Come on.

NILES. I know, but my whole understanding of — or misunderstanding of — nuclear — ah —

VITA. — little nuclear emergencies —

NILES. — emergencies comes from 1950s movies on the Late Show. I suffer from that sci-fi brain damage peculiar to the chronic insomniac.

ZAP. No way, I'm really chicken-livered, you know? Even when I was a kid, any picture the title was in shaky letters I couldn't go see it.

MARION. Well, I'm going to brave it. *(She exits.)*

NILES. Careful! There's a peculiar, spiny-looking plant that I'm certain was not there when we parked the car.

ZAP. That's gonna do it. I been down here three days, it hasn't bothered me; now I can't go out.

NILES. So what is the news?

ZAP. They're saying soon now. Hi. *(This is to Doherty as he enters.)*

DOHERTY. Yes, yes, yes —

NILES. Sorry for that absurd —

DOHERTY. No, no, no. The mission has seen everything. During the land-grant riots one of my colleagues was in his church when bullets came flying through the window. I'm afraid he packed his bag and left the keys to the church at the post office. I so much enjoyed your tirade. I love a good tirade, they're such fun. Talkers and tiraders. *(Singsong.)* "I love a tirade."

NILES. I'm afraid I do tend to fly off the handle.

VITA. Like an ax blade.

DOHERTY. I was struck by what you said. Teachers with concern are rare. People don't always care by your age.

NILES. Thank you.

DOHERTY. Yes, it's unusual, I believe. Oh, you mean age — well, you can't do anything about that.

NILES. Thank you.

DOHERTY. No, by your age *(Niles reacts.)* too many teachers have become cynical. Teachers and preachers. Dr. Don saw a lot of that, didn't you, Dr. Don? All that elbowing and getting ahead? Of course, he was at the top of his class; always dizzying to look down from those heights.

NILES. Are you? Congratulations.

DON. Thank you.

DOHERTY. Yes, one of the chosen. Many are called but only two are chosen. Dr. Indian Don and a bright young woman intern, Dr. Alice, who is not in my parish, being a Baptist. Not under my wing.

DON. I'm not under your wing, Father.

DOHERTY. No, you're making your way away.

DON. The first chance I get.

DOHERTY. Yes, he has to be in Santa Fe tonight. He's meeting the Great Man and the young woman intern, and the three of them are winging away to San Francisco. *(Sings lightly.)* "Open your *Golden* Gate..." You are naturally proud to be one of the chosen two.

NILES. And you think he shouldn't be?

DOHERTY. Pride indeed. Lambs, led to the slaughter. All very glorifying. Vanity, vanity.

NILES. But why not? Vanity is only human.

DOHERTY. Yes, but then, what isn't? Aren't we all very human, though? Sometimes I'm amazed at how very human everyone is.

DON. It has nothing to do with you.

DOHERTY. He's always telling me that. That's an impolite way of saying nobody asked you. And believe me, nobody did. I volunteered. *(Don storms out.)* I think the wonderful thing about people is that if you leave them alone they'll do what their heart knows is right. If you only leave them alone. *(Beat.)* Long enough.

DON. *(Entering.)* Where are the keys to my bike?

DOHERTY. Aren't they in your bike?

DON. You know where they are. Let me have them.

DOHERTY. Do I know where your keys are? He's always trying to trap me into telling a deliberate lie. No, I don't know where your bike keys are. Exactly.

DON. I'm not staying here. I'm not going to do what you think I should.

DOHERTY. I have every confidence you're going to do what you think you should.

MARION. *(Entering, a small memo pad in her hand.)* I got through; I have it.

ZAP. Oh, no.

DOHERTY. I've always felt —

ZAP. Excuse us, Father — Oh, boy. When do I play?

DOHERTY. Oh, you got through.

VITA. San Diego does exist.

MARION. Eleven in the morning.

ZAP. Oh, great.

MARION. I have the whole schedule. Your leg up to the final eight.

ZAP. *(Long pause.)* You better read it to me. What does that look mean? It's good? Same old…? You better read it.

MARION. Eleven in the morning, first match is Evans.

ZAP. Clyde Evans? *(Nod. A long pause — five seconds. Matter-of-factly.)* That's no sweat.

MARION. Then the winner of the Baley and Syse match. Then the winner of Bouton and Tryne or Carey and Luff. Luff is seeded eighth, believe it or not.

ZAP. *(Beat.)* Let me see. *(She hands him her note.)* "Zappala-Evans, Baley-Syse, Bouton-Tryne, Carey-Luff." I can take Evans in straight sets — 6–1, 6–1 if he lucks out. Baley-Syse is like a matching from the tadpole pool. Tryne gets mad, Carey is a fairy, and Luff — with all due respect to my fellow players, Luff is a cream puff. Evans, Baley, Syse, Bouton, Tryne, Carey, Luff. Woooo! Son-of-a — Woooo! I mean, I don't want to disparage true professionals who will, I'm sure, play up to their ability and with great heart, but this is a list of the seven most candy-ass tennis players I've ever seen. This is the Skeeter League. If I couldn't make the final eight in a — Where's Rose? Where's Charley Tick is the question. They got all those guys together on the other leg? What kind of a lopsided draw — Tryne does not possess a serve. None. Carey is, in all humility, probably the worst professional sportsman I've ever seen. What Paul Carey most needs is vocational guidance. Syse I have personally beaten four times without him winning one game. 6–zip, 6–zip. Zap! You candy-asses. Wooo! I gotta walk, I gotta walk. You charter the plane? *(Exits.)*

MARION. He's waiting on the runway.

NILES. Is it really that easy a field?

MARION. Luff could be a problem, but I don't think so. It's so much luckier than any draw he's had — nothing's sure, but it's very fair. *(Enormous yell offstage. Everybody gets up, looks out.)* No, it's just Zappy. He's okay. What do you know. What do you know. Son-of-a-gun.

NILES. That's remarkable. That's — *(Mumbles.)* wonderful. Something like that.

VITA. What, love? Are you okay?

NILES. That's wonderful, I said. Dizzy, nothing. *(Sitting.)* Did he leave his radio? Do we have a report?

VITA. Soon.

ZAP. *(Re-enters, furious.)* Is that what they think of me? This is my class? What I should do is say forget it. If that's all the respect you got — if I ain't better than this — what this is is a public embarrassment. They're lucky if I show after this.

MARION. It's the luck of the draw. It's names out of the hat.

ZAP. That's not luck, that is a massacre. *(Beat.)* Okay. Okay. What I gotta do here is not get overconfident. What I gotta prevent is getting the big head. My paramount problem here is going to be not falling asleep, which, when you're facing Charley Baley across the net, is not an easy thing to do. Evans, Baley, Syse, Bouton, Tryne, Carey, Luff. Puffballs. Puffballs. Massacre. I gotta walk. I gotta walk.

DON. Zap, do you have the keys to my bike?

ZAP. Hell, no.

DON. You don't?

ZAP. But I don't mind lying to you like a priest would. *(Don makes a move toward him. Zap dodges.)* I don't have 'em; if I had 'em, I'd take a spin. Watch out, "Brave with Arrow," I'm fleet of foot.

DON. Forget it. *(He stands glaring at the wall.)*

ZAP. I gotta walk, I gotta walk. *(He exits.)*

DOHERTY. It's always possible that you lost them. You tend to lose things lately. *(Beat.)* Now, he's going to be stoic. I used to think Ernie was calling him Elijah. I thought he saw in Don the prophet of the Lord, fed by ravens, slayer of the false prophets of Baal. It turned out he was calling him Kow-liga. Kow-liga was a wooden cigar-store Indian in some hill-billy song. *(Sings.)* "Poor old Kow-liga." I don't know why you think any of us would be opposed to your success. Could you see a motive for anything but rejoicing, Professor?

NILES. *(To Don.)* He really does do that, you're right. *(To Doherty.)* I'm sure it's no one's business but his.

DOHERTY. My point exactly.

DON: Oh, sure.

DOHERTY. He doesn't trust a word I say.

NILES. I don't see the point in badgering the boy. It's his decision.

DOHERTY. I'll have bad dreams about his silent indictment. Imagine knocking cancer research. I'm sure they need every man, woman, and Indian.

VITA. He might be the one who finds the answer.

DON. I think we will.

DOHERTY. We have great respect for your chosen field.

DON. When did you find out?

DOHERTY. Your great Dr. Noah Lindermann called me for a reference. I think he wanted to be reassured that you wouldn't scalp your co-workers at his renowned research center. I gave you a glowing recommendation. I was surprised to discover you'd visited there. You neglected to mention it. Wined and dined, no doubt.

DON. Enough.

DOHERTY. It sounds like quite a place, Marion. Warm climate. Highest-paid researchers in the country. He didn't neglect to mention that. Most of the researchers, the Great Man told me, prefer to live away a bit. Houses along the coast road. Pleasant drive to work. Sunset highway.

MARION. Sounds like Los Alamos. Highest standard of living in the state.

DOHERTY. If you judge by creature comforts, as everyone does nowadays.

MARION. Everyone in the state resents Los Alamos, but the milk resents the cream.

DOHERTY. Your Great Man said he'd been impressed with the way you presented yourself. Thought you'd be useful eventually in an *administrative position.*

DON. He didn't say that.

DOHERTY. He did. Said you had agreed.

DON. I said I'd do what was necessary.

DOHERTY. I can see you now, making a grant proposal: belligerent and sincere. I told him you cleaned up nicely.

DON. The place is better endowed than any other in the country.

DOHERTY. Yes. They're better at it. Drafting a woman and an Indian. It's a wonder he didn't grab a black and a Chinese. Oh, they're probably already there.

DON. You don't know anything about it, Father.

DOHERTY. About what? Grantsmanship? I know nothing about that? I think this may be the first time in history someone in the Catholic Church has been accused of not knowing how to make money.

MARION. I think they'll love you. I see a turquoise belt buckle and maybe one earring.

NILES. Why not?

DOHERTY. Why not, indeed? It sounds like a wonderful life. Clean surroundings, intellectual problems, no patients, no pain, no filth, no ugliness. Only success. Even the rabbits and the mice are white.

NILES. It remains his decision. You can't tell them what to do. No profit in it.

DOHERTY. Profit is the last thing I'm concerned about.

NILES. *(He holds his hand to his head.)* It isn't up to us to judge what's right for those —

DOHERTY. Judgment! Oh, my goodness. I quote chapter and verse on judgment. We are here, you and I, to show the light — teachers and preachers —

NILES. No, no. Who are we to say go one way or go another?

VITA. Don't get upset again.

DON. It's nothing to you.

VITA. Do you have a headache? You've had a little too much sun, maybe.

NILES. No, the — too much sun, I'd imagine. Just a passing fuzziness, it occurred a moment ago, outside. It passes. Don't look so alarmed. You're determined something should be the matter — what is the situation with our being held hostage here?

VITA. Soon.

MARION. Soon.

NILES. "Soon" means nothing. Soon is now. I see no reason why we couldn't pack the car. You hadn't intended to leave all this here, had you?

VITA. I thought perhaps not. We can put this in the car if you like.

NILES. I am sorry, I am irritable and I am antsy and quite cross and half-crazy, and I don't know at all why. But I do not intend to stay here any longer. Darling, do pick that up. *(She looks at him.)* You open your hand, put your hand on the handle. You close your — I'll do it. Take that. I'll do it. Excuse us, it's been real as the — and my hat. *(As she just looks at him.)* Leave it. Leave it. Get to the car.

MARION. You can't go anywhere until they lift the roadblock.

NILES. You think they'll gun us down at the checkpoint? I think not.

MARION. It wouldn't be out of character.

NILES. If they don't let us pass, then we will either run the damn roadblock or wait there until they do let us pass. One can apply logic with amazing results if one tries. *(Vita is taking the keys from his hand.)* What do you want?

VITA. I'll drive, you navigate.

NILES. I'll drive, thank you. Very — *(Mumbled word — supports himself against the wall.)*

VITA. Something is not quite right with you, my dear, and you're not going to —

(Niles slides to a seated position on the bench.)

DON. Has he eaten?

VITA. Very little; he hasn't been hungry, he said.

DON. Does he have diabetes? Does he —

VITA. No. I don't think so. He doesn't go to doctors — What, darling?

NILES. I thought I had passed out — Did I...?

DON. Straight out on the bench —

VITA. *(As they stretch him out.)* What's wrong?

ZAP. *(Running in.)* Boy, he has really spooked me. I can't go out —

MARION. Sit, doll. Not now.

DOHERTY. It's all right. Don knows what he's doing.

VITA. So tell me.

ZAP. He passed out? Maybe you should put his feet up.

MARION. Cool it, Zappy.

DON. Is he usually as nervous as he's been here?

VITA. Only the last month; the last week or so it's been worse. Every other day or so.

DON. The perspiring is normal?

VITA. Not usual at all. I assumed it was the heat.

DON. It isn't that warm.

VITA. You're talking to someone from Rhode Island.

DON. I've never had the pleasure. Does he drink?

VITA. No, almost never.

DON. Has he had a drink today?

VITA. He doesn't drink. No. Sorry.

DON. What drug is he taking?

VITA. Only Valium. There were three. I squirreled the rest away.

DON. *(Presses Niles's leg.)* You feel that? *(The other leg.)* That? Can you move it? *(Niles does.)* This one? Arm? *(Niles moves one arm.)* This one? *(Niles waves his hand.)* Well, what the hell, we'll try the sugar. *(To Marion, pointing to the sugar and lemonade.)* Put a lot of that in a glass of that stuff. *(Back to Vita.)* You're sure he doesn't have diabetes? At least it can't hurt.

VITA. What is it?

DON. Who knows.

VITA. What's his pulse?

DON. Exceeding the speed limit a few miles. *(Marion hands him a glass of lemonade, Don and Vita help Niles to a sitting position.)* Can you drink that?

NILES. Oh, Lord, no.

DON. Drink. It won't hurt you. *(To Doherty.)* You should keep a medical cabinet here. I've told you that before.

DOHERTY. If you have to take him to Los Alamos, you can use my car.

VITA. Why would…?

MARION. That's the closest hospital. It's at least two hours to Gallup.

NILES. I pray Gallup is a town and not a mode of transportation.

VITA. Do be quiet.

DON. Drink that.

NILES. I don't know why, but — *(Mumbles.)*

VITA. Don't talk.

NILES. I said, I have every confidence in you. I can't imagine why.

DON. That's all, now. Close your eyes if you want. *(To Marion.)* Do another. It's nothing. He's just faint.

ZAP. Oh, Jesus. *(Turns to go.)* I can't go out there, the ants will get me.

MARION. Sit.

VITA. He's out cold.

DON. No, no. *(Niles opens his eyes.)* Hello again. You don't have to open your eyes. Drink that. All.

VITA. What's wrong?

DON. *(Nods to Marion for another lemonade, checks pulse.)* It could be any of about ten things. All this flying off the handle is not his typical behavior?

VITA. Not at all, no.

DON. And not eating. *(Though they talk, their concern is still with Niles.)*

VITA. No, he's always been very predictable in his routine; very careful about his health.

DOHERTY. Until he made his dramatic denouncement to his class?

VITA. Yes.

DOHERTY. That must have been a surprise to you.

VITA: No, we went through his work together. I didn't completely agree at first, but I certainly saw his point. Actually, by the time he left the college, we were pretty much in agreement that it was the only thing he could do.

DOHERTY. All very brave. We always admire all that. And what are your plans after Singer's?

VITA. I don't know if we have any —

DON. *(Checking pulse.)* I think that's slowing down to a trot now. That's amazing. Feel that. What do you know?

VITA. It seems weak.

DON. No, it's good.

NILES. If this has anything to do with radiation poisoning, I'll sue Chin Rock's ass.

DON. Who knows. Could be the heat if you're not used to it. Could be some kind of slight stroke, I don't think so. Stress, nerves, some sort of mild hypoglycemic attack. Could be…

NILES. I flatly refuse to suffer from hypoglycemia.

DON. Pulse doesn't speed up like that and then come back that dramatically in many instances.

NILES. No, no, it's much too "the thing to have." I couldn't possibly.

DON. Everyone likes to say they have hypoglycemia; it's no fun if you do. No way to be sure without an examination and tests. They have the facilities to fix you up at Singer's.

NILES. *(To Vita.)* Could you bear my telling people — say at cocktail parties — that I'm feeling a touch palpitant from my hypoglycemic condition?

VITA. Grounds for divorce.

NILES. That's what I thought.

VITA. You're very tall to keel over in that way. You might hurt someone.

ZAP. Hypoglycemia. Is like you feel sweaty, and you get kinda faint, you don't have any energy?

MARION. I'll club you, I'm not joking.

ZAP. No, I'm cool. You're looking good, Professor.

NILES. I feel an utter imbecile. *(To Vita.)* I seem to be coming apart at the seams on you, don't I? Everything is coming unglued all at once.

VITA. Not quite.

NILES. Not quite all at once, or not quite everything?

VITA. Not quite unglued.

DON. Sit. You're not going anywhere. Finish that.

NILES. Vile.

DON. Have one more.

NILES. Oh, surely not.

DON. No argument. They're small.

NILES. Anyone care to join me? I hate drinking alone.

DOHERTY. I think I will, actually.

MARION. *(With the thermos.)* Would you like a little something in it?

DOHERTY. No, no. Not one of my vices.

MARION. You don't mind if I…?

DOHERTY. Not at all. Any number of precedents.

MARION: Vita?

VITA. No.

DON. Go ahead.

VITA: I think maybe I will.

NILES: *(To Don.)* That's amazing stuff.

DON. If we had a fifty-percent glucose solution, that reaction would have been instantaneous.

NILES. I refuse to believe all my histrionics can be ascribed to low blood sugar.

DON. It's…it's more complicated than that.

NILES. Things always are.

DON. *(Has scribbled on a notepad.)* Give this to Admissions at Singer's.

NILES: *(Reading.)* You really must be a doctor. This is completely illegible. There's a certain poetic justice. One would expect denizens of an "ivory tower" to have thin blood.

DON. Forget I said that. I wasn't thinking.

NILES. No, I thank you. I was walking around out there remembering. Though my student years were in earlier and what we like to think of as easier times — centuries ago, it seems — I remember having the same romantic impression of my professors' lives. Heaven knows, I'd never have gone into such a business otherwise. An edifice not at all unlike an ivory tower was my ignorant and egotistical hope those centuries ago. I actually envisioned a life of quiet reflection, strolling through the groves — the lot of it. We would go, a gentle band of enlightened teachers with quiet good humor, exchanging ideas with those younger minds entrusted to us, in a lively, perhaps even elegant symposium, with, we hoped, something like grace.

DOHERTY. But lately you experienced a — what did you call it? I liked that so much. You experienced a disturbance in your willful suspension of disbelief. Wonderfully articulate, those poets. It took me fifteen minutes to figure out what that could possibly mean. All those negatives. Disbelief. What a thing to require. But disbelief is rampant nowadays. People are running about disbelieving all over the place. But a willful suspension of disbelief is believing, isn't it? So a disturbance in one's willful suspension of disbelief is right in my wheelhouse.

NILES. Oh, dear.

DON. Comes with the territory.

NILES. When I started teaching I was a renegade, believed nothing, investigated everything. And subtly over thirty years I became absolutely dogmatic. This is true, that is false. *A* is better than *B*. *B* is superior to *C*. Look for *A* about you. Anyone today not able to accomplish *A* is no kind of artist at all. All very neat and formulated. And they copy it in their workbooks slavishly. *A* is better than *B*. Look for examples of *A*. They don't even realize they're being brainwashed. They don't care. The thing they most often ask is, "Is this going to be on the test?" Once, in a thousand students, someone says, "How do you know that?" "Why, good Lord, man, when you've looked at the art of the Renaissance for as long as I have, with utterly blind eyes, you'll know that too."

DOHERTY. So you blew the whistle on yourself; took yourself right out of the game.

NILES. The sporting move when I discovered I was more hindrance than help.

DOHERTY. Then, like a silly, you stopped eating and made yourself sick. You threw it all away and looked up and saw yourself standing at a crossroads, and you looked down the wrong road at the wrong future and you saw nothing, of course, there's nothing down that road. But you can't do nothing, man. You have a young wife, the possibility of a family, I would think. Anyone who writes for children must want that. *(Beat.)* What manner of person ought we to be? I'm afraid I'm not going to be able to refrain from preaching a little sermon tonight. The only good thing that can come from these silly emergencies, these rehearsals for the end of the world, is that it makes us get our act together. *(He takes the Bible from the altar.)*

NILES. I'm in no state to follow you to the end of the world just now.

DOHERTY. Fortunately, you have a remarkable sense of self-preservation. *(Looking through the Bible.)* Imagine storming out in such a beautiful rage and not saying: "And I quit." I wouldn't have been able to resist it.

NILES. I have that to look forward to.

DOHERTY. But you could go back next term as though nothing had happened.

NILES. I cannot go back. My only sure conviction is that teaching is harmful.

DOHERTY. I'm sure anyone as clever as you could find a way to teach that.

NILES. And how would that appear in the college catalog? Beginning Heresy?

VITA. Professor Harris on Heresy.

DOHERTY. Of course. What else? Heresy 101. But imagine the subterfuge necessary. You'll be like St. Peter meeting the early Christians in the catacombs outside Rome.

NILES. "Now, my children, this is the truth. Tell no one where you heard it lest we all be hanged for attempting to bring the whole bogus boondoggle down to its knees."

DOHERTY. Seven times around the wall, and on the seventh day they blew the trumpets and the walls fell down flat. My, my. I should have been a rabbi. I love those old Hebrew tales. Subversives were being hidden by harlots in every well.

NILES. If there was a way to survey my subject without comment, without comparisons. "This is a painting. What does it say to you? There will be no test, make friends where you like." Oh, dear. Given today's students, begging for structure, half the class would have breakdowns within a week.

DOHERTY. *(With a Bible.)* Ah ha!

VITA. What?

DOHERTY. This is the end of the world. *(Reading.)* "The day of the Lord will come as a thief in the night; in the which the heavens shall pass away with a great noise, and the elements shall melt with fervent heat. The earth also and the works that are therein shall be burned up. Seeing then that all these things shall be dissolved, what manner of persons ought ye to be in all holy conversation and godliness?" It seems appropriate tonight to remind ourselves of that. And you are a teacher. So you simply have to find a way to teach. One of those professions, I've always thought, one is called to. As an artist is called, or as a priest is called, or as a doctor is called.

ZAP. That "call," man, that's the moment, man. That's magic. That's magic, that's magic.

MARION. What, doll?

ZAP. No, that magic that happens and you know who you are, you know? Like, "I'm a doctor, is what I do." Or, "I teach kids." Or like Marion.

MARION. Hardly.

ZAP. No, no joke. She said — you told me — I want to show artists' work. Like Van Gogh's brother. He was —

MARION. Theo.

ZAP. Yeah. Or like when I found out I was a tennis player.

VITA. I love you.

ZAP. No, no joke. I went to church and lit a candle, man.

DOHERTY. You give thanks for that light.

ZAP. Really. I said my novenas, man, 'cause it had been like a — not a miracle that anyone would know except just me — but it had been like when those girls saw Our Lady of Fatima up on that hill. It was really weird. I was like in the fifth grade and I was watching these two hamburgers on some practice court, and they took a break and one of them hands me his racket. So I threw up a toss like I'd seen them do and zap! Three inches over the net, two inches inside the line. There wasn't nobody over there, but that was an ace, man. You should have heard those guys razz me. I mean, you know, they say, "Man, you stink." And all those things you can't repeat in front of a priest. They was really on my case. And I think that's the first time anybody ever looked at me. I mean, I was skinny, you've never seen — most of the girls in my homeroom had about twenty pounds on me. So this guy shows me a backhand grip and he hits one to me and zap! You mother! Backhand! Right down the line. And the thing is, that's where I wanted it. I saw the ball come at me, and I said I'm gonna backhand this sucker right down the line, and I did.

So then they took their ball back. Which I don't blame them, 'cause no high school hotshot is gonna get off on being showed up by this eleven-year-old creep that's built like a parking meter, you know?

But that was it. I hit that first ball and I said, "This is me. This is what I do. What I do is tennis." And once you know, then there's no way out. You've been showed something. Even if it's just tennis, you can't turn around and say you wasn't showed that.

So I went to church and said a novena for those meatballs 'cause they didn't know all the butterflies that was in my stomach, that they'd been my angels. But, man, on the way home, anybody had asked me what I did, right there I'd have said, "I play tennis." Didn't know love from lob, didn't matter. That's what I am. 'Cause once you know what you are, the rest is just work. *(Pause. Don nudges him with his foot.)* Whatta you kicking me?

DON: Get up.

ZAP. It ain't like I got a lot to do, you know? There's not even a paved area and a wall to hit a ball against.

DON. Get up off the bare floor. That's the worst thing you could do to your-self. *(Beat.)* Half the aborigines in the world have arthritis by the time they're twenty from lying on the bare ground.

ZAP. Don't start with diseases, okay?

DON. Are you relaxed? Your muscles are loose? You're hanging out? You feel loose?

ZAP. Are you kidding? I'm cold, I'm stiff; I'm about as loose as a fireplug.

DON. Lie on a bench, don't lie on the bare floor.

ZAP. Now, see, I'll remember that. I retain things.

(The helicopters return. Over their sound microphones blare: The Road Is Clear. The Road Is Clear.*)*

DOHERTY. Isn't that wonderful. Playing with their toys.

HELICOPTER: *The road is clear!*

DOHERTY. Listen to them. *(To the door.)* You've given us all our monthly dose of fear, now fly back to White Sands and gloat. Shame. Shame! Don't they love to scare us to death. Don't we love them to do it. Can't you feel the tingling? Isn't fear exciting?

VITA. I could do without it.

DOHERTY. Well, maybe you can. Most people are beginning to look for-ward to these little emergencies. These shows of power. They've always wanted a big terrible God of the Old Testament and now they have Him. They want to see the fiery cloud. Don't tell me they don't.

(The helicopters are making another sweep. Doherty goes out the door. They are directly above him.)

HELICOPTER: *The road is now clear!*

DOHERTY. The road is not clear! You're sick as cats! You've made the bomb your god and you're praying for the bomb to call in the number. Well, you'll get it if you don't watch out. The Archangel Gabriel will announce the second coming of the Son of Man, and this time his voice will be a siren. *(The helicopters go off.)* Oh, I get so angry with everyone. Look at how foolish I am. *(He comes back in, brushing dust off his shirt.)*

NILES. You shouldn't have been a rabbi. You should have been a foot-washing Baptist.

DOHERTY. They do, they worship energy. Dear, dear. We've regressed to the caveman, astonished by fire. Compare a diddly bomb on this diddly planet with the divine design of the universe. Some silly astronomer said to me on a radio program that the universe started with a Big Bang, and I said: "Yes, you know that, and I know who pushed the button."

MARION. You've taken to speaking on the radio?

DOHERTY. No, local talk panels about goodness knows what. The program's been running for twenty years; by now they're scraping the bottom of the barrel. My superiors aren't happy about it. They'd like to send me somewhere. But there's no place left to send me.

VITA. And you wouldn't go.

DOHERTY. Oh, wild horses. No, someone has to stay. If every rational person leaves, the vultures will pick the Indian clean. The Spanish and the Anglos have good hospitals, so what do they care if the Indian has shockingly inadequate medical facilities. With Don leaving, they'll have almost no help at all.

DON. Come on.

DOHERTY. We had hoped for an improvement after all these years.

NILES. I believe I see a drift back to your thesis. You don't let up.

DON. I was expecting it.

DOHERTY. As well you should have. The professor could tell you. You left the college because you thought you'd been bought. I'm sure you recognize the purchase of someone else.

NILES. You really are shameless. All those stories of his childhood, dragging a stethoscope around —

DON. That's one of his favorites.

DOHERTY. You sit there and don't overtax yourself. You know nothing of the situation here. The Indians have one hospital for the Navaho, the Zuni, the Hopi...

DON. The Jemez, the Zia, the Laguna, the Acoma, the Apache...

DOHERTY. The Indian doesn't go to the hospital until he's nearly beyond hope. Until this Noah Lindermann Don had been planning to travel from pueblo to pueblo.

NILES. Much as you do.

DOHERTY. Much as I do. "Seeing that all this world shall be dissolved, what manner of persons ought we to be?" That man is a doctor. He has been a doctor since he was five years old. The man has been called. If you think I'm going to let the devil take him away from his people —

NILES. Hardly the devil —

DOHERTY. Oh, many fancy disguises, and don't forget it. I've never talked to anyone so smooth, even on the telephone, in my life.

NILES. I'm sure you set great store by him, but what he wants to do with his life is no concern —

DOHERTY. The need here is something you can't comprehend.

NILES. Need be damned. Need is not the question.

DOHERTY. *(To Don.)* Weren't you called to be a physician? Didn't you kneel here at this altar with me and pray after you told me you had been called to help your people?

DON. I was eleven years old.

DOHERTY. Have you been called now to alter your course?

NILES. You really can not do this!

DOHERTY. Have you, have you? Did you hear a voice saying to you: "Leave your people and leave your land and go with this great television personality?" Did you?

DON. I discovered I have a very special talent for research; if that's hearing a call, then I've been called.

DOHERTY. No, you decided you can't turn down this opportunity for a better personal life. Maria knows it, your uncle is shouting it to the sky right now, and you know it too. He knows what manner of person he ought to be.

NILES. Then trust him to decide!

DON. You are tearing me apart!

NILES. *(To Doherty.)* You don't care a damn what he does for *him.*

DOHERTY. Your brightest star jumped in the bay. What would you have done if you had the chance? This is my brightest star. Ten seconds from now he'll be in midair over the water. What would you do?

NILES. You cannot hold power over another man; even for his own good. This is your foster child. You see your reflection in him. I've seen it with teachers a dozen times. I've done it myself.

VITA. Not now.

NILES. You want that for you. You may be right as rain, but you're doing it for yourself. I don't know if that's Christian, but it's certainly not kosher.

DON. Don't talk.

DOHERTY. No. Don't say anything for a moment. I'm thinking. *(Pause. He goes to the window and looks out for a long while. When he turns around, there are tears in his eyes.)* I don't know that it matters, but you're right. I was thinking of myself. Well, well…vanity, vanity. You seem to be almost fit, Professor. Don, you're to be congratulated. Now, I'm holding Mass not too long from now, and there are things I have to do. *(He picks up the tray with pitcher and glasses.)* Will you need this again?

DON. No, Father.

NILES. I may have been a bit severe for a disinterested stranger.

DOHERTY. No, no. I'm very thickheaded. Only approach, only approach. Very thickheaded me. But I'm right, young man, and you know it.

DON. I knew you'd think so.

DOHERTY. Right as rain you said — we don't get much of that here. You think we should let them make up their minds; I'm not above blackmail and bludgeoning.

NILES. We can only present the case. I imagine you've shown a rather remarkable example.

DOHERTY. No, no, too common. Working with the common people, as they call them in their ignorance, is very common. *(To Marion.)* Well. Those asinine helicopters said the road is clear. They were more truthful when they said the bridge is out. *(He carries the tray into the residence.)*

VITA. *(To Zap.)* You have a plane to catch.

ZAP. Yeah, the cars are moving. Oh, boy, now I don't want to go.

MARION. Sure, sure you do. Get our stuff; don't run off without the radio.

NILES. You feel they should check us all into a hospital to monitor the radon count in our blood. Not that they could do anything about it.

MARION. I'll settle for leaving.

ZAP. I'll drive; I'm too drunk to sing. Keep my mind busy.

MARION. *(As Doherty returns.)* So. Listen. We have to go. I'll see you.

DOHERTY. No, no…actually you won't.

MARION. Thanks, Father Doherty. You were a good friend…to…all of us.

DOHERTY. I take more than I give.

MARION. Don't we all? Vita.

VITA. Marion, good luck. Good meeting you.

MARION. Under any other circumstances.

NILES. I'm pleased about your draw.

ZAP. I can't think about it. Oh, uh — Father. Do you think you could bless me? I mean not so I should win, I wouldn't want to take advantage of the other players, but just so I shouldn't fall over my feet, you know, and make Marion look like a fool.

DOHERTY. Sure, sure. One of my specialties. *(Zap kneels. Doherty mumbles.)* May almighty God bless you in the name of the Father, of the Son, and of the Holy Spirit.

MARION. Take care of yourself.

NILES. I intend to. You as well.

DOHERTY. Don't forget to give Don the keys to his bike.

ZAP. Oh. He said hide 'em, don't tell me where you put them. I gave them to Marion. Come on. 'Bye, now. Vita; Professor.

VITA. 'Bye now. Nice meeting you, Zappy.

ZAP. Doctor.

DON. Zap. Ace 'em.

ZAP. Right on. *(Exits.)*

MARION. I almost forgot. *(She takes the keys from her purse, tosses them to Don. He catches them, looks at her for a moment. She goes.)*

VITA. How far is the airport?

DOHERTY. Only an hour and a half. He'll get a good night's sleep.

(There is a car horn.)

VITA. That's Zappy. I love him. He reminds me of my brother.

(They all move to the doorway, looking out. The horn fades away, honking repeatedly.)

DOHERTY. I cheated. I said, "Make him win." *(Pause.)* Look who's pumping water over there.

VITA. Is that the old woman who won't eat?

DOHERTY. Mrs. Valdez. I think she's changed her mind. I made a pact with her granddaughter. The little girl pretended to be deathly ill, and the old lady had to get up to take care of her. Deathly ill, deathly ill. I'm very good at applying Band-Aids, but sometimes the parishioners are only suffering from scratches.

(They turn away from the doorway.)

VITA. It's so beautiful here.

DOHERTY. You be careful. Most of the residents came just to look and never left.

VITA. I wouldn't mind that.

NILES. I can imagine us living here as well as I can imagine us living anywhere.

DOHERTY. You can't think right now. Who could? You're exhausted. Look at you.

NILES. Everyone keeps telling me.

DOHERTY. You need a good rest and you're going to get it. Then you're going to sneak back to work and you're going to raise Cain. That's not exactly the way a priest should put it, but...

NILES. Like Peter outside the gates of Rome you said. Peter was crucified upside down, as I remember.

DOHERTY. But in a good cause. Which reminds me, I've invited your wife to stay for Mass. It must have been years.

NILES. That's thoughtful of you, but —

DOHERTY. She accepted.

VITA. It was my idea.

VITA. I think I've forgotten the responses.

DOHERTY. They come back. It's like riding a bicycle, you don't forget. I speak Navaho, and they reply in Navaho. A little broken Latin will work in beautifully. *(Exits into the residence.)*

NILES. *(To Vita.)* Would you like to stretch your legs? Then we can come back.

VITA. I'd like that.

(Doherty returns. Puts the Mass kit on the altar steps.)

NILES. *(To Don.)* It won't hurt to walk a little?

DON. It won't do you any good. You should sit and rest.

NILES. Just a short turn. To the road and back.

DON. Why did you ask?

NILES. Thank you, by the way, Doctor. If I haven't said that.

DOHERTY. That's what he's here for.

NILES. Or there for.

(Doherty spreads the two cloths on the table that serves as an altar. Vita and Niles look at Don a moment, then exit into the garden. Doherty sets out two little vials — wine and holy oil, then two candlesticks and two candles.)

DON. *(After a long pause.)* I'm glad I saw you.

DOHERTY. *(Sets out two goblets, and covers one.)* Me, too. Don By-the-River.

DON. Tabaha.

DOHERTY. *(Sets up cross.)* No, no, By-the-River. Don By-the-River. Like the song. *(Sings lightly.)* "Don-by-the riverside." Dr. Don. I've been too fond, young man. Too fond.

DON. Me, too, Father.

DOHERTY. Yes, yes…well… *(He goes to the altar, lighting the two candles.) (Don is crying. He looks around the church, picks up his duffel bag, and leaves. Doherty turns from the altar and moves to the window. The motorcycle starts up. The sound fades away. Doherty turns back, looking to the altar. After a moment he checks his watch and walks slowly outside and begins ringing the bell to call the congregation to Mass as the lights fade.)*

END OF PLAY